The Postcolonial Studies Dictionary

The Postcolonial Studies Dictionary

Pramod K. Nayar

WILEY Blackwell

This edition first published 2015
© 2015 John Wiley & Sons, Ltd

Registered Office
John Wiley & Sons, Ltd, The Atrium, Southern Gate, Chichester, West Sussex,
PO19 8SQ, UK

Editorial Offices
350 Main Street, Malden, MA 02148-5020, USA
9600 Garsington Road, Oxford, OX4 2DQ, UK
The Atrium, Southern Gate, Chichester, West Sussex, PO19 8SQ, UK

For details of our global editorial offices, for customer services, and for information about
how to apply for permission to reuse the copyright material in this book please see our
website at www.wiley.com/wiley-blackwell.

The right of Pramod K. Nayar to be identified as the author of this work has been asserted
in accordance with the UK Copyright, Designs and Patents Act 1988.

Library of Congress Cataloging-in-Publication Data

Nayar, Pramod K.
    The postcolonial studies dictionary / Pramod K. Nayar. – First edition.
        pages cm
    Includes bibliographical references.
    ISBN 978-1-118-78105-0 (hardback) – ISBN 978-1-118-78104-3 (paper)
  1. Postcolonialism in literature–Dictionaries.   2. Postcolonialism–Dictionaries.
  3. Developing countries–Literatures–Dictionaries.   4. Literature, Modern–20th
  century–Dictionaries.   5. Literature, Modern–21st century–Dictionaries.   I. Title.
    PN56.P555N38 2015
    809'.911–dc23
                                                        2015004076

A catalogue record for this book is available from the British Library.

Cover image: Palestinian girl looks out from her home in the Rafah refugee camp, Gaza
strip, 2007. © Ibraheem Abu Mustafa/Reuters/Corbis

Set in 10.5/13pt Minion by SPi Publisher Services, Pondicherry, India
Printed and bound in Malaysia by Vivar Printing Sdn Bhd

1 2015

Contents

Terms

Acknowledgements

To Emma Bennett of Wiley-Blackwell, I owe the largest quantum of debt: for the enthusiastic reception she accorded the proposal and her sustained engagement with the project through the writing.

To the nearly half-dozen reviewers of the proposal, for their painstaking reading and valuable suggestions, this project owes immeasurable gratitude. I have tried to incorporate, wherever possible, those of their suggestions and recommendations that I found relevant.

Nandana Dutta, with her gently and clearly expressed reservations about the genre, read sections and offered incisive comments. Thank you for your splendid affection, observations and general confidence, ND!

Anna Kurian arched her eyebrows at the idea of a *Dictionary* ('is that a genre you *really* want to try? Oh well, okay, if you say so') and then plunged wholeheartedly into the project. Thank you, Anna, again, for the loving loyalty you extend (even) after over a decade of reading my manuscripts (and for that crucial tip about the *terra nullius* discourse).

Nandini, Pranav, parents and parents-in-law, with their bewildered tolerance and unstinting support of my obsessive work schedules, deserve awards for their patience! To them I owe, of course, both gratitude and apologies (but hey all of you, I am just embarking on the next project, so be ready!).

Friends at various stages unwittingly offered bibliographic suggestions – little did they know how I would store these bits and bytes! – and thus contributed to the material in this work: Rita Kothari, Narayana Chandra, Nandana Dutta (again) and Walter Perera.

To others' solicitous enquiries about my life, health and work (not in that order) I owe a huge debt, they tether me to the rest of the world and life: Ibrahim, Ajeet, Saraswathy Rajagopalan, Neelu (whose Joke Factory runs 24x7), Vasu and Bella, Molly Tarun, Ron (especially noted for her status messages on WhatsApp), Josy Joseph and Premlata.

Preface

Postcolonial studies today continues to examine the making of colonies and empires in history but also, more importantly, critiques the *continuities* of these older empires in the form of neocolonialisms and US imperialisms. It studies the 'remains' (Young 2012) of colonialism in the form of the legacies the postcolony (Mbembe 2001) has to deal with. Thus racialized power relations, subjectivity, identity, belonging, the role of the nation-state, cultural imperialism and resistance remain central to postcolonial studies today even as it tracks the genealogy of these structures, domains, concerns and crises from the historical 'properly' colonial pasts to the globalized, neo-colonial present.

Postcolonial studies, especially in the literary and cultural academic domains, has since the 1980s focused both extensively and intensively on discourses, whether literary, scientific or philosophical. Studying representations, narrative and rhetoric, the field has remained faithful, one could say, to the poststructuralist-discourse studies methodology, and has thus received considerable criticism from materialist critics. Subjectivity, identity and history in such readings have more or less firmly been located within a discourse studies framework, but often (it has been suspected, and not without cause) at the cost of due attention to questions of political economy and real material practices.

Since the late 1990s and the early decades of the 21st century developments in other fields, most notably natural sciences, philosophy and science studies, have begun to make their impact in the field of cultural theory. The writings of Lynn Margulis (1981, 2000), Scott Gilbert (2002), Pradeu and Carosella (2006), Rosi Braidotti (2010, 2013), Karen Barad (2007), Cary Wolfe (2010), Alphonso Lingis (2003), and collections such as Diana Coole and Samantha Frost's *New Materialisms: Ontology, Agency, and Politics*

(2010) have resulted in examinations of bodies, things and environment. These (re)turn us to material contexts, conditions and contests, especially to the ways these constitute subjectivity.

For postcolonial studies the impact of the new thinking in materialism is still nascent, although recent work by Dipesh Chakrabarty (2012), Elizabeth DeLoughrey (2012, 2014), Kaushik Sunder Rajan (2006) and others suggests an awareness of the 'return to the material' in other disciplines. When, for instance, Winifred Poster studies the new credit economy (2013) or Rita Paley the e-Empires of the globalized era (2004) they also study the new configurations of individual identity as cast within affect, labour, social relations, circuits of capital, bodies and biology – material realities, in other words – and thus contribute to a materialist understanding of postcolonial identity. Other lines of inquiry also open up in contemporary postcolonial studies, most notably of the electronic diasporas, globalization, secularism/post-secularism and the question of faith and 'fundamentalisms' (especially in the work of Saba Mahmood, 2005, 2009), neo-colonialism and biocolonialism.

It is possible that traditional postcolonial questions of racial discourse may be linked with material practices of torture and embodiment, of the crisis in corporeal and sensorial identity and the resultant crisis of subjectivity. One could for instance think of the Abu Ghraib tortures as inviting such a reading (Rejali 2004, Nayar 'Body of Abu Ghraib' [2014], 'Abu Ghraib@10' [2014]). Global biopolitics, as seen in studies such as those of Nikolas Rose and Carlos Novas (2005), Catherine Waldby and Mitchell (2006), Adriana Petryna (2002), enmeshes the materiality of bodies with the materiality of discourses. Material practices whether in medicine or industry that affect bodies and being bring back the significance of matter into debates about identity and subjectivity. Studies of industrial disaster, pollution, organ trade and politics move away from mere discourse to looking at real bodies, matter (such as poisons), to examine the differential valuing of bodies, and of life itself, across races and geopolitical regions. Contemporary issues of environmental health, animal life and human existence in fields as diverse as environmental studies, politics and medicine call for such a new materialism that refuses to position the human as discrete, arguing instead for its material connections with the material world. Thus in Cary Wolfe's provocative comparison of human extermination of animals to the Holocaust and genocide (2010) one could argue that we see links between racism and speciesism. By tracing material exchanges across bodies (trans-corporeality), the subsequent affective changes and relations and changing ontologies propel postcolonialism's concerns with race and discourse toward species and material embodiment: a posthuman turn to postcolonialism, if you will.

This *Dictionary* seeks to bring together in its explication of the terms and concepts in Postcolonial Studies both its historically inflected analyses *and* its contemporaneity, the emphasis being on textual analysis *and* political-materialist concerns, with perhaps a tad heavier weightage toward the former, understandably, given the fact that it relies almost exclusively on literary texts for examples and articulations of the field's premier themes.

PKN
Hyderabad
September 2014

aboriginal: The *OED* defines aboriginal as 'people born in a place or region' and refers to indigenous peoples of Canada, Australia and Americas – regions which eventually witnessed European **settler colonialism**. The term was used as shorthand for any 'non-European' and homogenized Maoris, the many Native American tribes, the numerous language groups and ethnic formations of these regions. James Cook (1728–1779), explorer, was one of the first to offer descriptions of the Maoris and the Australian indigenous tribes. The latter he deemed 'animals' because they expressed no interest in barter of commodities with the British, whereas the Maoris seemed eager to trade. In other parts of the world where colonies existed till the middle of the 20th century, the term was less in vogue. Europeans in India rarely used the term, preferring instead 'native races' with a pejorative connotation. (The concept of race itself emerged alongside the European drive for territories.) The term 'aboriginal' came into popular use in 1838 with the founding of the Aboriginal Protection Society, as a name for the indigenous peoples of colonized regions. It is only since the 1980s that the term 'aborigine' has acquired greater qualifications as Canadian Aboriginal, First Nation, Australian Aboriginal or, in the case of the USA, Native American. Today it is most often used to describe the indigenous tribes, populations and cultures of Australia and Canada. In some writers in the late 20th century aboriginal concerns about land rights and cultural identity have been aligned with similar concerns of Native Americans and tribals in other parts of the world. We see a literary instance of this alignment in Jimmy Chi and Kuckles' play *Bran Nue Dae* (1990)

The Postcolonial Studies Dictionary, First Edition. Pramod K. Nayar.
© 2015 John Wiley & Sons, Ltd. Published 2015 by John Wiley & Sons, Ltd.

where a recitation goes thus: 'This fella song all about the aboriginal people, coloured people, black people longa Australia. Us people want our land back, we want 'em rights, we want 'em fair deal, all same longa man' (2001: 345). Several oppressed groups and people – First Nation, aboriginals but also blacks – are brought together here. Groups such as the Kurds or the Romanis have also claimed the status of 'aboriginal' populations. Tribal and aboriginal literatures have mainly focused on the loss of their lands to white settlers, and the slow erasure of their ways of life as their young men and women get seduced by white cultures. Thus Kath Walker's 'We are Going' documents the aboriginals' loss of land, culture and people with the arrival of the whites. 'We are strangers here now', declare the aboriginals, about their own place because 'all the old ways/gone now and scattered' (1996: 223–234). Aboriginal writing makes use of many narrative conventions that seek to preserve its older modes of storytelling – the oral tradition – while mixing them, as does Thomas King (of Cherokee descent), with contemporary forms. Figures from aboriginal and Native American tradition, such as the Coyote or the Trickster, people these literatures. Very often, as in King's short story 'The One about Coyote Going West' (1996), we are given an alternate history of creation itself, where it is Coyote who makes the world, and then makes a 'mistake': the creation of the white man. In Narayan's *Kocharethi* (2011), the first novel by a tribal from Kerala, southern India, the author speaks of the temptations the city holds for the tribal youth, but also points out that far from an ideal life, tribal life is fraught with gender inequalities, not to mention exploitative relations with landowners and the state itself. In Australia the Aboriginals have a particularly traumatic history as a result of the forced institutionalization – under the Aboriginal Protection Acts dating back to the 1860s, initiated, supposedly, for their own good – including displacement, and the loss of their children ('the stolen generation', where Aboriginal children were forcibly taken away by the white administration and placed in foster care, from the early 1900s till as late as the 1970s). (See also: **settler colonialism**)

abrogation: When postcolonial writers reject a particular 'standardized' language, it is often described as abrogation. Famously identified as a postcolonial strategy by Bill Ashcroft, Gareth Griffiths and Helen Tiffin in their *The Empire Writes Back* (1989), abrogation is now a commonplace descriptor of the many varieties of English language usage that we see in Chinua Achebe, Salman Rushdie, Wilson Harris or Monica Ali and Zadie Smith more recently. Take for instance Amos Tutuola's title, *The Palm-Wine*

Drinkard (1952). Apparently an ungrammatical construction that deviates from the standard 'drunkard' in the Queen's English, the variant makes a political point about the rejection of an ideal or normative English in the title itself. Similarly, the mixing of English with Igbo proverbs (Achebe) or Hindi film songs (Rushdie) that breaks up the syntactic and semantic norms of English language use ensures that we recognize the malleability and flexibility of any language, and not its so-called 'purity'. Further, it also shows how non-European writers not only reject the 'standard' English of their former masters but also modify it to suit their purposes. As the Indian poet Kamala Das put it 'the language I speak/becomes mine, its distortions, its queerness/all mine, mine alone' ('An Introduction', 1996: 717). Abrogation in this sense goes along with concepts like **appropriation** and **creolization** in postcolonial writings. Abrogation's key contribution to postcolonialism's political stance lies not only in its rejection-appropriation dynamics of language but also in its shift away from the standard-non-standard idea of language and therefore of culture. With abrogation there is no longer a sense of the British Empire and its English being the centre, norm or standard and the colonies being the periphery, variant and inferior. A significant political point being made with abrogation is also that during colonization European languages were instruments of dominance and control: the abrogation of postcolonial writers shows they no longer allow such control. There is no 'right' or 'wrong' English, in this postcolonial abrogation of language. When, for example, John Agard criticizes the English for their sense of class and linguistic superiority, he gives this critique to an immigrant who says: 'mugging de Queen's English/is the story of my life' ('Listen Mr Oxford Don'). In the performance poetry ('Dub poetry') of Linton Kwesi Johnson and Jean 'Binta' Breeze English words are set to Caribbean and African rhythms in yet another instance of abrogation, 'reverse colonizing' (as Louise Bennett put it in the poem of the same title) and creolization.

Adivasi: Treated as roughly the Indian equivalent of 'aboriginal', the term refers to a large number of ethnic groups, mainly tribal, in the subcontinent. Often used interchangeably with 'vanavasi' (forest dwellers) and 'girijan' (hill people), Adivasis are believed to be the original inhabitants of the land. Tribes in central India, parts of the northeast and the Andaman and Nicobar Islands are grouped under this term, and in terms of political categorization are listed under 'Scheduled Tribes' of the Constitution. Their retention of older ways of life and the increasing threats to their land and culture as a result of developmental projects has pushed the Adivasis into the limelight, most notably in the case of the Narmada river projects. Faced with the threat of displacement (to make way for dams, mining projects and roads, in particular), they have become politicized and campaigns for tribal rights, especially land rights and cultural rights, are now frequent. However, it must be noted that several of these tribes have had political experience right from the colonial period and tribal rebellions against the British occurred through the late 18th and 19th centuries, most famously in the central Indian region. The Lushai, Bastar, Kuki, Tamar, Bhil and Munda rebellions are some of the more famous, with the Munda rebellion becoming the subject of a book, *Chotti Munda and His Arrow*, by Mahasweta Devi (translated by Gayatri Spivak). As a consequence their geographical isolation and cultural identity have also been disturbed – most famously in the case of the Jarawas of Andaman Islands, whose lands and lives are at risk from tourism in the region. Efforts are underway to preserve their cultural traditions and languages. One of contemporary India's most significant cultural projects, 'Project for Tribal and Oral Literature', by the Indian Academy of Letters, has to do with the preservation of Adivasi tribal languages and literary traditions. Led by G.N. Devy, it aims at preserving fast-disappearing languages of the tribes. Devy also heads the People's Linguistic Survey of India, a project in cultural rights aiming to document the several hundred languages and dialects, oral traditions, with the explicit purpose of databasing linguistic and speech communities, building bridges across languages and protecting linguistic diversity.

Afro-Europe: Arising from an acknowledgement of the role of Africans in the colonial empires, most notably in the form of their employment as soldiers in the European armies, and the increasing migration from Africa to Europe in the 20th century, 'Afro-Europe' is 'Black Europe', a version of the Black Atlantic, made famous by Paul Gilroy's work of that title. Through the period of colonialism, and especially in the world wars, Africans fought in European armies in Burma, Singapore and other places. Critical work emerging in military history has begun to document the stories, processes of recruitment and lives of such soldiers (Koller 2008; Moorehouse 2010). Journals such as *Afroeuropa* undertake studies of 'blackness' in Germany, the rise of black Spanish identity, diasporas and racial tensions. Recent fiction has attempted to examine the lives of blacks in occupied France and their encounters with German racism (Esi Edugyan's *Half-Blood Blues*, 2011, would be an example).

agency: Agency in critical and social theory is taken to mean the ability, capacity and freedom of an individual to make choices for her/his life and to carry through with these choices within existing social structures. Within postcolonial studies the focus has been on the non-European individual to make such choices and the possibilities of realizing those choices in the colonial or post-independence (*post*colonial) contexts. Postcolonial studies notes that the native individual under colonialism has been for so long humiliated, rejected and marginalized that s/he loses all faith in her/his abilities to carry forth a plan of action or make decisions. Institutionalized marginalization, in the form of racism for example, denies the social and political structures in which an individual can assert choices or make decisions. The continued absence of opportunities to fulfil one's potential means the loss of agency in such a situation. Fanon, for example, in *Black Skin, White Masks* (1956) notes how the African man begins to despise himself, losing his sense of masculinity, and his faith in his native cultures because the colonial powers have symbolically and often, through torture, physically emasculated him. Under such conditions the African does not believe he has any agency. Insults, torture, humiliations and contempt dehumanize the man, who loses his sense of self and his confidence in his agency. When such a man seeks to reassert agency he needs to enact a set of choices, however terrible the consequences of such choices might be. Fanon identifies tribal dancing and violence as two modes through which the colonized subject seeks to exorcise his frustrations and anger, and thereby purge them in order to acquire a measure of agency. We also see violence-as-agential in Thomas Keneally's novel *The Chant of Jimmie Blacksmith* (1972). Jimmie (himself the child of an aboriginal woman and a white man), tired of being emasculated and denied agency, goes on a murder spree killing white men, women and children. His rage, which of course leads him to destruction at the hands of the colonizer, might be read as a desperate act of agency where the only choices he can make are of murder and violence. Some critics, such as Homi Bhabha (in 'Of Mimicry and Man', 'Sly Civility'), have, however, argued that even under colonialism the native individual did manage to effect agency in an insidious and devious fashion. Mockery, ridicule, quiet disobedience and carnivalesque play-acting – mimicry – as we see in the case of Wole Soyinka's *Death and the King's Horseman* (1975) or Derek Walcott's *Dream on Monkey Mountain* (1970), are modes of asserting agency. Gandhi's mode of asserting agency was in the passive resistance offered to the colonial excesses of beating, arrests and protracted incarceration. Thus Gandhi shifted the terms of agency away from violence and forceful assertion of rights to passive resistance and gained a moral upper-hand as a result. Symbolic resistance, even so-called superstitious cultural practices, according to commentators like Bhabha and Ranajit Guha (1982, 1987), are indeed the colonized subject's modes of asserting agency, although these are covert rather than overt as was the case with Jimmie Blacksmith. That said, it is arguable whether symbolic expressions such as mimicry are truly agential since these do not really change existing social and political conditions. If agency is the ability to alter the course of one's life in accordance with one's own wishes and needs, then symbolic resistance or articulations offer only a certain emotional triumph without altering the real material conditions. Women writers in the postcolonial canon have argued against mere symbolizations of the 'motherland' or 'African woman' because, as novelist Mariama Bâ proposes, such a 'sentimentalization' and nostalgic praise circumscribes the woman's role to motherhood and/or lover, effectively limiting their agency in the postcolonial patriarchal culture (in Schipper 1984).

alterity: A term that acquired considerable value in contemporary critical and social theory from the 1980s, alterity is 'otherness'. Popularized in the work of the philosopher Emanuel Levinas in the 1970s, it originally meant a sense of the non-self, of something that is outside of, and therefore different from, the self. It is now used as one of a semantic pair with 'ipseity' (the sense of one's self, self-awareness). Alterity is what enables us to distinguish ourselves from the world, to see the world as outside us and our consciousness. Within postcolonial studies the term is deployed to convey the sense of a radical racial-cultural otherness and the *processes* through which this 'otherness' is constructed. There are several layers to this postcolonial use of the term. First, colonial culture constructs the native as the radical Other of white cultures. Edward Said in *Orientalism* (1978) argued that the European sense of self is constructed only in its pairing with this African, Arab or Indian Other. Second, this African or Caribbean Other is not simply Other, it is an inferior Other. The African or Indian native is primitive, pagan and non-modern as opposed to different from the modern, advanced, Christian white. Thus within the pairing of the self-Other, colonial cultures place a certain set of values on each of the categories: the European self is *superior to* the African Other. Third, African, Islamic and Hindu cultures become objects of study in colonial science, philosophy, literature and psychology. 'Alterity' in this sense is the reduction of the native individual and culture to a mere object, lacking any will or consciousness and one which can be examined, studied and pronounced upon by the colonial. Fourth, constructions of alterity in the colonial context take recourse to stereotypes: the savage, irrational, emotional native versus the calm, rational and systematic white. Fifth, such constructions of Otherness become institutionalized, resulting in practices such as racism where the different skin colour of Africans or Indians is evaluated as a sign of their inferiority to the whites. Sixth, once alterity has been institutionalized it can then justify colonial conquest, modernization-civilization projects (wherein the European self seeks to improve the primitive colonized subject) and governance (since it is assumed that the colonized subject is incapable of governing him-/herself). The institutionalization of alterity enables the European to present him-/herself as saviour, benefactor, ruler and modern and therefore crucial to the colonial enterprise. In texts like Rudyard Kipling's *Kim*, Kipling presents the older, more learned lama as dependent upon the stripling Kim. The implicit suggestion is that the older Asian is the less competent member of the team, especially since the other member of the team is a European. Kim's own sense of self, which is still in formation at his young age, is bolstered by his awareness of the subject's dependency. The Africans in Rider Haggard's fiction, as in Joseph Conrad's, are the inferior Others to the whites, to be ordered, punished and even brutalized. They are presented as governed by superstition, and as irrational and therefore unequal to the whites. Robinson Crusoe, who has begun to see himself as the master and king of the uninhabited island, is able to reinforce this sense of himself when he 'acquires' Friday and determines that Friday is the slave-Other to him. Alterity, as analyzed by postcolonial writers and critics, simply makes the non-European the inferior Other so that the European can dominate, educate, improve, marginalize and chastise the Arab, the African and the Indian. Increasingly, however, this reading of English literature about the colonies as merely documenting racial and cultural alterity has been called into question. Numerous critical works have demonstrated how England constructed itself through an incorporation of European, Asian and other cultures into itself. That is, colonialism was not structured around a simple us/them binary but was a more complicated movement through and across multiple cultures. England's literary genres were born out of a hybridization with European forms (Aravamudan 2005), and genres like the *Bildungsroman* were often recast within the colonial context (Esty 2007). Its material culture of domesticity, socializing and even national identity hinged upon the import and consumption of products such as tea, tobacco, Kashmiri shawls from the colonies and distant places (Knapp 1988, Kowaleski-Wallace 1994,

Zutshi 2009). The idea of Englishness was constructed around acts of heroism, vulnerability and philanthropy in the colonies, as well as through the case of slavery (Ferguson 1992; Richardson 1998; Fulford 1999). Finally, England's own cosmopolitanization in the later 19th and early 20th centuries (but dating back to the early 19th century) was contingent upon the inflow of immigrants and an increasing multiculturalization of, say, London (McLaughlin 2000).

ambivalence: This term acquired critical currency in postcolonial studies mainly through the works of Homi K. Bhabha (the essays collected in the volume, *The Location of Culture*). Bhabha adapts the psychoanalytic concept to refer to the odd fascination and phobia that co-exists in the colonizer's attitude toward the colonized. Bhabha argues that the European colonial wishes at once to reform the native into being more like him (Bhabha, it must be noted, is specifically addressing the masculine gender here). This stems from the colonizer's fascination with the native and the belief that the native can be reformed. However, beneath this fascination and belief is the fear that the native cannot be reformed. Or, more accurately, the colonizer is worried about the form the colonized subject might take once he has been reformed according to European ways. On the one hand, therefore, the European wishes to make the natives more white, more Western, more Christian, more modern. At the same time, the colonial would rather the native stayed the same passive colonized subject with his exotic culture and old ways of life because this subject was predictable and manageable. A 'modernized' native subject might not be a quiescent subject any more. Bhabha ('Of Mimicry and Man: The Ambivalence of Colonial Discourse') thus proposes that all colonial discourse is schismatic as a result of this ambivalence toward the native. This shift engineered by Bhabha has crucial consequences for the ways in which we see colonialism itself. Colonialism is no longer the confident, strident, all-knowing and coherent set of goals, processes, ideas and policies. Instead, we now come to see it as divided, uncertain, unstable and undermining itself with its dual feelings and ideas toward the colonized subject. Ambivalence is the mark of the erosion of colonial authority in Bhabha's interpretation. E.M. Forster's *A Passage to India* (1924) gives us characters who exhibit just such an ambivalence toward India. Mrs Moore, who wishes to understand India better, is more generous and compassionate toward India and humanity in general, but is also overwhelmed by, and not a little afraid of, the country and its people. Adela Quested, who in Forster's words wishes to 'see the real India', is unable to overcome her prejudices about or desire for (since Forster never makes it clear what happens in the Marabar Caves) virile Muslim men which lead her to believe that Dr Aziz assaulted her in the caves, and yet cannot resist the desire to know the unknown India. It is possible to discern in Conrad's classic, *Heart of Darkness*, a similar ambivalence. Conrad shows how, having treated the Africans as 'brutes', the white Kurtz himself becomes a brute. When Marlow sees Kurtz he appears an animal. Further, when the novel ends Marlow sees the 'heart of darkness' not in the interiors of Africa but in London itself. The novel seems to reflect not on the colony as a setting but on the effect the distant colony has upon the white man and the imperial metropolis. Similarly, in Arthur Conan Doyle's 'The Sign of Four', 'The Speckled Band' and other texts London and English culture are shown as being corrupted by the arrival of people and products (opium, jewels) from the colonial peripheries. One could read these texts as embodying an ambivalence toward the Empire because the English are now re-evaluating the imperial project and seeing within it not simply glory and profit but degeneration and evil for England itself. There is an acknowledgement that the colony is essential but this is tempered by the awareness that England now needs to *fear* the colonies.

anthropology (colonial): While the 'science of humanity' (anthro = human) has been around since ancient times, the colonial period saw a particular kind of academic interest by European anthropologists in non-European cultures, both present and past. The work of Franz Boas (1858–1942), Bronislaw Malinowski (1884–1942), Claude Lévi-Strauss (1908–2009), Margaret Mead (1901–1978) and others from the 19th and early 20th centuries produced extensive work on non-European kinship, family systems, rituals, religion, totems and taboos, and cultural practices. The aim was to develop laws and propositions about the nature of these people. Tribes and ethnic groups, their languages and lifestyles were documented by European anthropologists in Asia, Africa, Australia-New Zealand and the South American continent. Their works were treated as authentic, objective and authoritative interpretations of the 'native' cultures. It was also part of the myth of colonial anthropology that the European observer was detached and objective in her/his process of documenting the tribes (who were simply, the 'object' of inquiry). Differences in culture are viewed through the prism of race, and those characteristics of African or Asian society that did not conform to the European idea of the 'modern' were treated as primitive. Since the 1980s there has been considerable work on the link between anthropology and colonial hegemony, mainly from Michael Taussig (1987), Abdul JanMohamed (1983), Talal Asad (1973) and others. These revisionist histories of the academic discipline of anthropology show how the knowledge produced about these subject races by colonial anthropologists (in respectable institutions such as the Royal Anthropological Society or the Asiatic Society) found its expression in legislation, administrative measures and civilizational missions of the European. These anthropological studies were not in any way objective or scientific but (as work on the narrative strategies of anthropology show, notably in James Clifford 1988, Clifford Geertz 1983) only assumed the objectivity of the European observer. Postcolonial critiques of colonial anthropology argue that the methods (the fieldwork strategies used by anthropologists), methodology (the normative standards and theoretical frameworks set up to 'measure' and observe people) and representations (interpretive documentation of the observed data) enabled the colonials to construct particular models for the non-European races and cultures. Colonial anthropological studies, for example, of so-called 'criminal tribes' in India in 1871 resulted in the enactment of legislation that categorized them as criminals as a result of which members of the community could be arrested for no other reason than that they belonged to that community. These studies were also firmly entrenched in European ideas and prejudices about other cultures. Anthropology thus created hierarchies of races, cultures and nations, where categories like 'non-modern' or 'primitive' were affixed to Asian and African nations and automatically assigned the descriptor 'modern' to Europe. Anthropology in fact helped construct the idea of the 'primitive'. A timeline was produced within the discipline wherein Asia and Africa stood at the early stages of development and civilization and Europe at its later ones. When such categories and hierarchies were put in place they also ensured that Europe would be able to 'naturalize' its role as protector, guardian and teacher of the world: these roles would be consistent with imperial projects. Colonial anthropology might therefore be seen as a major classificatory project in which categories and definitions of criminality, deviance, progress and primitivism were constructed for the furthering of Empire (Thomas 1994). Anthropology pretended to furnish the evidence in 'scientific terms' for the racial-cultural hierarchies on which colonialism depended. Yet both anthropology and colonial discourses carried the same prejudices and beliefs: neither was in that sense truly 'scientific' or objective. Thus anthropology as an academic discipline was important not because it studied humanity closely but because it enabled the construction of racial and cultural hierarchies and thereby offered a rationale for the domination of 'weak' races/cultures by 'strong' races/cultures. Anthropologists and scientists who provide data on land use and geological eras ignore, however, the impact of Western modes of dealing with the land and the colonial projects. In the work of Jean and John Comaroff (2001) and more recently, Elizabeth DeLoughrey (2012, 2014) and Nicholas Mirzoeff (2014), there has been a focus on the scientific discourses, particularly the environmental, in history. In these studies of the 'anthropocene' (defined as the era in geology, about 250 years now, caused by human intervention and practices such as the burning of fossil fuels) and its representations, Mirzoeff and DeLoughrey discern a colonial ideology. Mirzoeff proposes that an 'anthropocene visuality' ensures that histories of environmental degradation and exploitation have been obscured from visualization. Biogeographies, databasing of weather and ecologies, classification of plant and animal lives are part of this process of anthropocene project because they deliver an illusion of a knowable world while obscuring the destructive practices of human life on the planet. DeLoughrey proposes that almost all visual representations of the planet might be linked with the rise of global surveillance of the 20th-century post-World War II era and tracked back to the 19th century colonial mapping of the world's resources and peoples. Even notions of global consciousness, ideas of ecosystems and other such systems thinking, have their origins in US nuclear testing projects.

apartheid: The term means 'separation' in Dutch. Historically apartheid has its origins in the land policies in South Africa. Black farmers were not allowed to own land beyond a specific acreage and the overall land available for black farmers in the country itself was very low. This automatically meant that much of the land was under the control of the whites, although their actual numbers made them a minority in the country. From here the policy of segregation moved into other areas, such as demographics, as the government began to prepare records of racial types. Transport systems, work permits and public spaces were all organized around white and non-white (within which, over the years, the government developed sub-categories to include blacks but also Indians). Townships were organized around racial lines and non-white populations evicted from areas designated for occupation by the whites. The struggle against apartheid in South Africa, spearheaded by organizations like the African National Congress and leaders like Desmond Tutu and Nelson Mandela, was an extended one. The struggle attracted swift and brutal reprisals and Robben Island prison became a symbol of white oppression for the number of prisoners – including

Mandela – incarcerated there. After the official end of apartheid in South Africa, a Truth and Reconciliation Commission was set up to inquire into police atrocities, during the course of whose processes *testimonios* by former prisoners and policemen, judges and civilians emerged that offered a traumatic history of the country. In Critical Race Studies and postcolonial studies apartheid serves as a code word for racial discrimination, hegemony and violent anti-racism struggles. Thinkers like Frantz Fanon used features of apartheid policy, such as the spatial demarcation and segregation of cities, to read the various discourses (architecture, space, demography) of racism. A vast body of apartheid literature, which includes the *testimonios*, prison writings by Mandela and others, activist writings such as those of Ken Saro-Wiwa (Harlow 1992, Payne 2008), and protest poetry, now exists and constitutes a key component of postcolonial studies. Post-apartheid fiction such as that of J.M. Coetzee seeks to understand the dynamics of race in the aftermath of a history of violence, discrimination and struggle.

appropriation: as noted in the entry above, **abrogation** referred to the postcolonial process of rejecting a standard, normative and superior language. Abrogation is a preliminary stage to appropriation. Appropriation is the slow takeover of European culture by the former colonized subjects. When, for instance, a Salman Rushdie or a Caryl Phillips writes fiction using the English language, England's landscape or English cultural practices but does so in order to reflect upon its flaws, shortcomings and politics, we see postcolonial appropriation in operation. Chinua Achebe, Amos Tutuola, Raja Rao and Ben Okri all use the novel form for their writing. The novel, as critics argue (Watt), is a European form that arose as a consequence of particular social, economic and political contexts in the early 18th century but with an increasing emphasis on individuality, individual consciousness and the individual self (Slaughter 2006, 2007). When the postcolonial Okri appropriates this European genre he does not, however, simply re-use it. Instead Okri, in *The Famished Road* (1991) for instance, breaks the tedium of the realist novel – Europe's major form – with bursts of surrealism, dream sequences, magic and delirium. The Abiku character in Okri's fiction disrupts the realist mode of the novel. Abiku is made to function as an oracle, a traditional folkloric device in many African cultures. This can be seen as a mode of literary appropriation where the European novel, once adopted by the postcolonial, is adapted and therefore is no more recognizable as the colonial master's genre or device. Abiku, despite being a child, therefore speaks in aphoristic fashion: 'The world is full of riddles that only the dead can answer' (75). And elsewhere,

'There are many riddles amongst us that neither the living nor the dead can answer' (488). By giving the child-character such heavy responsibility as an oracle Okri unravels the conventions of the realist novel with his **magical realism**. Coetzee's *Foe* (1988) goes one step further. Coetzee takes the most canonical-colonial Englishman-character, Robinson Crusoe (from Defoe's 1719 novel) and inverts the story by having a female castaway Susan Barton, a silent Friday and a cantankerous Cruso who, in contrast to his fictional predecessor, has no enterprise or enthusiasm. The Robinsonade genre that arose from Defoe's novel is turned right on its head by Coetzee here with his female adventurer, reluctant and debt-ridden novelist (Foe) and unenterprising Englishman, Cruso. Norms and standards of what the novel is, what it should do, and the 'great tradition' are summarily rejected and the genre itself modified to accommodate the themes, politics and styles of non-European cultures. Strategies such as magical realism in the postcolonial text might therefore be seen as modes of appropriation of the European genre or medium but also, importantly, as strategies of resistance to a dominant cultural practice (writing), lexicon (British English), tone (neutral), and point of view (third person) in order to create a postcolonial hybrid genre.

archive (colonial):   The colonial archive is not, in the view taken by postcolonial studies, a mere encyclopaedic collection of data about cultures collected by European powers and governments over the period between 1400 and the mid-20th century. Rather the archive is a politically powerful device put in place by the colonial authorities. Data is raw material but the information is the interpretive frame through which (i) specific kinds of data are collected and (ii) the data collected is then made to generate meaning. Unless the framework is in place the data cannot be made to yield meaning. Thus the colonial archive is a method of interpretation within which certain kinds of data are stored and which then yields certain kinds of meaning. In this way archives of phrenology (the 'science' of measuring shapes and sizes of heads in order to determine individual-racial characteristics in the 19th century) were created with a set of assumptions where the shape/size of the cranium was believed to reflect moral, intellectual and other characteristics of the individual (Bank 1996). The data collected based on the these assumptions is then taken as the yardstick to put in place administrative, legislative and other policies to further control the colonized subject. In his work *The Imperial Archive* (1993) Thomas Richards proposed that the archive represents a 'fantasy' of knowledge over the entire world, producing data about every aspect of non-European cultures, from geography to cultural practices, what he refers to 'accumulation of discrete facts'. Various bits of local knowledge were gathered into the archive and ordered into patterns to enable comprehension. Richards thus sees the unification of the knowledge of the world into a comprehensive system in an archive as a key feature of the imperial process itself. The 'survey', as the anthropologist Bernard Cohn (1997) pointed out, was central to the British colonial system, whether it was the linguistic survey, the zoological or the archaeological. What Richards and Cohn point to is the politics of knowledge-making, where there is no 'innocent' gathering of facts and details, but rather a careful organization of information with the larger goal of control. Museums, maps, surveys (for which specialized institutions such as the Archaeological Survey of India and the Zoological Survey of India were established), administrative reports and even personal accounts of travel, such as Mungo Park's, contributed to this imperial archive (on museums see Barringer 1998). The imperial archive might be usefully thought of as a textual colonization of the world.

arithmetic (colonial):   Imperialism had a quantificatory impulse. The survey, the census and the account book were crucial tools in organizing knowledge about the colony. From the earliest travelogues in the 17th century we see such an impulse in operation. Since trade was the single most important factor in the early travels of the West toward the rest of the world, location, winds (for ships), weights and measures, currency – and their equivalents in European measures – were appended to most travel narratives of the period. Thus English writings on India by John Ovington, Thomas Herbert, John Fryer (all 17th century) list Indian units of distance, currency, and weighing units with their English equivalents so that future travellers and traders might be able to navigate through India better. By the 19th century, with the imperial structure established in colonies, the administration felt it necessary to map boundaries (of their empire but also within it), organize taxation based on land and produce and systematize people. This resulted in land surveys of which one of the largest was the Great Trigonometrical Survey of India, starting in the 1780s (Edney 1997). (On the imperial 'survey' mode, see Cohn 1997). Population statistics were compiled, even as land use, produce and profit were computed for tax purposes. People were also ranked in terms of caste or official hierarchy. In schools mathematics curricula were also instruments of cultural control and transmission, with examples in sums coming from cricket or distances being computed in miles (Bishop 1990). Local modes of computing intimately connected to the local cultures and environment were ignored in favour of 'Western' mathematical processes. Rationality, objectism (seeing the world as a set of discrete objects) and the importance given to economic worth characteristic of Western maths were often at odds with local ways of dealing with abstract issues of 'value', 'reality' or relationships which could be read in spiritual, moral or quasi-religious terms and symbols. Western symbols also replaced local ones, thus leading to the hegemony of these symbols, along with their attached mathematical processes, as 'universal'. Contemporary studies have shown us how counting and economics have existed in the Arab, South American and Asian contexts since antiquity. These may not have the same focus – for instance, the emphasis in Western maths or science on application (Bishop) – but nevertheless constitute ways of knowing and measuring the world.

***assimilado*:**   A term and concept specific to Portuguese colonies in Africa, it is also a unique one in the sense that it indicates a colonial policy that consciously determined to make the colonized subject assimilate into the European country/culture. Initiated into legal processes around the early decades of the 20th century, this project, under the auspices of the Portuguese government's Department of Native Affairs, aimed to classify native/colonized people into those who were supposedly 'advanced' on the European civilizational scale and could be 'assimilated' into European culture, and those who were not. The *assimilado* was one who had adopted Christianity, Portuguese language and culture. S/he was then deemed to be a role model for other colonized people to emulate. As in the case of the Eurasians in India (born of Englishmen and their Indian wives) in the 19th century, the *assimilado* was considered a valuable cog in the imperial machine. And, like the Eurasians in India, the *assimilados* were given government jobs, although full-scale political rights were never a reality. In the latter decades, however, the Portuguese made it more difficult to acquire this *assimilado* status (again, like the Eurasians in India who, after 1900, were treated as 'half-castes' and as emblems of the ruling class's shame, and so began to be excluded). The *assimilado* represents the formal colonial attempt to create cultural hybrids.

barbarian/barbaric: Originally from the Greek, the term meant 'those who did not speak Greek'. There is therefore a *linguistic* foundation to the term; other races, especially those with a different or 'alien language', are represented as barbarians. Often used interchangeably with 'savage', the term signifies any individual/group outside the bounds of civilization. The barbarian in English literary history took many forms. Stories of wild men who lived in forests and on the peripheries of the world, people without 'culture', cannibals and others whose norms of behaviour did not fit Western/European views of society were called barbarians. John Mandeville's travelogue from the 14th century spoke of monsters. Montesquieu's 'Of Cannibals' (1580) crafted a lasting stereotype of the wild man as the cannibal (Hulme 1992). Shakespeare's Caliban in *The Tempest* was a savage. Spenser's Saracens were barbarians mostly interested in wealth (Souldon in *The Faerie Queene*, 1590, 1596, for example). People from Barbary (North Africa) were also called barbarians. In later European literature the Native American was either a primitive savage given to cannibalism and horrific cruelties (which is manifest in English writings in the 1780s period, during and after the American War of Independence). Gothic novels from Charlotte Smith (*The Old Manor House*, 1793) and others fictionalized the cruelties of the Native Americans against British soldiers. Captivity narratives (of Europeans at the hands of Native Americans) reinforced the stereotypes. The barbarian in colonial discourse occupied the lower end of the evolutionary scale. Those who didn't cook their food, or did not possess writing, were deemed to be barbarians in anthropological works by Claude Lévi-Strauss and others. But a different image of the barbarian/savage was also

The Postcolonial Studies Dictionary, First Edition. Pramod K. Nayar.
© 2015 John Wiley & Sons, Ltd. Published 2015 by John Wiley & Sons, Ltd.

inaugurated in Rousseau and later writers in the form of the 'Noble Savage'. This was the image of the savage who had a kernel of the human within. The black was also a barbarian, but one who still held the potential to be civilized according to the European Enlightenment's humanitarian project across the colonies. Hence numerous poems about slavery in Hannah More ('The Sorrows of Yamba'), Robert Southey ('Madoc'; 'The Dirge of the American Widow' and the sonnets on slavery), as well as the abolitionist tracts of William Wilberforce, portrayed the black and the Native American as possessing the same human and humane qualities of Europeans, in terms of melancholy, familial affections and others. In Hayden White's analysis (1972), the wild man who once occupied the peripheries of the globe disappears because the peripheries were, by the end of the 19th century, explored and mapped. The wild man therefore becomes internalized in the writings of Freud and Jung who posit the 'wild savage' in all humans. For postcolonial writers and critics the barbarian was a stereotype that enabled the European to define themselves. The barbarian was non- or pre-modern, primitive and savage in contrast with the European who was modern and civilized. In postcolonial writings the figure of the barbarian is deployed to great effect by J.M. Coetzee in *Waiting for the Barbarians* (1980). Here the white imperialists raid the indigenous settlements, torturing and killing the so-called barbaric natives. The Magistrate who begins to worry about the ethics of imperial domination is himself tortured by his countrymen for supporting the barbarians. When the novel ends, the imperialist forces have fled, although there is no sign that the barbarians are invading. Coetzee's powerful novel inverts the European symbol of the barbarian by showing how the entire story of cruel barbarians out to decimate the whites becomes a useful myth to enforce violent measures upon the natives and revealing how the whites are the true barbarians. The savagery in the novel is all 'performed' by the whites, and thus overturns the stereotype of the savage, ungovernable native.

Black Atlantic: The term originates in the influential work of Paul Gilroy in his book of this title (1992), although the construction of European consciousness around the black presence dating back to the 18th century had been already studied by David Dabydeen in his *Hogarth's Blacks* (1985). For Gilroy ethnic and national identities were reworked through travel and exchange. He argues that the black intellectuals of the 19th and early 20th centuries learnt from their travels in and engagements with European cultures and traditions of thought. Using the image of the sailing ship – which is also a reminder of the slaving voyages – Gilroy proposes that transculturation is what constituted black identity. But Gilroy is also emphatic that European consciousness was hybridized due to its exposure to African cultures. While Gilroy accepts that fear, suffering and terror is at the heart of the African experience (due to slavery), he acknowledges that it also produced a 'double consciousness', for it gave the slave both suffering and the possibility of emancipation (here Gilroy is reading the work of Frederick Douglass). Gilroy thus rejects any argument about national or racial purity, seeing cultural identity as the effect of travels, traversals, contests and conflicts. For Gilroy black culture was not simply the periphery to the European centre (a traditional reading that argued for the binary centre-margin structure of the Europe/non-Europe relationship). Instead, Gilroy proposes, European modernity was dependent upon Europe's cultural exposure to new cultural forms and practices, such as black music. Similarly, for the blacks, European ideas of emancipation ensured that the rise of an intellectual tradition was not bound up only with suffering or exploitation. Both European and black cultures in Gilroy's analysis are transnational in origin, and neither has any cultural purity. In terms of influence, Gilroy's theories reject the emphasis on cultural purity and absolutism and are more in tune with postcolonial views (Bhabha 1992; Gandhi 2006; Young 1995, 2001) of hybridity and cosmopolitanism. What Gilroy's work also demonstrates is the reciprocity of cultural exchanges even when across politically unequal races. In the travelogues of Caryl Phillips (*The Atlantic Sound*, 2001) we see the Black Atlantic manifest as a literary theme. Phillips travels from St. Kitts to Britain and finally to the USA to replicate the 'triangle' of slave voyages. Like Gilroy and Phillips, Saidiya Hartman's *Lose Your Mother* (2007) seeks to study shared cultural memories, on either side of the Atlantic. Hartman's work tracks her family's ancestry, and the larger trade and slave routes through which slaves from Ghana made their way to the coast prior to embarking on the Middle Passage. Hartman notes (thus complicating Gilroy's arguments about a 'black Atlantic') that people in Ghana did not wish to remember the slave practices – dungeons, the identity of trading families, collusion with the whites, etc. – and so practised a cultural amnesia. Here, Hartman discovers, Ghanian identity consists of *not* recognizing the victims and perpetrators of the Middle Passage. If the USA and UK are cultures 'made' through the cultural exchanges effected through the slave trade then, Hartman demonstrates, contemporary African culture is simultaneously constituted through the memories, scars, absences and identities of the slave-past. Gilroy's Black Atlantic also becomes multi-layered when somebody like Hartman, based in the USA, a cosmopolitan and 'First Worlder' now, seeks a 'memory citizenship' with Ghana. Like Gilroy, and despite her failure to find a full citizenship in the memory archives of Ghana, Hartman offers a cosmopolitanization of atrocity memory (Nayar 2013).

black consciousness: During the course of the 19th century in the USA African American intellectuals, notably Booker T. Washington, Frederick Douglass and Marcus Garvey (who declared: 'Africa for the Africans'), called for a return to African cultural practices. They argued that the white man's culture had combined with slavery to cause the African American to not only forget his African roots but also to feel contemptuous of them. Even the benevolent paternalism of the whites, they argued, ran the risk of marginalizing the African and black roots of the identity of African Americans. Retrieving African folk culture, story-telling forms, philosophies, and music among diasporic Africans in the Caribbean and the USA, they believed, would demonstrate the uniqueness of African culture, reverse the alienation of the blacks from their own culture, bring together blacks of different origins and lead to a sense of pride in being black. A 'back to Africa' move was mooted where some thinkers advocated a physical relocation to their nation/land and culture of origin while others saw it as a return to African ways of thinking and living, one that would give the descendants of slaves in America a sense of their history. The Harlem Renaissance drew upon this movement, and philosophers like Alain Locke were instrumental in raising their voice for 'black pride'. In Africa itself the black consciousness movement was integral to the anti-apartheid struggles. It emerges in the writings of Frantz Fanon, Leopold Senghor and later Steve Biko and others in the anti-colonial struggle, as they sought to retrieve a sense of their culture among colonized Africans in Africa. Biko has been credited with actually using the term 'black consciousness' and for coining the slogan 'black is beautiful'. The term may also be aligned with the Pan-Africanist movement he initiated. Black consciousness sought to use available African myths to rediscover its heritage – remnants of this campaign might be seen in the plays of Wole Soyinka in which African spirits and folk demons are characters. The poetry of James Matthews during the height of the anti-apartheid struggle exhorted Africans to prepare for war, demand their rights and be proud of being black. Besides Matthews, Don Mattera, Sipho Sepamla and others wrote and sang of the degradation of the African's life in apartheid and called out to their fellow blacks to 'quit stuttering and shuffling' (Mandlenkosi Langa, 'Banned for Blackness'). Black consciousness campaigns have served as useful models for ethnicity studies (Stuart Hall) and studies of modernity's complicated history (Paul Gilroy). Philosophical writings and cultural studies have also found their intellectual antecedents in the black consciousness movement. Black consciousness in academia has now enlarged its scope to include aboriginals and ethnic groups whose histories of exploited cultures bring them together as 'people of colour'. Kwame Anthony Appiah (1992) has suggested that a certain Pan-Africanism that allows African Americans, Afro-Caribbeans, and Afro-Latins to align with continental Africans and thus find cultural resources from either side of the Black Atlantic could become an international project and prevent what he thinks of as a self-isolating black nationalism in any of these regions.

cannibal: The term, and stereotype, enters the racialized vocabulary of Europe with stories of a species of man-eating humans in the 14th-century writings of John Mandeville and later Christopher Columbus. Mandeville's fictitious travelogue listed the cannibals as one of the many strange and grotesque species of humanity and monsters he supposedly encountered. Like monsters that were traditionally said to occupy the peripheries of the known world, i.e., Europe, cannibals were originally associated (Hulme 1992) with the Caribbean islands (or Caribs as they were known). Cannibalism in European discourses of travel and literature such as Montaigne's 16th-century essay 'On Cannibals' served as the single most dominant marker of all things primitive and pagan. Cannibalism apparently was the polar opposite of European civilization, and the real experiences of James Cook in the South Seas where he encountered cannibals added to the cultural hierarchy of 'savage' and 'modern'. Cannibalism marks, as Maggie Kilgour's 1990 study tellingly argues, the division between 'inside' and the 'outside' through the notion of incorporation. Cannibalism was therefore the marker of cultural boundaries (as we can see in the essays collected in Kristen Guest's volume, 2001). As a transgression of the ultimate taboo the trope of cannibalism in European literature served a crucial purpose: of dismissing not just Caribbean but also African and even Asian cultures as primitive and savage. Thus cannibalism served the colonial discourses of cultural hierarchies very effectively. It also served as a justification for, first, racial oppression and second, the civilizational mission (the French termed it 'mission civilisatrice') whereby the Europeans felt compelled to 'uplift' the savages from their

The Postcolonial Studies Dictionary, First Edition. Pramod K. Nayar. ·
© 2015 John Wiley & Sons, Ltd. Published 2015 by John Wiley & Sons, Ltd.

mire of superstition and evil practices. This project or mission of course involved the destruction of the subjects' cultures. Postcolonial readings (in collections like Barker et al.'s *Cannibalism and the Colonial World*, 1998) of cannibalism in European texts therefore see the entire trope as a part of colonial discourses about the European Other that facilitated racial control and cultural conquests based on very thin evidence about actual practices of cannibalism. Shakespeare's 'Caliban', critics propose, serves as an anagrammatic reminder of 'cannibal', and is, expectedly, a savage. In his classic work of colonial enterprise and European conquest, *Robinson Crusoe*, Daniel Defoe's eponymous protagonist is worried that the island he is marooned on is populated by cannibals. Crusoe witnesses cannibals in action and rescues Friday from certain death. Friday, if he was ever a cannibal, does not demonstrate a taste or craving for human flesh. In the postcolonial era J.M. Coetzee's *Foe* rewrites the Crusoe story and has its female castaway, Susan Barton, ponder over Friday's food preferences (although she discovers that he has been violated irreversibly – his tongue has been cut out) as well. Even today the obsession with what foreigners eat – with denunciation of races and cultures that eat creatures and foods deemed unacceptable by some other cultures – extends, Maggie Kilgour has argued, the colonial era's interest in using food habits as cultural markers of 'insiders' and 'outsiders'.

captivity narratives: These have a long history in English and European writing. The capture, forced conversion to Islam and slavery of American and British soldiers/sailors by Barbary pirates was an important theme from the 17th century. Captivity writings by Abraham Browne (1655), Robert Knox (in Sri Lanka, 1659–1678), Mary Rowlandson (by Native Americans, 1682), John Foss (1798), William Ray (1808), Maria Martin (1809), Eliza Fraser (in Australia, several versions published by her in the 1830s) and several others were hugely popular through the 19th century. These narratives focused on the trial of Christian faith in adverse circumstances, redemption through this faith, white slavery and the cruelty of the non-European Other. Stereotypes of cannibalism and savagery abound. Later editions embellished these narratives, adding layers to the theme of savagery (both intra-tribe as well as that directed toward the European captives) and primitivism. But also underwriting the woman's captivity narrative – Rowlandson, Fraser – was the implicit anxiety over **miscegenation**. As Kay Schaffer has noted, such narratives contributed to the colonial discourse of racial difference when they portrayed the 'engagement between the innocent, saintly, white female victim and her encounter with a savage "otherness" at the margins of the British Empire' (2001: 363). From India, accounts of white women besieged during the 'Mutiny' of 1857 contributed similarly to the anxiety over miscegenation, English femininity and racial purity (Sharpe 1993). More recent work by Linda Colley (2010) treats captivity narratives from the British Empire as revealing another, more human, side to imperial expansion where soldiers and sailors imprisoned and tortured demonstrate the vulnerability of the island nation.

Carib: One of the two groups of people central to European constructions and encounters with the Caribbean Islands since the age of Columbus, the Caribs were always seen in contrast with the pastoral Arawaks. Representations of the Caribs, as Peter Hulme has shown in his study (1992), encompass many of the stereotypes of the colonized, native or non-European. The discourse divided the local inhabitants into the fierce, barbaric cannibal Carib and the Arawaks, who conformed to the ideal of the 'noble savage'. European representations focused on the fierceness of Caribs – their propensity for violence, stealing, for instance – right from the 15th-century narratives. But, as Hulme notes, the Caribs were also the people who defended their territory and culture against the Spanish – unlike the Arawaks who simply could not resist the European invaders. The natives who were willing to accept the Europeans were quickly, in supposedly ethnographic studies, labelled Arawaks and those who did not were classified as Caribs. Thus the representations had something to do with the nature of the European-native encounter as well. Associating 'Carib' with 'cannibal' in an absurd semantic shift, the Europeans painted the Caribs as the real problem of the Islands, as intruders, invaders and those who did not belong there (whereas the relatively quiescent Arawaks did, in European rhetoric). The Europeans could then take it upon themselves to protect the mild Arawaks from the fierce Caribs, and thus play out the key role of benevolent protectors. Later, scientific, religious, ethnographic, lexicographic – once the meaning of Carib is defined as 'cannibal', then the Carib is a cannibal, by circularity of definition – and other discourses were invoked in order to demonstrate the 'true' nature of the Caribs. Hulme's study of colonial discourse shows how linguistic and anthropological categories, such as the Carib, operate within political subtexts of imperialism.

cartography: For postcolonial studies maps have held particular significance as instruments of colonial control, of spatial organization of their homelands, and as symbols of divisive forces. Maps in postcolonial studies (Rabasa 1999, Edney 1997) are seen therefore as representing not only colonialism's epistemological conquest of the lands but also as artefacts that are iconic of appropriation and political control. Early Modern maps were organized around a **centre-margins** form, with Europe occupying the centre and with the rest of the world arranged at the periphery. Explorers and voyagers predicated their quest for new lands, routes and civilizations on maps, and this mapping of the world led to the European '**discovery**' of the New World and Asia. Maps therefore were inspirational texts, even when inaccurate or completely erroneous, because they textually organized the world into the 'known' and the 'unknown', calling upon the Europeans to explore the unknown. The measurement of the world necessary for map-making relied upon European models of geography and mathematics – with latitudes, longitudes and navigational aids. Maps subsequently produced gave European names to newly 'discovered' places, and thereby established European textual, epistemic and material control over these spaces. Such acts of naming ignored the local inhabitants' names for their places. In fact the maps were constructed based on the assumption that the newly 'discovered' lands were 'empty'. This was particularly the case with Australia and Canada where the presence of local people and cultures was completely ignored in favour of a discourse of *terra nullius*, from the Latin 'land belonging to no one' and translated as 'empty lands', although the entire discourse of 'empty lands' (without the specific term) dates back to the European interpretations of the *New World* (the Americas) from the 17th century. European settlers, notes Lawrence Buell about North America, saw the land as 'primordial' or empty (and their descendants saw it as 'wilderness', he notes!) whereas humans had arrived 'millennia before', just as nonhumans had existed as 'somebodies' on that continent before the Europeans (Buell 2005: 67). Buell is pointing to the spatial imagination of the Europeans. Maps marking these spaces as empty were therefore presented to the European public as ready for settlement by Europeans (native settlements, being primitive, could easily be dismantled and destroyed). Map-making was professionalized in England with institutions like the Royal Geographical Society. Maps were also used by the 19th century to construct models of civilization, climates and disease. Maps were maps of difference, of the colony from Europe in numerous domains, from disease and climate to culture and people. James Rennell, who would go on to become the architect of the Great Trigonometrical Survey of India in the 18th century, compared African topography to the 'skin of a leopard', and thus exoticized Africa as a wild space. Travellers like Francis Buchanan,

Mungo Park and James Cook enabled the making and redrawing of maps by sending in updated information from their expeditions. Maps were also part of the 'survey modality' (Cohn 1997) of colonialism, pinpointing places, people and events. Maps were totalizing projects, combining with their scheme, topographies, routes, people and resources, all made available at a single glance. Zoological, ethnographic, archaeological, botanical and mineralogical surveys of lands were conducted in most of the colonies across Asia and Africa. Archaeological surveys determined which monuments (in the colonies) were significant and therefore needed to be preserved – maps here therefore determined the history of the local culture by creating a hierarchy of artefacts and symbols. Later, regions like the Indian continent were divided into nations by maps drawn by Europeans. The map in Rider Haggard's adventure fiction (*King Solomon's Mines*, 1885; *She*, 1887) set in Africa, usually represented in the opening pages, was a key device: it mapped Africa as a woman (to be seduced, conquered) but also as a space of wealth (hidden, but there for the Europeans to lay claim to). For the European readers, the maps of the colonies marked a visual schema of the progress of their empire, the expanse of territory and the demographics of the conquered peoples. Creighton Sahib in Rudyard Kipling's *Kim* is a Director of the Survey of India (an institution set up in the 19th century to map the subcontinent), but works essentially as a spy to thwart the Russians at the 'Great Game' – the battle for the Himalayan regions – and Kim is drawn into the Game. Kim of course repairs the map as well in what works as a symbol of imperial reorganization of the colony. For postcolonial authors Amitav Ghosh (*The Shadow Lines*, 1988) and Kamila Shamsie (*Kartography*, 2002) maps are expressions of collective and cultural memories of horrific events like the Partition of the Indian subcontinent, communal violence and civil war (Mallot 2007).

catachresis: A term in classical rhetoric where a word or figure of speech has been inappropriately used, or whose meaning has been stretched to make a new figure. A common example in idiomatic expression would be 'winter of discontent' where the descriptor of a season, or weather, is extended to imply an emotional state. The season and the emotion really have nothing to do with each other. In the school of criticism called Deconstruction the term was used to indicate how the 'original' word remained incomplete and had to be placed in new contexts. The postcolonial theorist Gayatri Spivak (1990) used the term to indicate words that supposedly describe large groups of people but where examples of these people cannot be found. Generic names and descriptors like 'the worker' or the 'brown woman' are examples of this usage, what Spivak terms 'master words'. They are oppressive terms that idealize types although we cannot find examples of the 'true' worker or brown woman. For Spivak catachresis is a value-coding process where, using types such as the above, entire groups of people are brought into a category, mobilized and classified. Thus, once the term 'worker' or 'woman' is used there is no need to seek individual examples. All individuals are assumed to approximate the features, behaviour and qualities of '*the* worker' or '*the* woman'. Catachresis, in this reading, is the imposition of a typology, an identity and functions to homogenize people irrespective of their key or distinctive features.

citizenship (cultural):   A concept popularized in the writings of Toby Miller (2001, 2008), cultural citizenship refers to the building of solidarities and the conservation of cultural ties and lineages through activities and practices like education, festivals and religion. Cultural citizenship is non-formal and beyond the rules and domains of political and administrative control, and is therefore distinctive from political citizenship (which concerns voting rights) and economic citizenship (which concerns employment and social benefits) that emanate from government regulations. In the postcolonial context cultural citizenship marks diasporic and migrant communities in the First World. Faced with new contexts and cultural practices communities seek to preserve their cultural traditions. As historians and cultural commentators (Lal 2003) have demonstrated, migrant communities displaced from their countries of origin tend to adhere more closely to their original cultural practices. Such a cultural citizenship might therefore be seen as a response to increasing globalization and migration where communities and individuals encounter sustained displacement and new neighbours and cultures. Cultural citizenship among migrants, exemplified in novels such as Monica Ali's 2001 novel *Brick Lane* (set in Spitalfields, London) involves the belonging and bonding forged through everyday, routine and commonplace sharing of music, sports, fashion and food. Ali's account of the various foods on display, the clothes on clotheslines, the call centres, shows how a Bangladeshi community tries to recreate an aura of home in racist London. These contexts of cultural citizenship establish the bases of belonging, especially for newcomers to the area, but also for long-term residents who constantly live in the past. Ali uses the term 'artificial biradri' ('biradri': family or brotherhood) to signify the sense of belonging through shared cultural practices among the Bangladeshi migrants of the area, and this might be seen as a synonym for cultural citizenship.

citizenship (ecological):   Articulated as a distinct category by philosopher Andrew Dobson (2000, 2003), ecological citizenship (not the same as environmental citizenship, which draws upon existing traditions of liberal rights-based citizenship) coheres around the theme of ecological footprints – essentially a mode of measuring the human demand on natural resources, the amount of natural resources any human population in a particular area/nation consumes in order to survive. It examines the ecological footprints that individuals, communities and nations leave. Dobson argues that ecological citizenship, unlike any other form of citizenship that is linked to nation-states and geopolitical borders, is non-territorial. Further, the responsibility to leave sustainable (as opposed to unsustainable and therefore damaging) ecological footprints will always be asymmetrical and non-reciprocal because the ecological footprints of some countries/ cultures will adversely affect other nations. Ecological citizenship works at the level of the everyday: how we lead our daily lives determines the kind and extent of ecological footprint we leave behind us. Dobson sees the primary duty of ecological citizenship as the obligation to ensure sustainable ecological footprints and an equitable distribution of ecological space. Later writers have appropriated Dobson's ideas to establish connections between global/cosmopolitan citizenship and ecological citizenship (Sáiz 2005).

census: In technical terms a means of measuring population, the census has a specific role and purpose in colonial history. Colonial administrators used the census in order to prepare racial and ethnic profiles of their colonized subjects. The census has been seen by scholars such as Bernard Cohn (1997) as a colonial device. The subjects were organized according to economic status, education, size of families, religious affiliation, territorial location, etc. The census reduced the complexity and diversity of the colony into statistics and maps, into understandable, at-a-glance and manageable data. It comprehensively mapped the population into convenient segments based on 'reliable' categories which acquired the sheen of scientific truths. Measuring heads, ankles and limbs in some cases, quantifying income in others, the census represents the colonial power's arithmetical imperative of reducing uncontrollable vastness into governable numbers, charts and maps. Ostensibly directed at better governance – where the colonial master 'knows' his subjects well – the census also functioned as a surveillance mechanism. Specific tribes and communities in India, for instance, were identified and branded as criminal tribes (a tag that existed into the mid-20th-century post-Independence India). Legislation and surveillance mechanisms were instituted to 'check' these tribes.

centre and margin: The terms represent a traditional model of empire where Europe represented the centre and the colony, the margins. Colonial discourse drew upon a medieval cartography of the earth wherein monsters inhabited the regions outside the borders of the known world (Cohen 1996, Campbell 1996). Civilization, development, Enlightenment, progress, modernity and 'culture' were the characteristic and prerogative of those who resided at the centre. Primitivism, savagery and pre-modern lives marked the beings or creatures who occupied the margins. Colonialism built on this model and stereotyped the so-called margins of the known world as the uncivilized colony. In effect the centre-margin model was a hierarchy of cultures and civilizations in the European discourse about non-European spaces. Yet, these margins and peripheral regions were also places of conquest, desire and adventure as the European sought to explore new sea routes, islands and continents. Going beyond known frontiers was a mark of the European character, from Mandeville to contemporary science fiction. The centre-margin model fixed the races and cultures in unchanging, constant **essentialisms**. This mode of reading the colonial discourse (exemplified by Edward Said's *Orientalism*) tended to see only one model of imperial relations, built on a **Manichean allegory**. However, with new developments in postcolonial studies we have learnt to read the cultural expressions of the colonial period as complicating the centre-margin model, and that Manicheanism was not the defining characteristic of the Empires. From Massinger, Marlowe, Shakespeare and Dryden in the Early Modern period to Wilkie Collins and Arthur Conan Doyle in the late 19th and early 20th centuries writers from the centre have documented the arrival of goods, people and ideas from these so-called uncivilized peripheries. Thus Alexander Pope in *The Rape of the Lock* (1712) wrote of the 'unnumber'd treasures ope at once, and here,/the various off'rings of the world appear' (1963: 227–230). Spices, cotton, china, tea, religious views, paintings, shawls, 'curios', animal heads, tribal artefacts, jewels from the Orient or the South Sea islands (the periphery to the central: London) were objects of conspicuous consumption (Jardine 1996, Thomas 1994) and brought the colony, in the form of its produce, into English homes. Sailors, lascars, acrobats, painters, ayahs and soldiers from the colonies were common sights in the English metropolis since the 17th century (Fisher 2006; Vizram 1986, 2002), and Indian travellers, from statesmen to philosophers and princes, visited England for extended periods from the early years of the 19th century, and were spectacles in Oxford, London and other places (Banerjee 2010, Nayar 2012 'Beyond the Colonial Subject'). Industrial exhibitions such as that of 1877 provided the English public with glimpses of the colony. There was, in the 19th century, the colony at the heart of the imperial metropolis (Catherine Hall 2002; Burton 1998). When Collins in *The Moonstone* (1868) wrote of the 'moonstone' from India: 'here was our quiet English house suddenly invaded by a devilish Indian diamond – bringing after it a conspiracy of living rogues, set loose on us by the vengeance of a dead man' (36–7), the rhetoric suggests that the centre-margins model was not entirely valid since there were considerable exchanges and transactions between the two. Another process through which the dichotomy was (unwittingly) collapsed was the nativization of Europeans. Englishmen who, through the 19th century, took to native ways of dress and eating, and even married native women, displaced the cultural and racial hierarchies through such acts. The intellectual affiliations of A.O. Hume, spiritualists such as Madame Blavatsky and reformers like Annie Besant with Indians through the 19th century also disrupted the traditional racial models of uncivilized native/civilized European (Gandhi 2006).

chutneyfication:　A term popularized by Salman Rushdie in *Midnight's Children* (1981) to describe the indigenization and transformation of the English language and history, the term has a culinary root. 'Chutney' is a common Indian side dish, tangy, and essential to the flavour of the main meal. Rushdie's appropriation of the dish to describe the postcolonial speaker's use of English adds a degree of complexity to the question of language use itself. Rushdie suggests that it is the indigenization that really adds the tangy, acerbic taste to the former colonial language. It implies mixing, spicing-up, and a whole new stylization, where the side dish, standing as a kind of adjunct, becomes central to the full savouring of the main dish. In more political terms 'chutneyfication' implies a resistance to the hegemonic nature and dominance of the former colonial master's language, a nativization and therefore agency, and finally a hybridization. It indicates that new forms of the English language emerge not within England but within the former colonies. Rushdie, like other later writers, wished to write in an English closer to the way it was spoken by Indians and the postcolonial nation, not bound by the grammar, syntax or diction of England. Chutneyfication achieves what some critics consider cultural transcoding especially when appropriated, in postcolonial contexts, for political protests and social campaigns (Nayar 2011), using a dominant and elite language, imbuing it with vernacular, native and local meanings and codes to generate a certain cosmopolitan concern: human rights and women's rights. However, other postcolonial critics, such as Harish Trivedi (1991, 2011) have noted that the 'chutney' constitutes an 'optional extra' at a meal, just a 'relish', but with very little nutrition or sustenance (2011). Therefore, chutneyfication is only an exoticization, like the dish, of a new brand of English (Hinglish – Hindiized English) used by authors like Rushdie to cater to Western readers (for a critique see the collection by Kothari and Snell 2011). Scholars of regional literatures of the subcontinent, such as Francesca Orsini (2002, 2009), have noted that the influence and impact of English is not a recent phenomenon, and indeed even the Hindi public sphere and its popular cultures (say, popular novels) modified itself. New forms of writing, registers of language and attempts at standardization emerged as early as the 19th century in the 'Hindi public sphere'. The impact of English (and other European languages, but predominantly English) on native language cultures has produced a fair amount of anxiety over the loss, and death, of these other cultures – a process often called 'linguistic imperialism' (Phillipson 1992), a subset of cultural imperialism. (See also: **vernacular**)

colony/colonialism: The term 'colony' originates from the Latin 'colonye', meaning 'to cultivate', and referred to the Roman Empire that colonized large parts of the world including Europe and England. The Greek term for 'colony' described 'settlement'. Thus various parts of England were 'colonies' or outposts of the Roman Empire. In the 16th century Richard Hakluyt used the term 'plantation' to describe the settlement – botanical and human – in the 'New World' ('A Discourse on Western Planting'). An important insight into this semantics of settlement, colony and cultivation comes from Andro Linklater (2014) who argues that it is the individual ownership of land that is at the heart of colonization (ironically, the Aborigines in Australia and Canada, and the Native Americans in the Americas did own their land, and had done so for generations, but not in the eyes of the Europeans, who saw the lands as **terra nullius** and **terra incognita**!). 'Colonialism' in postcolonial studies is used primarily to describe the European conquest, settlement and systematic administrative control (by which we mean institutional structures of governance, legal apparatuses and military dominance) over territories in Asia, Africa, South America, Canada and Australia (Ireland and America were also England's colonies). The term has been associated primarily with *European* empires of the 19th century although there have been empires for centuries before that of Europeans, most created through the desire for wealth, resources and religious expansion. The Roman, Assyrian, Babylonian, Ottoman, Chinese, Japanese and Russian empires are a few of these (Burbank and Cooper 2010). Colonial empires, such as England's or Europe's in the 19th century, were based on actual physical settlement by the English. Colonization itself was, very often, a violent process of subduing the indigenous and native populations before the setting up of administrative, military and economic structures to retain this dominance. Colonialism had very strong economic bases: the colony provided the raw material and labour for English manufacturing industries, the market for its goods, the clerks and soldiers for its administration and army. It was also founded on a clear racial binary: the advanced, progressive and modern European ('Us') versus the backward, primitive and non-modern native ('them'). This us/ them binary, according to postcolonial studies, indicates how Europe needed its non-European Other for its own sense of identity. For literary, historical and cultural studies, colonialism comes in for attention particularly for its cultural impact. Colonialism brought with it its own practices – religion, education, language – that were, slowly or violently, imposed upon the subject races of the colony. This was accompanied by an erasure of native histories and a condemnation of native beliefs and practices (such as religion) as primitive. Colonialism also demanded a careful construction, within discourses, of not only the racial binary but also the rationale for the continued presence of the colonial: the improvement of the native. Colonialism's cultural role involved the acquisition and codification of knowledge of the native in disciplines like anthropology, archaeology, literature and others. Postcolonial literature has examined various features of colonial rule, just as postcolonial critics have unravelled the multiple layers of colonial discourses, in gender (McClintock 1995; Nussbaum 1995; Sinha 1995; Stoler 2002), history and anthropology (Cohn 1997; Metcalf 1989; Dirks 2003; Bayly 1999), literature (Leask 1993; 2002), law (Singha 1998), and medicine (Arnold 1993; Harrison 1999). In Chinua Achebe's fiction and Wole Soyinka's plays (*Death and the King's Horseman*) we see the exploration of the cultural impact of colonialism: the native loses his territory, language, religion, belief systems. In Tsitsi Dangarembga's *Nervous Conditions* (1988) a school girl finds colonial history's representation of her community difficult to digest (literally). Mudrooroo points out the contradictions in colonial history where the benevolent colonial master began his career in violence. In Derek Walcott ('A Far Cry from Africa'), Salman Rushdie (*Midnight's Children*, 1981), and V.S. Naipaul (*A House for Mr Biswas* 1961, *The Mimic Men* 1967) we see colonialism's legacy of hybridized natives. In most of these authors the violence of colonial history is a constant theme. The study of colonialism, since the 1990s, has extended to the study of newer forms and manifestations of the Empire. (See also: **Empire – new figurations of, e-Empire, neocolonialism, *terra incognita*, *terra nullius*)**

colonial discourse: The term comes into prominence in the 1980s with postcolonial studies paying attention to the modes of representation in European, colonial writings (across genres, from biomedical reports to fiction, administrative tracts to travelogues) and arts. 'Discourse' in poststructuralist theory refers to the conditions – political, social, administrative and linguistic – that enable certain kinds of things to be said. It describes the hierarchies of power in which certain figures – doctors, police, kings, administrators – determine what may be articulated and what will be silenced. Colonial discourse, as first examined in detail by Edward Said in *Orientalism* (1978), is the study of European representations of non-European cultures and peoples. It posits a power relation wherein the colonial power had the authority to represent (put into narrative, into language) and make pronouncements about its colonized subjects without always seeking authenticity or validation. Colonial discourse validates itself and thus, in the absence of any contest (from the native) about its claims or propositions, establishes itself as the 'truth' about the colonized subjects. Colonial discourse may thus be defined as a set of European representations of the colonial power's subjects that enables the political, economic, cultural and social practices of racialized power relations between colonizer and colonized peoples. Colonial discourse in the numerous studies that followed that of Said is seen as offering particular kinds of images of the non-European: as savage, effeminate, primitive, vulnerable, child-like, superstitious, illiterate, apolitical, etc. It represented the land as empty (*terra nullius*, in the case of Americas, Canada and Australia), savage (Africa), once-glorious-but-now-decadent (India). Such representations, in the manner of all discourse, circulated powerfully and became (i) the rationale and justification for colonial rule since, according to this unchallenged discourse, the natives are savages and incapable of ruling themselves;

and (ii) accepted by the natives as the true representation of themselves. This second was a very insidious means of imposing colonial rule because the discourse, once it was accepted by the subject, presented the colonial rule as necessary, benevolent and natural. Thus 'empty' Australia could be 'occupied' and 'settled' by the British, 'savage' Africa could be 'tamed' and 'decadent' India could be hauled back up the civilizational ladder, if the colonial discourse is to believed . A good instance of this power and reach of discourse is the Waitangi treaty that the British signed with the Maoris in 1840. In the British view the Maoris with this Treaty handed over all their legal rights to their lands, although, of course, the Maoris did not see it this way at all. When the British emphasized the sacrosanct nature of the written document – which the Maoris' culture did not privilege over the spoken word – they effectively rejected native beliefs in common ownership of the land in favour of the European belief in private property. Later the British could declare sovereignty over the Maori land based on this document itself. Another consequence of the discourse can be traced to the *self*-representation of the English – as heroic, just and fair – that they themselves imbibed and which enabled them to train their young men and women to become colonial rulers. The travel writings of Mungo Park, the explorer, offered the heroic-Englishman-battling-inimical-African-landscape image to the English youth. Baden-Powell's tracts on boy scouts offered the English schoolboy a role model as empire-builder. A major strand in postcolonial studies has been devoted to the unravelling of the political and social subtexts of discourse, arguing that such discourses have material effects because they are both manifestations of and the driving force behind the power structures of empires. Shakespeare's representations of the savage Caliban or of the hypersexed Cleopatra, Marlowe's of the tyrannical conqueror Tamburlaine, Defoe's of the speechless savage Friday, Brontë's of the Creole Bertha Mason, Conrad's of the animalesque Africans, are instances where the colonial discourse portrayed the native subject in particular ways by either ignoring other aspects of their culture or degrading these. Later studies, notably by Homi Bhabha, have pointed out that colonial discourse was not simply about the imposition of one point of view or idea. It was often **ambivalent** and uncertain, and reveals itself as divided in its opinions and views of the colony. Forster's ambivalence toward India, where he seems to fault the English for their arrogance (although he does caricature the Indian Godbole), is an example. Contemporary readings now detect this kind of ambivalence in English literature's subtle and hidden critiques of imperialism.

Commonwealth Literature: The descriptor derives from 'Commonwealth', or more accurately, the British Commonwealth, which includes former colonies of the British Empire. 'Commonwealth Literature' is the writings coming out of the former British colonies. This literature might be said to have become more popular with the founding of journals devoted to the area (*Journal of Commonwealth Literature*, 1965; *World Literature Today*, 1971; *Kunapipi*, 1975) and the 1964 Leeds Conference. The contribution of these developments cannot be overestimated, for they initiated what we now see as postcolonial studies: asking questions about the centrality of English literature to the newly independent nations, the dominance of English as a language, the necessity of addressing and examining nationalist thought and non-English/European literary texts and traditions, and the methodology of reading literature itself. 'Commonwealth Literature' addressed not only colonial legacies but also local concerns and anti-colonial, nation-building themes in literary texts. Writers of the pre-independence era were also classified under this heading or under 'world literature'. However, the tag 'Commonwealth' indicated the continuing political context of literature: the continued connection with the colonial past. From the 1980s it was argued that the term was inappropriate since the British polity or government had no hold over the formerly colonized and the power relation implied in the term no longer existed. That is, the label 'Commonwealth' was based on the shared political past of having been a colony. Further, as Salman Rushdie famously pointed out in 'Commonwealth Literature Does Not Exist' (1991), people and cultures from diverse backgrounds were forced into a ghettoized category called the 'Commonwealth'. Slowly the term postcolonial, more indicative of the socio-political reality (post-colonial, implying after the colonial), came to replace the term 'Commonwealth Literature'. 'Postcolonial' writing increasingly moved toward addressing problems of the newly independent states, the bicultural (native and European) legacies of these societies in Asia or Africa, the tensions of local identities and local legacies (of feudalism or tribal conflict), the establishment of a distinct native culture within the framework of new forms of government (democracy, socialism) and the constant engagement with the contemporary world system of neocolonialism. It is possible to see the shift from 'Commonwealth' to 'postcolonial' as the shift from mere anti-colonial sentiment, relatively binaristic identities ('us' versus the European 'them') and nation-building in the former to negotiating new social challenges, including the assertion of multiple and fragmented identities, fundamentalism seeking to return to older identities, and globalization in the latter. Its social and cultural contexts include, as Aijaz Ahmad noted (1992,

1997), the Vietnam War, the Algerian Revolution and the Civil Rights campaigns in the USA. We could add the Paris student strikes of 1968 to this list of events that called for probing the complicity of European and Anglophone/Francophone texts with unequal power structures, oppression and identities. Colonial and neocolonial texts concealed and furthered the cause of racialized relations and the Empire. It is in this intellectual engagement with literary and socio-political histories of Empire and Asia-Africa-South America that 'Commonwealth' literature becomes postcolonial literature. There is another dimension to the term emerging since the 1980s: while earlier it would indicate literatures of former colonies written in European languages the term 'postcolonial' now includes literatures written in native, i.e., non-European languages. Further, several of the authors in Gikuyu or Hindi would rather identify with 'Gikuyu literature' or 'Hindi literature' than with the label 'Commonwealth'. It is now taken to include American, national or regional literature (Australian, Canadian) but also aboriginal writings, and the ethnic literatures within First World nations. Local languages themselves had to negotiate with the arrival of the English language, the printing press and the literature (Orsini 2002, 2009).

comprador colonialism: The word 'comprador' is from the Portuguese, and means 'purchaser'. These were the middle-men, or brokers, who served as facilitators for the Europeans to trade in the colony. The natives who served as brokers, interpreters, slave traders (especially in Africa where the Africans of some tribes/groups sold others into slavery) or even business partners are seen, in contemporary studies (Ronald Robinson and the Cambridge School of historiography) as integral to the structure of Empire in a 'collaborative model' of imperialism. *Kim's* Hurree Chunder Mookherjee would be an instance of a kind of native that actively colluded with – for various reasons, including privileges or monetary gain – the English administration, and therefore a comprador. Tribal chieftains and kings who helped the Europeans find markets, raw materials or simply animals for the hunt were also, in a sense, central to the imperial machine. In the postcolonial writings of Arundhati Roy or Ken Saro-Wiwa native business houses and even the state in places like Africa or India are seen as compradors – helping MNCs and foreign interests acquire major stakes in natural resources, influencing financial policies, education and even defence. The postcolonial writers argue that the comprador class compromises the sovereignty of the country and extends the colonial exploitation of native lands and peoples through these business alliances that masquerade as free trade or foreign aid. Postcolonial studies also sees the influence of Western theory in postcolonial theorists as evidence of a cultural complicity with the Western/ former colonial rulers. This complicity severely compromises the project of intellectual decolonization of even postcolonial theory because it replicates the hierarchic relationship of colonialism, where all knowledge flowed from the West and the natives merely copied, assimilated or adapted it. Such a comprador class, postcolonial writers have argued, also sets the postcolonial writer apart from her/his native traditions and people. Frantz Fanon wrote of the native intellectual classes as being complicit with the colonial regime in the same way as the bourgeois class, since both, in the final instance, enabled the dominance (whether in business or in intellectual domains) of the European.

conquistador: Portuguese and Spanish term for 'conqueror', the conquistadors were the first explorers of the New World in their famous voyages of the 15th and 16th centuries. Several voyages were for trade routes to the East (Vasco da Gama's to India and Magellan's to the Philippines are two of the better known). Not all of the conquistadors were Spanish or Portuguese, however, and foreigners enlisting in the armies took on local names, of which the most famous is perhaps *Amerigo* Vespucci (Italian), who was an observer on several Portuguese voyages to South America. Some of the conquistadors, as professional warriors, became the subject of heroic tales. Hernan Cortés, who was responsible for the conquest of the Aztec Empire (completed when he took the capital Tenochtitlán in 1521), and Francisco Pizarro, who conquered the Incas (and is associated with the native woman, Malintzin or 'La Malinche' in one of the earliest cases of cultural and racial hybridity), were arguably the best known of the conquistadors. Many of the conquistadors also negotiated with their sponsoring monarchs to set up colonies and/or trading rights with the places they arrived at. From the very beginning the conquest included conversion to Christianity, sanctioned in the case of Spaniards by the papal bull from Pope Alexander VI.

contrapuntal reading: A formulation made famous by Edward Said (invoking a term from music), it is close to what Terry Eagleton treated as 'reading against the grain'. The critic's task, argued Eagleton and later Said, was to examine and bring to the surface the deeper meanings of a literary text, and show how these deeper meanings are actually complicit with exploitative structures like racism or colonialism. Literary texts are cultural texts, and contrapuntal readings uncover the contexts of cultural production, whether Empire or tourism or disease, that manifest in the form of literary symbols or tropes or themes. Contrapuntal reading is the process through which a text is treated as always already embedded in the prejudices, beliefs, myths and biases of its contextual culture. These might be hidden beneath literary representations or clever tropes. The critic needs to unravel these hidden beliefs and demonstrate how the texts were modes of enforcing racial, patriarchal, or class differences and hierarchies. Thus contrapuntal reading perceives literary texts as active devices in the making of colonial, racial, patriarchal or class hierarchies and consequent oppression or exploitation. When, for example, Said reads *Mansfield Park* contrapuntally in *Culture and Imperialism* (1993) he shows how Austen is linked not to the European Romance tradition or other literary texts but to colonial structures like England's Caribbean plantations with their racialized relations. Images of sickness in the writings of Shakespeare, James I and economists like Thomas Mun, demonstrates Jonathan Gil Harris in his contrapuntal readings in *Sick Economies* (2004), are actually codes for the anxiety of the foreigner-as-contagion. Alan Bewell (1999) discovers in his study of the English Romantic poets that, beneath the focus on the loveliness of English Nature and the countryside, there is a palpable anxiety over the tropical illnesses that have entered England. *Dracula*, show readers like Martin Willis (2007), Bollen and Ingelbein (2009), is a novel about the foreigner as racial/cultural Other, and as a foreigner about to invade *England*, although it is ostensibly about vampirism. Contrapuntal readings reveal cultural anxieties and affiliations, and often locate literary texts in social and political contexts of race, colonialism and Empire.

cosmopolitanism: Initiated as an idea by Immanuel Kant in the age of European Enlightenment, but dating back to the ancient Greeks, cosmopolitanism is at once a philosophical idea, an ideology, and a choice of lifestyle today. As a philosophical idea it proposes that there is a universal humanity, and humans can be citizens of the world through the sharing of moral codes, intellectual ideas and compassion. For postcolonial studies the concern with cosmopolitanism has been a more indirect one. In the European tradition, cosmopolitanism manifested as a form of universal humanitarianism, where the upper-class, elite European could assume upon himself (it was a gendered role) the task of being the benevolent protector of the distant Others, or colonial subjects, in the world. This translated into colonial interventionary projects. Interpreters of Victorian/colonial cosmopolitanism, such as Amanda Anderson (2001), John McBratney (2010), and Lauren Goodlad

(2010), have argued that the cosmopolitan attitude implied a certain 'reflective' distancing (Anderson) from both cultures, while in many cases it was responsible for a dual vision: outward at the Empire's boundaries (which they sought to extend) and inward at rural England (McBratney) – and thus was responsible for a globalization and for generating a geopolitical aesthetic (Goodlad). Philosophers see cosmopolitanism as central to ethics (Appiah 2006) and the question of hospitality toward strangers and foreigners (Derrida 2000, 2001). One approach to the study of cosmopolitanism comes from the diaspora studies of Robin Cohen, who sees in the new alliances and transnational engagements by, say, indentured labourers, forced migration and voluntary displacements the beginnings of cosmopolitan identity-making. Within postcolonial versions of cosmopolitanism, especially as they appear in literary texts, Neelam Srivastava (2008) identifies an 'imperial cosmopolitanism'. Here formerly colonized subjects wilfully and cheerfully surrender their identity in order to become more acceptable to and adapt to First World lives, cultures and identities. It is an assimilationist move, and one that is celebrated by several postcolonial writers like Rushdie, Bharati Mukherjee, and Neil Bissoondath, among others. This becomes, in Srivastava's reading of characters like Solanki in Rushdie's *Fury*, an extension of the colonial-era cosmopolitanism where the native subject, in order to survive, surrendered her/his cultural identity in exchange for a Westernized one. A second kind of postcolonial cosmopolitanism is discernible in Hanif Kureishi, Amitav Ghosh and Vikram Seth, according to Srivastava. This is a more 'responsible' (Srivastava's term) cosmopolitanism wherein the postcolonial, even when located in another nation-state, is deeply engaged with the problems and contexts of her/his native land and culture. Srivastava's reading here approximates to a form of vernacular cosmopolitanism (Pnina Werbner) and what Emily Johansen identifies as a 'territorialized cosmopolitanism' (2008), which is based in specific if dispersed places and where the cosmopolitan is ethically and morally committed to both the world at large and a local/specific place. Here an inclusivist worldview is not at the expense of a local commitment and, as Johansen argues using the fiction of Amitav Ghosh as an instance, a concern for the decaying democratic fabric and secular ideals of the 'home' country. It also entails a scrupulous evaluation of globalized projects and the local costs of such globalizing processes.

cosmopolitanism (vernacular):   A concept mooted by anthropologist Pnina Werbner (2006), vernacular cosmopolitanism has been defined as the coexistence of the local and the parochial alongside the transnational, translocal and the universalist. It is treated as a resistant strategy to the totalizing cosmopolitanism of the globalizing process where the author or cultural practitioner is able to wed universal aesthetics to local concerns and politics. It focuses on the nature of cultural interactions of peoples and communities as manifest in literary and other works to see how global arte-facts intersect with local conditions, products and ideologies. Thus in the fiction of Amitav Ghosh, commentators note (Luo 2013), we can see a 'rooted' cosmopolitanism or a more territorialized version of cosmopoli-tanism. Celebrity humanitarian projects mostly exhibit this variety of cos-mopolitanism, where the celebrity moves from local conditions, develops a discourse of local involvement (and a history of this involvement), utilizes her/his star status and joins global campaigns. However, such a vernacular cosmopolitanism often elides the very nature of global regimes that produced the suffering in local conditions that are now to be ameliorated by the celebrity and the global humanitarian project. Thus vernacular cosmopolitanism's dialectic of local/global contains, in the literal sense, the ambivalence at the heart of the global humanitarian regime whose own antecedents lie in colonial pasts, but which have to be ignored by the celeb-rity who emerges from this context but seeks global visibility and role (Nayar forthcoming).

Creole/creolization: 'Creole' originally referred to a form of language derived from pidgin that had evolved into the language of a speech community in a locality. (Robert Pinksy beautifully defines it as '*Creole* comes from a word meaning to breed or to create, in a place', in a poem titled simply 'Creole.') 'Creolization' as a concept was first popularized by Edward Kamau Brathwaite in *The Development of Creole Society in Jamaica* (1971) to describe the cultural and linguistic effects of coloniza-tion. He defined it as the 'cultural action' of 'culturally discrete groups' wherein 'two or more distinct cultural and racial units' interacted to 'form a "new" construct, made up of newcomers to the landscape and cultural strangers to each other' (296). Brathwaite was describing the hybrid nature of language and art that emerged within Caribbean culture as a result of the mixing of pre-colonial and folk forms/language/genres/styles with the English language and culture. He proposed that the African and European cultures mixed first in a hierarchic fashion – superior European, inferior African – as a result of the colonial process. The African therefore began to subsume his own culture and adopted that of the European mas-ter. However, over time, the Europeans also started acquiring fragments of African culture. Creolization is visible in most colonized cultures where (i) anti-colonial struggles consciously revive, in, say, **nativist** movements, pre-colonial folk forms as a response to the cultural hegemony of the European master, (ii) through a long period of contact, exchanges and interactions between the native and European (colonizer's) culture, new forms of language, register and cultural practices emerge. Creolization must be seen as neither strictly the colonizer's nor the colonized's cultural practice. It is somewhere in between these two, and therefore can be seen as a hybrid form, an entirely new form that is constituted by its two 'origins' but whose present state or character is productively messy so that the origins are irrelevant to the performance today. The circulation of the European novel form or Romanticist ideas and poetry in many parts of Africa, South America and Asia introduced the genre to native writers, several of whom adopted it as a welcome medium for their writing. In India, for example, Bankim Chandra Chattopadhyay and the diasporic Toru Dutt experiment with the novel as a form (although India's narrative traditions did not include this form). The early poets in English from the subcontinent – Toru Dutt, Michael Madhusudhan Dutt and later Sarojini Naidu – were deeply influenced by the English Romantics. Through the 20th century we see Rap and Hip Hop enter the English pop/rock music scene even as African performance poetry, like Dub poetry (Jean Binta Breeze, Linton Kwesi Johnson, with the latter famous for his 'inglan is a bitch'), was retrieved by African, Caribbean and African American performers. Creolization is now seen increasingly as an inevitable effect of globalization, even though this process dates back several centuries. The work of Lisa Jardine on the Renaissance and Dirk Hoerder on the history of migration demonstrate how even supposedly Eurocentric phenomena like the Renaissance were made possible due to extensive cultural linkages, exchanges and creolization in architecture and the arts. Salman Rushdie, Chinua Achebe, Wilson Harris, and Amos Tutuola are authors who have combined the linguistic registers of the English language and the English novel with Asian and African folk, pop culture and narrative traditions to produce hybrid/creolized works that are unique in their own right. Thus the Indian satirical poet Keki Daruwalla says in his poem 'Mistress':

> You can make her out the way she speaks;/Her consonants bludgeon you;
> Her argot is rococo, her latest 'slang'/Is available in classical dictionaries …
> No, she is not Anglo-Indian …/She is Indian English, the language that I use

When Walcott wonders how he can abandon either the English language that he loves or the African languages that are his legacies (in 'A Far Cry from Africa'), or when he tracks his identity to multiple origins ('I have Dutch, nigger, and English in me', 'The *Schooner Flight*'), he is speaking of the tensions of creolization but also gesturing at the productive effects of cultural mixing that give him, as a poet, multiple sources on which to draw. (See also: **transculturation**)

cultural imperialism: Other forms of imperialism, such as cultural (Edward Said) and linguistic (Phillipson), have also come in for attention in postcolonial studies, especially since the 1990s. Critics claim, for instance, that due to the specific strategies of language use (English during the colonial era, and today on the internet or as the language of global trade), local languages are given short shrift and slowly die out. The overwhelming power of Western consumer products, ways of thinking about beauty or fashion and even organization of workspaces (in American-controlled MNCs across the world) ensures a certain amount of cultural homogenization that erases local cultural forms – this is called cultural imperialism. The adoption of the novel form by non-European writers (Achebe, Raja Rao, Ngugi) is an instance of the domination of English/European culture. Native forms of storytelling – the *katha*, the folk song, the *kissa* – were forgotten as a result. Modes of remembering a culture's past were similarly forgotten as the griot's song was no longer treated as 'history', since history-writing demanded the following of conventions as laid down by the Europeans. Cultural imperialism as examined by writers and literary critics such as Ngugi, Said and Mudrooroo point to the disappearance of native ways of thinking about the world among the formerly colonized people as a result of long decades of Western education. Chinua Achebe's fiction was one of the earliest to document the deleterious effects of cultural imperialism when tribes began to lose their young men to Western ways of thinking. Proverbs were forgotten, local relationships and markers of respect ignored, new languages acquired that cited the Bible and English writers instead of folk tales and local myths, the young men's heroes were British soldiers and statesmen while the headman and even the patriarch of the family were ignored resulted eventually in a complete break from the village/tribe and family. Cultural imperialism here is not so much about the economic exploitation of the local subjects as it is about the devaluing of native traditions and the luring away of the young men from these traditions. Cultural imperialism works through hegemony and consent rather than through force and coercion. Naipaul, Rushdie, Walcott, Dangarembga and other writers portray non-European characters who wish to speak and look like their Western masters and have contempt for the culture they grew up in. Even the names of houses in the former colony are named after the English manors and European estates, as Rushdie satirizes in *Midnight's Children*: 'Buckingham', 'Sans Souci', 'Versailles' and 'Escorial'. Western/ American consumer culture is seen within postcolonial studies as an excellent instrument of cultural imperialism because this culture offers the formerly colonized subject the (Euro-American) role model and then the wherewithal to emulate it. Contemporary studies in media demonstrate how today's business outsourcing and call centre labour (Shome 2006; Poster 2013), requiring accent training in Americanisms and a cultural literacy about America – cultural imperialism in a new key – result in new forms of hybridity in the global age. In formerly colonized peoples even their racist tendencies and prejudices are 'imported' from their European masters, suggests Sri Lankan expat novelist Yasmine Gooneratne in *Relative Merits*: 'Cultivating English modes of living and thinking, the members of my father's clan had imbibed a very proper English prejudice against Jews, 'frogs', 'chinks', 'niggers', 'japs', 'huns', 'fuzzywuzzies', 'wops' and 'wogs' of every description' (1986: 84).

Dalit: The term became commonplace after the 1970s and 1980s in India as a descriptor of the so-called lower castes. It derives from the Indian language, Marathi, in which 'dala' means 'of the earth' and thus symbolically captures the oppressed ('ground into the dust') conditions of certain castes in India. 'Dalit' is now the standard term for the historically marginalized and oppressed castes, but is not usually applied to the tribals. The so-called 'lower castes' in the Hindu social hierarchy were denied basic rights and dignity – education, land ownership, privacy – and were always treated with horrific cruelty, notably by the 'upper-caste' Brahmins. Social reform movements during the 19th century by people like Jotiba Phule sought to educate the Dalits on the necessity of abolishing the caste system and the role education plays in this effort. During the anti-colonial struggle the debate between Gandhi and the leader of the 'oppressed classes' (as they were called), B.R. Ambedkar, was centred on political rights for these castes. Ambedkar rejected Gandhi's spiritualization of the caste system (Gandhi called them 'harijan', or the 'children of God') and sought political, social and economic rights. The Constitution of India, adopted in 1950, banned the practice of untouchability. In the decades following Indian independence Ambedkar and later organizations like Dalit Panthers fought for basic rights, arguing that the Dalits had always been second-class citizens, even in pre-colonial India. The Dalit Panther manifesto of 1972 also defined 'Dalit' in a more expansive fashion, 'a member of Scheduled Castes and Tribes, neo-Buddhist, the working class, the landless and poor peasants, women, and all those who are being exploited politically, economically and

The Postcolonial Studies Dictionary, First Edition. Pramod K. Nayar.
© 2015 John Wiley & Sons, Ltd. Published 2015 by John Wiley & Sons, Ltd.

ABCDEFGHIJKLMNOPQRSTUVWXYZ

in the name of religion'. Ambedkar's numerous writings and speeches on the subject are now part of both revolutionary and reformist literature in politics and culture. The rejection of Hinduism is central to a major strand of Dalit politics. With affirmative action policies more Dalits have entered the educational and occupational sectors (those run by the state) but cultural and social acceptance is still some way off. Recent debates have centred around the role the English language plays in the social mobility of these castes. A vast body of writing in the local languages, especially poetry (Namdeo Dhosal), exists ('Dalit Literature') and a substantial amount of work is now available in English translation. Memoirs and autobiographical writings (Bama, Sharan Kumar Limbale, Narendra Jadhav) have formed a large chunk of Dalit writing, and critical studies foreground the political and cultural significance of these texts for offering an alternative to 'elitist' mainstream Indian literature. The aesthetics of Dalit writing, arts and other cultural practices have also come in for some attention since 1990s as articulating a **subaltern** aesthetic.

Dark Continent: The history of this term is often attributed for first use to Henry Stanley, the African explorer, in his *In Darkest Africa* (1890). It was used to describe Africa, and mainly to convey the sense of mystery about the interior places and inhabitants. This air of mystery was compounded by the fact that the continent proved so difficult to explore and map. Although Defoe had written (in *Captain Singleton*) of Europeans who walked from one coast to another, the larger part of the continent remained mostly unknown. However, the myth of the Dark Continent served an important imperial purpose: it justified the bringing of enlightenment by missionaries, educators and statesmen into the country. In contrast with the irrational beliefs, cannibalism and superstitions of the Africans, there was Christian light, modernity and rationality. Patrick Brantlinger traces a genealogy of this myth of the 'dark continent' (1985) that departs from the above explanations. He argues that the landscape of Africa was 'darkened' within English writings because it was the scene of horrific torture, suffering and death of Africans at the hands of slave traders. Africans themselves participated, for profit, in the slave trade and thus the locus of dark deeds and evil was shifted to Africa and away from England in English abolitionist writings. Exploration writings depicted the European explorers as struggling against a dark, evil and obstacle-ridden landscape before returning to their homes, and light. Scientific writings located the Africans at the very lowest end of the human evolutionary scale. Novels set in the region drew attention to the savagery of the natives, and the white man's descent into the metaphoric nether regions of civilization, facing danger, generated the romance of the 'dark continent', so that, in keeping with the tradition of the romance, the Englishman/European emerged as the hero. For Brantlinger the myth of the 'dark continent' was a European invention that enabled the Europeans to project their fears and fantasies onto Africans. Thus Conrad's classic novel is only one of a long line of texts that sees Africa as 'dark'. Exemplary texts in the genre remain Rider Haggard's, complete with voodoo, excessive feminine sexuality and tom-toms.

decolonization: The term refers to both the loosening of colonial-imperial connections and control of the European nations over settlements and colonies in Northern and Southern America (from the late 18th century through the 19th) and the more culturally focused process whereby former colonies, especially in Asian and South American nations, seek to attain intellectual, philosophical and political independence from the Europeans and from European legacies. The American colonies' rebellion by European settlers against British rule and the subsequent attempts to develop a distinct 'American' identity might be seen as the first decolonization movement of the modern era. Decolonization also involved, at least in the British case, a tweaking of the imperial structure whereby several of their territories in Canada, Australia and Africa were designated partially autonomous 'dominions'. In postcolonial studies it is the second meaning that accrues more importance: the cultural-intellectual-philosophical attempt to escape colonial forms of thinking. Ngugi's controversial *Decolonising the Mind* (1986) argued that as long as the African writer wrote in European languages s/he would be inevitably writing for a European audience. Several other anti-colonial writers from as diverse a group as Mahatma Gandhi, Frantz Fanon, and Kwame Nkrumah, and literary figures like Mudrooroo, Ngugi wa Thiong'o, Raja Rao and Chinua Achebe, have in their works spoken of the intellectual colonization achieved by the Europeans and the need for decolonization. Decolonization is necessary, if we were to evolve a consensus here, in order to escape the clutches of European ideas which have come to permeate the culture and vision of the former colonized subjects. As a result of European intellectual hegemony wrought through instruments like law, education, religion and literature, the Asian and African subjects began to see themselves through European eyes, and therefore as inferior, primitive and non-modern. Further, and more insidiously, such subjects become complicit in the colonial project because they have assimilated the colonial master's ideas. Even nationalism of the anti-colonial struggle, Partha Chatterjee argues, is derived from European models. These views remained well in place after political independence from Europe. Decolonization during the anti-colonial struggle works within a nationalist project where native cultural forms, myths and beliefs are revived. Later, after political independence, decolonization took the form of a retrieval of these older, pre-colonial myths and images in order to establish a continuity of native traditions and cultural practices that are uncontaminated by the Europeans and their intellectual legacies. The nation itself begins to be envisaged in these mythic terms (although, ironically, the political-administrative structures of these newly independent nations in Asia and Africa are legacies of the colonial era). The revival of African philosophy in the works of Kwame Anthony Appiah, folklore in Wole Soyinka, the turn to nativism in Indian literature, the determined attempts to write in their own language and idiom in Raja Rao, Ngugi and Achebe, and the pride in aboriginal traditions and cultures in Mudrooroo, Kath Walker and Jackie Higgins can be seen as attempts at literary decolonization where the non-European legacies are highlighted and built upon for national, ethnic or regional identities. One of the tensions in postcolonial theory/studies itself has to do with decolonization processes. Critics and commentators like Arif Dirlik (1997), Harish Trivedi (1991), Aijaz Ahmad (1992, 1997) and others have suggested that postcolonial theory is itself complicit with Western modes of thinking because critics like Bhabha, Said and Spivak have been trained in the West, their language and register (by which it often means the postcolonial critic's jargon) are indebted to the West and their audience is also Western. Ethnic writers, suggests Dirlik (2002), carry the burden of providing ethnographic knowledge to the Western reader, hence even creative work becomes complicit with the West in that it is seen as an 'authentic' source of the non-European's cultures. Such critics propose that as long as postcolonialism uses the methodological or even linguistic (i.e., the English language) tools of the colonial master they cannot achieve true decolonization. Finally, the decolonization project of intellectual, cultural, economic and political independence of the postcolonial nation-state is seriously undermined by the globalization process of the late 20th century because the latter imposes what is usually a set of First World standards, norms (whether in economic policy or political treaties) and cultural products which erode the autonomy of the Third World nation. Many African writers have followed Ngugi's decision (to write in Gikuyu): Algerian Rachid Boudjedra (Arabic), Senegalese Boubacar Boris Diop (Wolof) and Angolan José Luandino Vieira (hybrid of Portuguese and Kimbundu).

dependency complex: Octave Mannoni (1950, English translation 1964) in his study of the psychology of colonialism proposed a typology of psyches of the colonizer and the colonized. The European, he argued, was prone psychologically to dominate and control. The African, on the other hand, sought protection. The colonial situation, said Mannoni, enabled these psyches to develop. Since the colonial situation sanctioned power to the white man, his psyche developed as that of a master. The African, beaten and oppressed, turned dependent upon the white man for survival and confidence. The white man comes to be seen by the dependent native in the role of guardian, protector, punisher and father. Mannoni explains rebellions by colonized subjects as the effect of the dependency complex. Whenever the subject believes that the protector figure is likely to abandon him, he fights to retain the white man. That is, the black man cannot survive without the authoritarian master. The rage during such rebellions was not, said Mannoni, against the white man, but an expression of the fear that the white man would abandon the child-like native. This theory of the innate dependency of the black man was rejected by Fanon. Fanon argued that the dependency and the inferiority complex were not innate features of the black psyche. The fear and anxiety of the black man proceeded from very real material conditions of beatings, police brutality, arrests and violence on the part of the white man. It is the absence of a secure life for himself that makes the black man anxious and angry. Thus Fanon refused to accept the black man's sense of inferiority as psychological in origin, instead locating it in the social, political and economic contexts of colonial rule. In a scene from Paul Scott's *The Raj Quartet* Ronald Merrick is interrogating the Westernized Indian Hari Kumar/Harry Coomer in prison. Merrick tries to sexually abuse Hari Kumar. During this one-sided 'confrontation' Hari Kumar tries to maintain his dignity but is quite unable to. Now, in terms of class he is superior to Merrick, as Scott makes clear, with his English education and social standing. But the very structure of the colonial administration leaves him at the mercy of his socially inferior Merrick: it is his racial identity that offers Merrick the context he needs to abuse Kumar. Hari Kumar's inferiority complex here is not the result of his Indian class identity or education: it is the direct effect of the racialized nature of their relationship.

diaspora: In the original Greek the term meant 'to disperse', referring to the dispersal of pollen and spores of plants that then take root and flourish elsewhere, in a new soil. The dislocation and subsequent relocation of the Jews in Biblical and religious history is taken as the paradigmatic instance of diaspora, especially in the pioneering work by William Safran (1991). Safran isolated specific features of diasporic communities that continue to have relevance today: collective memory, the anxiety over acceptance by receiving societies, the idea of an original homeland, idealization of this homeland and the existence of an ethnic-communal consciousness. Later writers like Robin Cohen discovered the need to expand the concept to include the experience of numerous ethnic groups, whose conditions of displacement and migration might have involved less cruelty and have had significantly less impact on the natal society (Cohen 2008). The term now describes a forced or voluntary movement (the theme of voluntary migra-tion was Cohen's contribution to the early debates) of people from their homelands into a new place. Diaspora and migration are now treated, espe-cially in the light of extensive anthropological and migration studies, as a key feature of almost the entire human race, and as the causal factor in the populating of new regions of the earth over a vast historical period, starting with the supposed origins of mankind in Africa. Diaspora is the context not only for racial mixing through **miscegenation** – and therefore for new races and ethnicities emerging in the world – but also for cultural hybridization, producing new forms of art, music, architecture and literature. Thinkers like James Clifford (1997) argue that we need to distinguish between people who live in borders areas/borderlands and in diasporic conditions. Clifford goes on to propose that we need to pay attention to histories of displace-ment, suffering *and* adaptation, and not just to these communities' 'projec-tion' (his term) of an origin. For Clifford diaspora consciousness is produced positively through identification and engagement with transnational historical, social, political and cultural forces that move away from simple questions of home and origin. More recently one of the founders of dias-pora studies has called for greater attention to 'global diasporas' (2008). Cohen here maps diasporic populations in terms of the kind of contexts in which displacement occurred. Thus, the categories of diaspora are organ-ized less around geographical territory than around contexts. Beginning with the Jewish diaspora under Christianity and Islam, Cohen maps catego-ries like victim diasporas (Africans in America), labour-imperial diasporas (indentured Indians in the British Empire), trade and business diasporas (Chinese and Lebanese). However, questions of home and homeland, especially in the case of Israeli and Sikh diasporas, continue to find resonance in such recent studies. Within postcolonial studies, diaspora comes in for attention on two fronts. First, as we see in the writings of colonial-era authors, it is the condition of colonialism itself. Second, it is the condition of numerous ethnic groups and peoples who move, willingly or under coercion, away from their homelands to other places. Slavery and indentured labour, about which people like David Dabydeen have written fiction, was an instance of forced movements producing a diaspora of Africans in the Caribbean and the Americas. Migration by people from the Third World nations into the First, characteristic of the 20th century and documented by Bharati Mukherjee, Shyam Selvadurai, Timothy Mo, Maxine Hong Kingston, Michael Ondaatje, Amy Tan and others, is another kind of diaspora produced by the voluntary displacement of people from their homelands. The literature of diaspora is characterized by nostalgia for the lost homeland, the dynamics of 'home' and 'foreign', assertions of ethnic identity even as they seek to assimilate new cultural practices and beliefs (tensions of acculturation), the anxiety of loss and suffering, the necessary adaptation of new identities that combine more than one cultural heritage (**hybridity**) and, increasingly, a cosmopolitanism where the migrant cele-brates multiple belongings. In Dabydeen's *A Harlot's Progress* an 18th-century black 'harlot' sells his traumatic story to abolitionists for money. Poems like Derek Walcott's 'The Sea is History' thematize the process of black diaspora – the slave voyage – that involved the forced displacement and resettlement of black populations from Africa into the Caribbean and then the Americas. Many authors also sought to capture in their fiction the intergenerational conflicts of migrants where the earlier generation in the UK or America preferred to retain their 'original' identities but the latter generations were more British than, say, Pakistani or Indian. Bharati Mukherjee's fiction (*Jasmine*, 1989) spoke of the difficulties of the Indian migrant in adapting to an American culture. Naipaul (*A House for Mr. Biswas*) gestured at the determined manner in which descendants of inden-tured labour fought to retain a vestigial Indianness through **cultural citizenship**. Monica Ali (*Brick Lane*) shows how migrants form communi-ties within metropolises like London and thus attain a sense of belonging in an alien country. Hanif Kureishi fictionalized the differences in approaches to cultural adaptation between generations of migrations (*The Buddha of Suburbia*). In this novel Karim watching his father thinks: '[with] fifteen … [years]… lived in the South London suburbs … [my father] stumbled around the place like an Indian off the boat' whereas Karim himself 'knew all the streets and the very bus routes' (1990: 7). The poetry of Agha Shahid Ali is full of nostalgia for the country he has left behind, and the non-fiction of Salman Rushdie celebrates the multiple belongings of the migrant. Pico Iyer's fiction and non-fiction are about global Indians, cosmopolitan and adaptable to any culture in the world. Diasporic authors are often accused of being excessively nostalgic and 'freezing' their homelands in time. They seek to market a particularly exotic view of their 'charming' homelands because their work is meant for Western readers (as described by Lisa Lau 2009; Graham Huggan 2001). Diaspora literature, in the last decades of the 20th century, has however altered significantly. In the case of authors like Kamila Shamsie or Mohsin Ahmad, for instance, the binary between 'home' and the 'world' is effaced in favour of a more complicated relation of the global with the postcolonial. Often characterized as 'post-migratory litera-ture' (the term originated with Caryl Phillips), the works of these authors map the emergence of new communities, new affiliations in heterogeneous and transnational contexts. It is not all about nostalgia and acculturation. Characters in these authors retain their cultural identity in new contexts, and resist an easy cosmopolitanism, although there is no nostalgia for the lost (left-behind) tradition either. There is, therefore, a 'bilateralsim' between the global and the postcolonial (Gamal 2012). Thus Mohsin Hamid's protagonist Changez in *The Reluctant Fundamentalist* crafts an identity that is not reducible to the Pakistan/West binary. Instead, his iden-tity retains the Pakistan identity and to this is added a whole range of cultural affiliations: Vietnam, Korea, Taiwan, Iraq and Afghanistan. That is, Changez affiliates culturally in a post-9/11 'West' with those nations against which the USA has launched wars. What the novel demonstrates is the blurring of the binary of home and abroad as Changez's 'migration' is not simply from 'East to West'. In more troubled regions like Palestine-Israel, to be an assimilated Arab in Tel-Aviv is not adequate, as Yasmina Khadra's *The Attack* (2006) demonstrates. Dr Amin Jaafari is arrested, tortured and placed under constant surveillance because his wife has blown herself up in Tel-Aviv. The tragedy of the novel lies in the fact that Jaafari had always seen himself and his wife Sihem as having been assimilated and accepted into Israeli society, and the discovery that his wife had retained her belief in the Palestine cause comes as an utter shock to him. Here the immigrant (who saves lives, incidentally) then acquires an education at the hands of both the Israeli police and the Palestinian fighters. (Critics note that novels originat-ing in the Euro-American context often depict the Middle Eastern/Muslim woman terrorist in a sympathetic manner; McManus 2013.)

discovery: The term has historically come to mean the mapping of new travel routes, lands and peoples by Europeans. Thus the term indicates a hierarchy of discoverer-observer and discovered-observed wherein Columbus 'discovers' the Americas and the natives residing therein. The indigenous tribes of these regions are never described as having discovered Europeans: discovery is always a one-way traffic from the Europeans to and about the non-Europeans. A key image and theme in European colonial writings about Africa, Asia, Australia and the Americas, 'discovery' is to be read alongside its effects: colonial conquest, settlement and dominance. European discoveries of the 'new world' were quickly followed by wars over territorial acquisition amongst the several European nations. Dividing up the natural resources the Europeans established kingdoms but – and this is important – decimated the native/indigenous populations and their cultures. Thus 'discovery' in the postcolonial sense is a tragic term for it refers to the depopulation and deculturation of these regions and their subsequent resettlement by the white races. This discovery theme was always in close conjunction with the theme of European heroism, whether of Columbus' errant and turbulent voyage to the Americas, the quest for the NorthWest passage or the journeys of the Livingstones and the Parks seeking the origins of the rivers and lakes of Africa in the 19th century. The narratives showed the European as honourable, stoic and courageous and the natives as vulnerable, non-modern, savages. Discovery narratives also documented, as in the case of Columbus, Walter Raleigh and others, the encounter with the indigenous people. The tropes and images used by these narratives became the lexicon with which later writers and commentators described the non-Europeans. The term suggests a ranking of cultures and people: those who wait to be discovered and the Europeans who discover them, and thus create specific identities as well: the objects of observation (the non-Europeans) and subjects performing observation (Europeans). Europe fashions itself through this dialectic of observer/observed. In the late 20th century similar journeys of discovery and conquest have been underway for the North and South Poles and outer space. Postcolonial revisions of the discovery trope has included demonstrating the uncertainty of the explorer, the courage of the natives, and the alienation (rather than the joy of a 'new world') of the new arrival. A stunning Margaret Atwood poem about Susanna Moodie, one of the first Europeans in Canada, concludes with this sense of alienation, desolation and unhappiness: 'the moving water will not show me/my reflection./The rocks ignore./I am a word in a foreign language' ('Disembarking at Quebec', 1997). Atwood leaves it unclear as to whether the alienation is due to the hostile nature of the receiving land/people or the baggage she carries from her European past into the new world. The 'I' in the poem is in a language foreign to the receiving land, so they do not validate her identity, and since all identity requires a validation from the world, she becomes just 'foreigner'.

dislocation/displacement: The term can refer to several forms of physical movement: of the Europeans to the colonies, of the Africans as slaves to the Caribbean and the New World, of migrant postcolonials to the First World, and of refugees. The dislocation of Europeans to the colonies is at the heart of the imperial project. The Europeans explored new territories and, in several cases, settled there (Canada, Australia), often in miscegenated relations with the natives. The convicts of England were also displaced into the Australian continent when it was developed as a penal colony. The Africans were taken into the New World, but with little choice in terms of occupation, place of stay or, of course, going away from Africa at all. Within postcolonial literature the term 'dislocation' most often refers to the sense of cultural and social alienation experienced by the migrant when seeking to adapt to a new society/country. The diasporic individual leaves home, but in a sense always remains connected to the home even when settled in an entirely new place. Second-generation migrants, however, do not undergo the same intense experience of alienation, having been born and adapted to the new culture, with new forms of **cultural citizenship**. In some cases the displacement from the home/country becomes essential because of the intolerance and oppression there. Hanif Kureishi, for example, speaks of displacement from Pakistan and his family as essential because these can be 'claustrophobic': for the individual with different attitudes and orientations, the First World represents freedom to be oneself (2001: 6). Here displacement is less about alienation than empowerment and individual agency. Rushdie and Bhabha celebrate displacement as productive because, they claim, it gives the individual the opportunity to acquire a new, hybrid identity. Amitava Kumar therefore writes of a world of sexual freedom (among other freedoms) associated with the West in Kureishi's fiction (2001). However, the diasporic novel itself has moved beyond the simplistic hybridity of the earlier generation into what is being called 'post-migratory' fiction (See: **diaspora**).

double consciousness: In Richard Wright's *Native Son*, Bigger asks himself 'did not white people despise a black skin?' He thinks he wears a 'badge of shame' as a black man, that he 'had no physical existence at all'. The entire powerful passage captures the psychological tension of a black man unable to deal with his blackness except as a negative condition of existence, because he *believes* he is despised. The passage is an exemplary illustration of Du Bois' theory. African American thinker W.E.B. Du Bois used the term 'double consciousness' in *The Souls of Black Folk* (1903) to signal the state of the blacks in America. Du Bois argued that after centuries of slavery and subjugation the black man could only see himself through the white man's eyes. The black, the subject of contempt and pity, says Du Bois, is conscious of being both 'American' and 'Negro'. Du Bois is speaking of the internalization by the blacks of white attitudes and prejudices. As a result of this internalization, the black man believes himself primitive, oversexed and savage – the beliefs the whites held. This instils a sense of inferiority but also causes the blacks, as individuals and as a race, to see the white man as the superior race. For the black man the struggle is to 'merge' the two selves into one coherent whole. What Du Bois also emphasizes is that neither of the two identities – American or Black – needs to be abandoned. Is it possible, Du Bois wonders, to be simultaneously a 'Negro' and an 'American'. Du Bois is anticipating the postcolonial struggle with identity where the formerly colonized owes her/his legacies to both Western education-acculturation and the native heritage. The African brought up within the American slave system and so to 'lose' his cultural roots over generations (their music was prohibited, they were given new, Christian names) has no 'native' culture to turn to. Although the early generations saw Africa as their true home and their (proscribed) culture as their true culture, they were forced to abandon both. In addition, later generations grew into an American culture that did not give space or significance to the African traditions within America itself. Thus, for them to see any historical or emotional connections to Africa as homeland was extremely difficult – they saw themselves only as they were conditioned to seeing themselves: as descendants of slaves in white America. In psychological terms this results in low self-esteem and a disruption of cultural continuities with the community's history – a condition that Frantz Fanon also would theorize in his *Black Skin, White Masks* (1956) when he spoke of the alienation of the black man in colonial Algeria. Fanon too proposes that as a result of colonial rule the black man loses all sense of his culture and identity and sees the white race as the one to be emulated: to speak like the white man, says Fanon, is the high point of the colonized's life. He thus puts on a white mask. Du Bois' theory of black consciousness is exemplified in one sense in Morrison's *The Bluest Eye* where the girl-child believes in the Western ideal of beauty (blue eyes), and has no sense of the black norms of femininity. In his writings Richard Wright admits that he experienced the 'contradiction' of being both Western and a 'man of color' but that this makes him more 'self-conscious' of his environment even as he is able to be critical of the West. Later theorists like Paul Gilroy would extend in a different way Du Bois' concept to argue a case for black (and American) identity as transcending national (African, America) borders and being generated through cultural exchanges, what Gilroy termed a '**Black Atlantic**'. Where Du Bois saw double consciousness as debilitating Gilroy, Stuart Hall and the postcolonial thinker Homi Bhabha saw it as productive, where the latter generations could speak, as Derek Walcott would, of a dual legacy. Gilroy therefore argued that the transatlantic exchange was integral to the making of a black identity.

e-Empire: A term that refers explicitly to the informational capitalism of the latter decades of the 20th century, the 'e-Empire' as Rita Paley defined it (2004) is a 'fluid and intersecting set of forces, practices, technologies, and events' … [it] comprises communicative networks, electronic commerce, modes of production, and global financial markets' (2004: 111). Paley's work clearly gestures at new interpretations of empires (Hardt and Negri 2000, Cooppan 2008) and its forms of labour (Terranova 2000). She argues that eBusinesses encompassing the globe are possible through the new digital technologies. Paley notes how these electronic ('e') Empires extend the Roman and British Empires into Wall Street in their rhetoric. Paley's work examines the rise of the new 'creative' classes, the new territories of markets and wealth, even as the new technologies effect an elimination of 'geographical boundaries, client base and global sales and marketing' (122). The nation-state becomes obsolescent in such a context. Paley, like Daya Thussu (1998), Oliver Boyd-Barrett (1998) and others (whom she cites), treats media conquests of the world by transnational media corporations as a component, or version, of such e-Empires. Like Hardt and Negri, Paley sees the e-Empire as a shadowy network which retains the configuration of 'command and control' although it might not have an identifiable centre or point of origin and end. (See also: **neocolonialism, Empire – new figurations of, globalization, postnational**)

ecological ethnicity: A concept popularized within postcolonial critiques of development by Pramod Parajuli (1998), it refers to the territorialized, localized ethnic identity of tribes and communities.

ABCD**E**FGHIJKLMNOPQRSTUVWXYZ

The Postcolonial Studies Dictionary, First Edition. Pramod K. Nayar.
© 2015 John Wiley & Sons, Ltd. Published 2015 by John Wiley & Sons, Ltd.

Ecological ethnicity sees the indigenous tribe or community as purveyor of authentic knowledge of the terrain due to its ancestral links with the land. It foregrounds human identity as intimately linked to the local land forms, ecology, weather and mineral, animal and plant life. Writings by Wangari Maathai, Ken Saro-Wiwa and others offer examples of ecological ethnicity. Maathai, for instance, in her account of her childhood *Unbowed: A Memoir* (2007), points to the ecology of her village and the sustenance it provided in the form of *managu* berries for her and the entire village. Later she contrasts this ecology of her childhood with the present when she notes that one cannot see these berries any more, the consequences of both overcultivation and pesticides. Ecological ethnicity here is the location of bodies of her community in connection/conjunction with the land, agricultural practices, natural and cultivated products, and a rhetoric that draws from this embeddedness, an instance of what has been called 'emplaced rhetoric' (Gorsevski 2012). In the writings of C.K. Janu (*Mother Forest*, 2004), a tribal activist from Kerala, India, we see a similar emphasis on the land-human life-identity linkage. Janu tells the story of tribals who have lived in the same region of the subcontinent for centuries so that their customs, language, myths and rituals – their very identity – are embedded in the climate, topography and fauna-flora of the space. Ecological ethnicity is most clearly visible in such bioregional writing. Debates around ecological ethnicity have been foregrounded in studies of development in Third World nations, globalization and the capitalist nations' control over farming practices, funding of research, among others. The work of the Comaroffs (2001), Rob Nixon (2006–7) and anthropologist Anna Tsing (2007), in particular, have drawn attention to disappearing ways of life of indigenous communities as a result of changed ecology brought on by globalization. Given the tensions of globalization's exploitation of Third World resources and the reiteration of ecological ethnicities in response to this exploitation there remains a certain amount of scepticism in the valorization and romanticization of tribal life and the so-called golden age of the locality. The writings of Vandana Shiva (1988) in the case of India, for instance, treat the ancient world as eco-friendly while quietly ignoring the other dynamics of, say, caste or patriarchy that prevailed in similar exploitative forms as well. More worryingly, this form of identity politics retains the serious risk of closing off localities and cultures from each other and erasing long and complicated histories of intercultural exchanges.

ecological imperialism: First elaborated as a feature of colonization in a book of the same title by Alfred Crosby (1986), the term refers to the biological colonization of Asia and the Americas. Crosby refers to the Spanish invasions of the 16th century during the course of which most native tribes and the Aztecs were wiped out due to the diseases the Europeans brought with them. Influenza, syphilis, smallpox were the key diseases in ecological imperialism and in the Massachusetts area smallpox decimated entire Native American tribes. Thus it was European pathogens rather than European military prowess that destroyed the native populations. In addition, new animal and plant species – with pollen – that accompanied the Europeans contributed to the potent mix of pathogens and altered the ecology of the 'New World' radically. But the reverse of this pathogenic movement can also be seen in history when Europeans picked up malaria, cholera and other diseases from the colonies. Botanists Joseph Hooker and Joseph Banks set up hothouses and enclosures for tropical plants in English botanical gardens in the 19th century, and thus brought the exotic life forms home to the metropolis. As Alan Bewell has shown in his work (1999), the English Romantic poets were obsessed with the increasing presence of tropical diseases among returning English sailors, soldiers and travellers. The idea of ecological imperialism marks a shift in the way both colonization and globalization are perceived. Pathogens and vectors cross geopolitical and national boundaries and produce a new dynamic of encounters. In the era of global capital, ecological imperialism has taken on new forms. Patenting of indigenous plants by Euro-American corporations, the trade treaties that create Western monopolies over crops in African and Asian farm lands, and the genetically modified seeds and crops the Third World is often forced into purchasing – which then alter the ecosystem of these countries for ever – all constitute ecological imperialism of the new era. The writings of Wangari Maathai, Ken Saro-Wiwa, and Vandana Shiva have addressed the issue of ecological imperialism in 20th-century contexts.

education (colonial):   When Elio Antonio de Nebrija presented his book on Castilian grammar to Queen Isabella in 1492, the year of Columbus and the 'New World', the Bishop of Avila declared that the book would be useful when Spain conquered the 'barbarians' who, in order to be properly brought under Spanish yoke, would need to be taught the European language (Mignolo 2003). Postcolonial studies' interest in colonial education examines the contexts in which it was introduced in the colonies, the uses to which European languages were put (to cultivate native elites in the service of the Empire), the supplanting of native languages and knowledge-systems by European ones and the persistence of European languages in the postcolonial era. Studies such as Gauri Vishwanathan's (1989) have demonstrated how native elites readily appropriated European languages (Vishwanathan is specifically looking at English in India) in order to reinforce their social authority and build relations with the colonial master (Allender 2007). Others writing in the vernacular languages also engaged with the new language of power (English) and attendant literatures (Orsini 2002, 2009; Naregal 2001). Ideas of modernization and reform came into native societies at least partly due to their exposure to Western ideas made available in the new education system. Thus on the one hand the native elites colluded with the imperial educational apparatus in reinforcing European and their own social dominance, but on the other they developed notions and concepts of independence – this latter development among Western-educated college students would eventually become the source of inspiration for the anti-colonial struggle in India at least. Textbooks and literary representation in the English/European education system offered depictions of the native as weak, vulnerable and unable to govern himself. Over a period of time, through assimilation, the native exposed to these representations began to believe them, and so agree to the colonial master's rule. Education thus enabled a consolidation of the Empire through the native's active consent. Further, the education system set up the European and his culture as the standard for the natives to aspire to and emulate. Through the supposedly more 'rational' European system the natives would, according to Charles Grant (1792), a pioneer in English education in India, become more rational and develop a sense of duty. Native elites readily accepted this argument and India's Raja Rammohun Roy, a celebrated visitor to Victorian England later in his career (Zoustopil 2010), would write to Lord Amherst in 1823 that the establishment of a college with English and Western education was very welcome because it would aid in the 'improvement of the native population'. A considerable portion of the European's educational policy depended on the complete rejection of native systems of learning, including his language and literatures. The Oxford University Press publication program in South Africa, as Caroline Davis shows (2011), pursued a liberal publishing agenda, including in the vernacular languages, and actively shaped Bantu education programs, although the textbooks never challenged apartheid. Thus, ostensibly involved in a liberatory education program, the Press continued to endorse the state's agenda because the textbook market was central to the Press's financial survival.

effeminacy: Gender roles, of femininity and masculinity, of both the colonizer/ruling race and the colonized subject race, were central to colonial discourse. In many cases, especially in Bengal (South Asia), colonial discourse constructed a binary of the ultra-masculine white man and the effeminate native man. The stereotype of the effeminate native dates back to the 17th and 18th centuries and the European travellers' depictions of such an emasculated type. Thus Robert Orme in *The History of the Military Transactions of the British Nation in Hindostan* (1763) wrote of the Indian as 'the most effeminate inhabitant of the globe' (also in James Mill, T.B. Macaulay and others). 'Effeminacy' was a signifier of several practices within heterosexual relations – including subservience of the husband and the overall lack of patriarchal authority. Kate Teltscher has noted that the stereotype of the effeminate Indian emerged within a cultural context, within discourses of diet, sexuality and religion (2000). The effeminate Bengali 'babu' was the object of ridicule, especially in the 1880s and 1890s. This kind of depiction served the useful purpose of portraying the native male as weak and consequently unable to take care of his woman – a lacuna that the masculine Englishman would fill. Thus, the effeminate native was the necessary anterior moment to the construction of the masculine *Englishman*. This latter construction was itself necessitated by the rise of the woman's movement in England, the demand for suffrage and the 'New Woman' model of English femininity. Reports of the cross-dressing and homosexuality of the English men in Arabia and other places (embodied in figures like T.E. Lawrence) heightened anxieties back home about a weakening English masculinity in the colonies (Hyam 1990). But there was another context, an indigenous one, as well. The Bengali elite, having lost their landlord-feudal lord status in the colonial economic system, set themselves up as the learned, professional-administrative class. The 'babu' as the bookish, learned Bengali man emerged from this context, and fed into the colonial stereotype as well. The discourse of effeminism added a new layer to colonial discourse, as the racial divide of white versus brown was now reconfigured as the white masculine male versus the brown effeminate, or unmanly, male (Sinha 1995). Sinha's argument shifts the debate about English masculinity away, crucially, from the English context toward the colonial context: it is in the engagement with the Bengali elite, mostly Western-educated and professionally employed, that English masculinity really comes into its own. Baden-Powell's initiative in creating the Boy Scouts movement was born out of a felt need of drafting young English boys into the larger project of imperialism, by making men of them from a very early age – and therefore set them apart from the effeminate Bengali (*Scouting for Boys*, 1908). The English boy had to learn very early to obey and to command, develop a sense of imperial responsibility and of course be conscious of an imperial masculinity as well – traits to be developed through sports and hunting. Baden-Powell's writings on hunting, scouting and sports might therefore be read as part of the larger project of 'toughening' up the English boy so that he may one day rule.

Empire – new figurations of: Traditionally the Empire was a geopolitical structure with a capital city that undertook major decisions, regulated the finances and economy, and in general took administrative control and responsibility for the vast territories under its charge. This Empire was also run with the effective use of military and law enforcement apparatuses like the army, the police and the judiciary. In *Empire* (2000) Michael Hardt and Antonio Negri analyze a whole new form of the Empire. The new Empire is decentred and nebulous, rhizomatic, anonymous and near-ghostly – and this is the present stage of capitalism. There is really no control-city with financial and administrative decisions centred in one place. In their famous definition it is a 'non-place'. Rather the decision-making and the controls are so diffused that it is impossible to track them. The new Empire is run not by one city or power but by conglomerates and associations of corporate entities, whose main stake/stock holders are also, very often, anonymous. The new Empire's territory does not have definite boundaries. Its territory is the world as such, and it grasps all available sources without racial, national or geopolitical borders. The new Empire is not run only through military and political power. Central to the new Empire is free-trade agreements and economic embargoes, a more shadowy system of exploitation. Integral to the Empire is the co-optation of difference. As has been pointed out (Cooppan 2008), while older empires rested on insurmountable difference (racial and cultural) the new Empire absorbs difference into itself. Thus the celebration of cultural difference is characteristic of the new Multinational Corporation (MNC): it turns this heterogeneity, variations and difference into its iconography as it spreads its tentacles across the world. But also crucial to the new Empire is its cultural imperialism where particular cultures – sometimes referred to as coca-colonization in direct reference to America's shadowy corporate power over the rest of the world – such as consumer culture or entertainment culture insinuate themselves into the rest of the world. With this the old aim of Empires (profit) continues but through the active collaboration of the world that has been, through media and advertising of consumer culture, converted into the craving consumer for the Empire's products. These products are themselves not always manufactured within the Western country, as the sites of production are dispersed, but the profits still flow into the coffers situated in Europe and America. The new Empires do not visibly create racial hierarchies. Indeed, as Hardt and Negri note, the new Empire's 'faces', such as a corporate organization like, say, Microsoft, try very hard to present themselves as multiracial and multicultural. The corporate organization is a 'machine for universal integration', as the authors put it (198). If the traditional Empire sought out and put down resistance from a different culture, the new Empire absorbs this diversity into itself and thus neutralizes the possibility of resistance. With the old-fashioned Empire there was the possibility of resistance, because there was a visible target (say, London) and organization (the East India Company and the British government). But in the new age of Empire there is no such visible face or organization, only a nebulous coalition of forces – the IMF, NATO, G8 – that wield power in invisible ways, through shadowy networks. The old Empire worked through conquest and control. The new Empire, although it has not entirely abandoned old forms of warfare, works through quieter forms of coercion (economic embargoes) and consent (cultural imperialism) in which media-orchestrated spectacles play a vital role. Hardt and Negri nevertheless continue to see the proletariat and the working classes around the globe – which they designate 'Multitude' – as the insurgents who will bring about revolution. The collapse of this massive Empire is possible precisely due to its structure, they argue: its diffuseness. Migrant workers in multinational, transnational flows constitute, they propose, a powerful force. (See also: **globalization, neocolonialism, e-Empire**)

Enlightenment (European): Dated to the late 17th and early 18th centuries in European history, the Enlightenment is the age of epistemological expansion and innovation. The expansion of knowledge was, incidentally, accompanied by major modes of organizing knowledge, whether in the form of the classification of plants, dictionaries (by Samuel Johnson) or encyclopaedias (by Diderot). The Enlightenment was accompanied by massive territorial expansion into Africa and Asia by European powers. It was this expansion that gave Europe the opportunities to study the world and its many cultures. In keeping with the Enlightenment obsession with systematizing knowledge, the world too was classified and organized, in the form of racial and civilizational hierarchies where European culture was contrasted with that of Asians (who once had an advanced culture but had now stagnated) and Africans (who were primitive). The myth of the 'noble savage' that gained currency during the Enlightenment and according to which a particular kind of primitive innocence was valued, was part of this process of organizing the world's people. On the one hand Enlightenment thinking spoke of universals – rights of man, for example – and yet on the other it foregrounded difference (of races and classes) in the colonies. Universalisms enabled Europe to ignore cultural differences and unite the diversity of the world under its imperial flag. Alternate forms of thinking – whether in science or religion – were not only ignored but also systematically destroyed and Western views, in the form of curricula and public discourses, put in place. Yet this ignoring of differences was accompanied by a firm belief that Europe needed to civilize the Other – which essentially suggested an implicit acceptance of difference. New views of Nature also emerged during this period. As knowledge of the racial-cultural Other grew, there arose a theory of humanitarianism, which argued that since Europe was the civilizational and moral superior to the Asians or Africans, it had the moral responsibility to improve the 'savage'. While this philosophy had its share of detractors (who questioned Europe's self-declared right to interfere in the lives of others), it gained considerable currency among colonial powers and institutional mechanisms were set up to achieve this end (of the 'improvement' of the non-European). The Enlightenment's **Eurocentrism** is now held as a principal explanation for the expansion of its cultural hegemony over the colonies, because it held up its cultural practices as superior to, and hence the standard for, the colonial subjects. More importantly, the Enlightenment's belief in Europe-led progress and standardization became the justification for territorial expansion and control over the so-called savage peoples of the world. Postcolonial critiques of the Enlightenment have noted the paradoxes whereby difference is both ignored and highlighted, universal humanism preached but not practiced (Carey and Festa 2009). Yet, as Dipesh Chakrabarty notes (1997, 2000), concepts of political modernity such as equality before the law, human rights, the public sphere, among others, that are central even today, owe their roots to the Enlightenment.

environmentalism: Colonial rule invariably meant the wholesale exploitation of natural resources of the colony by the European. Oddly, even during this process of exploitation the colonial rulers often expressed concerns over extensive deforestation and animal slaughter. They also objected to native modes of hunting and agriculture because, they argued, these were not conducive to protection of the environment. Laws were passed, for example in India, about 'reserve forests' with restricted access and use, in a bid to conserve the land and the animal life thereon. Colonial hunting narratives of the 19th century make the mandatory derisive remarks about the cruelty of the native hunting traditions, even as their own were described as 'sporting' because they at least gave a chance of survival to the animal/bird. Colonial environmentalism was a wholly different order where the conservation of the colony was seen as part of the colonizers' imperial duty. In the 20th century commentators like Ramachandra Guha and Martinez-Alier (1998) have begun to speak of an environmentalism native to local cultures. Guha and Martinez-Alier propose that environmentalism in Third World countries usually emerges from the condition of acute resource shortages for a vast majority of the population, since the resources are controlled by businessmen, landlords and the state. The general population in such contexts refuses the model of development as planned by the state (in collusion with large business interests), opting for local and traditional modes of agriculture and fuel use (fossil fuels, for example) and claiming the right to their traditional lands as part of their ancestry and cultural rights. Those who barely survive in inimical conditions such as these, whose agriculture and labour are directed at subsistence rather than profits, have a wholly different environmentalism, the authors suggest. Postcolonial histories of the environment have demonstrated the tensions of colonial administrators when it came to exploiting the colony and their own positions on ecology. Writings by Ken Saro-Wiwa and others have drawn attention to the continued exploitation of oil and other resources of African, Arab and other nations by corporate bodies located in the West. The Ogoni people, Saro-Wiwa noted in *A Month and a Day: A Detention Diary* (1995), received nothing even when their land's oil reserves were being exploited by Shell Oil with the active collusion of the corrupt Nigerian governments. The North-South divide on environmental issues that comes to the forefront during international summits on global warming has its origins in this 'environmentalism of the poor'. The environment is now seen as a domain in which the First World, having exploited it for centuries in the guise of industrialization or modernization, now places the onus of cleaning it up on the Third World, imposing sanctions on the use of fossil fuels or carbon emissions. Rob Nixon and others have examined how the First World's policies, whether in mining or disposal of radioactive waste, are anti-poor and are racialized. 'Slow violence', in Rob Nixon's words (2006–7), is that which is perpetrated on Third World nations through First World environmental policies, whose effects are not immediately visible but remain 'scientifically convoluted cataclysms in which casualties are deferred, often for generations'. More recently Dipesh Chakrabarty (2012), writing about global climate change and postcolonial studies, has pondered the 'universal' nature of climate crises, and therefore the necessity, perhaps, to think beyond the regional. In numerous postcolonial nations debates about development have asked questions about the environmental costs of, say, big dams and genetically modified (GM) crops. For postcolonial studies the dilemma has been the need to be pro-poor in terms of fuels and agricultural practices, while subscribing to global standards on emissions and pollution. There is a clear gender agenda to this postcolonial environmentalism (Wangari Maathai, Bina Agarwal, Mahashweta Devi and others) because women are seen as the earliest victims of anti-environment policies but also because women are viewed as having a greater involvement in the everyday interaction with nature (Agarwal 1992). (See also: **ecological ethnicity**)

epidermalization: A term used by Frantz Fanon in *Black Skin, White Masks* to speak of the colonial and European focus on the colour of the skin, white, black or brown. Identity, says Fanon, is believed to rest in the body. The black man, seen within colonialism as a black first and a human later, begins to feel trapped within his skin, and his colour. His entire inferiority complex, as a result, lies on his skin for him. Internal states of feeling, consciousness, rationality and attitudes all become associated with the surface, the skin, in such a condition. Fanon further argues that racism's primary site of torture, violence and humiliation is the epidermis, the surface, and only later the identity or consciousness of the individual. Wole Soyinka's poem 'Telephone Conversation' gives us an instance of such an epidermalization. A black man seeking accommodation in London identifies himself merely as 'African' on the telephone with the future landlord. The landlord seeks clarification: 'How dark? Are you dark or very light?' The black man qualifies: 'West African sepia'. He then dissects his body in terms of shades of the colour black: facially, brunette, but palm and soles of feet peroxide blonde, but his bottom, he apologetically admits, is 'raven black' (1964: 80–82). Soyinka suggests that for the white landlord everything about a potential tenant might be gleaned, predicted and calculated in terms of degrees of skin colour. What is being sought is the exact racial identity within the large category 'black': West African? Arab? Aboriginal? Historically, as Kim Hall (1995) has noted in her work, 'fair' and 'dark' begin to acquire moral and even theological connotations in the Early Modern period when the descriptor 'fair' used to describe the English/European race effects a conflation of skin colour and moral virtue ('fair' as in 'just'). Felicity Nussbaum (2009) notes that through the 17th and 18th centuries Arabs, Caribbean islanders, South Americans, Africans from the West and East of the continent, even Indians, were gathered under the rubric 'black', with little attempt to distinguish further categories of cultural identity or even 'shades' of blackness. That is, the categories, 'Oriental' and 'Black', like 'the East' and 'Africa', were not always clearly defined in this scheme of epidermalization. Due to colonialism's epidermalization complex issues and layers of individual and cultural identity are reduced to, or essentialized as, skin colour. However, it must be noted that such an epidermalization is not only a colonial construction. Several postcolonial societies and cultures like India attribute greater value to fair complexions, and studies of contemporary cultures of beauty, such as Nivedita Menon's (2008), draw attention to the enormous emphasis on fair skin for women.

epistemic violence: Building on the work of Michel Foucault who was interested in the way knowledge is sought, codified and ordered in every age – every age has its own modes of knowledge-formation, and Foucault called this an 'episteme' – postcolonial theorist Gayatri Spivak in her key essay 'Can the Subaltern Speak' (1988) developed the idea of epistemic violence. Spivak argued that knowledge production has its own forms of violence, especially when the colonial white races produce knowledge about the colonized/formerly colonized subjects. Whatever knowledge is produced by the Westerner then becomes established as truth, to be consumed by both the Western audience and the natives alike. Knowledge-making, or epistemology, was intimately connected to the violence of colonial conquest, domination and dispossession of the native subjects. The native subjects were produced as objects of knowledge to be inquired into, categorized and pronounced upon (as the Other of the West) by the West, and their own native knowledge-systems were rejected as irrational and irrelevant. Turning specifically to representations of Third World women in the writings of white feminists, Spivak sees the distortions and stereotyping of the brown/black women as vulnerable and lacking all agency as a form of epistemic violence that allows the white woman to go on speaking on behalf of this helpless 'sister'. Here Spivak makes a crucial alignment of imperialism with patriarchy. For the Western feminist the widow in India was a helpless victim of the ritual of *sati* (widow-burning). This interpretation of the native woman's helplessness came out of the Western mode of perception and thinking about the native subject. This epistemic violence on the part of the colonial was matched by the native patriarchy's construction of the widow as a willing participant in the ritual of *sati*. Thus, both imperialism and native patriarchy silenced the native woman and prevented any production of knowledge about herself by herself. Epistemic violence in Western feminism also relies on a homogenization of Third World women, unifying all of them under the rubric of the helpless black or brown sister. The brown or black woman exists only within the ways of perception deployed by the white woman, her (the native subject's) own ways of seeing and understanding the world have been systematically destroyed under colonialism. Within postcolonial texts the idea of epistemic violence plays out as both oppressive and emancipatory, especially in writings by Third World women such as Taslima Nasreen, Tehmina Durrani and Mariama Bâ. The woman of the house is spoken for, represented by and thereby effectively silenced by patriarchy. Other forms of epistemic violence include Western **cartographic** constructions of colonies like Australia and the New World (as ***terra nullius***) that consistently ignored the knowledge and perceptions the native subjects had of their land. (See also: **agency, essentialism, strategic essentialism**)

eroticization: Closely aligned with the trope of the 'torrid zones', the eroticization of the native was a key feature of colonial writings, as much contemporary feminist postcolonial criticism (Yeğenoğlu 1998; McClintock 1995) has demonstrated. Various forms of eroticization of the colonial and the colonized subject occur in English writing. Eroticization converted the native woman into an object of desire, danger, or one worthy of pity. Descriptions of Turkish and Indian dances in English texts belong to the first mode. In some, this mode takes an interesting tangent. The European woman casts herself as a fantasy object by appropriating the attire and mannerisms of the native woman, which are seen as seductive and erotic. Defoe's Roxana performs a Turkish dance and attracts the attention of the men at a ball, thereby eroticizing herself and reiterating the stereotype of the seductive Turkish woman. This is also true in the case of Mary Montagu in her *Turkish Letters* (1763) where she spends a considerable amount of time describing herself in native costume. In the second mode, the sensual native woman is to be distrusted. Montagu, for example, paints a picture of a liberated Turkish society where the veil is not only the representative of concealed erotic promise but also of lascivious intent. Here eroticism, especially of the native woman, is seen as an index of her loose morals and hypersexed nature. Often the entire space of the 'torrid zone', a standard mode in 19th-century colonial fiction (the 'station romances', for instance), also served the purpose of cautioning newly arrived Englishwomen about norms of socializing, marriage and domestic arrangements. It was very easy, suggested the fiction of Alice Perrin, Flora Annie Steel and others, for the English woman to lose sight of her role as a white female, especially in the company of numerous young men. Thus the potential sexuality of the white woman in the colony was deemed a threat to the imperial grandeur and authority. In the third mode of colonial eroticization poems and novels that depict the harem in William Beckford (*Vathek*, 1786), Thomas Moore (*Lalla Rookh*, 1817), Felicia Hemans (*England and Spain*, 1808) and several others focus on the harem as a space of iniquity, vice and unbridled sexuality, but also as a space where the native woman is incarcerated against her will, thus suggesting a restraint on her erotic potential (Byron's *The Giaour*, 1813; Johnson's *Rasselas*, 1759). Therefore eroticization, especially in this last instance, served to illustrate the native culture's tyranny against its women (Saglia 1997), as a preliminary, it could be argued, to the theme of the 'colonial rescue mission', a theme that has continued well into the 21st century with the West's rhetoric about Afghani and Iraqi women who need rescuing. Even feminists who rarely saw eye-to-eye with the hypermasculine military establishment, in the post 9/11 'war on terror' extended support to the US efforts in Afghanistan because they (suddenly) discovered the Taliban's impossible cruelties to its women. Thus, Western feminists who had up to that point been sceptical of the white man's efforts at saving the Arab/Hindu/Muslim woman, ended up reiterating the older colonial ideology. However, as commentators astutely noted, this was made possible because there was a 'studied silence about the crucial role the United States had played in creating the miserable conditions under which Afghan women were living', and they 'regularly failed to connect the predicament of women in Afghanistan with the massive military and economic support that the USA provided, as part of its Cold War strategy, to the most extreme of Afghan religious militant group' (Hirschkind and Mahmood 2002: 340–1). (See also: **torrid zones**)

essentialism: In contemporary critical and cultural theory 'essentialism' is the reduction of complex phenomena such as human nature or culture to a set of elements or features which are then taken to be the defining features of the human individual, race or culture. It relies on an assumption that all individuals in that group share the same features and that therefore a set of, say, four elements describes all the individuals in that group. It ignores variations of these characteristics but also excludes other aspects of that individual or group. Colonial discourse relied heavily on such essentialisms wherein a race or ethnic group was first represented as possessing certain key features and then those very features were 'applied' to all members of the group. Africans, therefore, in European writings were consistently essentialized as savage, primitive, superstitious and hypersexed. These became the characteristic features of all Africans, and there was no reference to the rich folklore, music, oral literature, religion or philosophies of the African continent. Any African individual would therefore be expected to possess these properties because s/he was an African. Essentialism served a crucial purpose for colonial administrators. It fixed the colonial subject in an unalterable condition, with no variations and therefore would offer no surprises. The colonial comes to acquire comprehensive knowledge of the native through such an essentialism. Cultural categories such as 'inferior' or 'pre-modern' races were essentialisms that then enabled the colonial to prepare policies based on these 'core' features of the native subject. Shakespeare's Caliban (*The Tempest*) is a monstrous creature, ugly and irrational. Essentialism is the assumption that these physiognomies or body-shapes represent the 'true' or 'core' nature of the creatures. Colonial discourse also essentialized the colonial master as the just, chivalrous, stoic and valorous man, the English woman as the true 'memsahib', feminine, supportive and Christian. All English personnel in the colonies would be essentialized with these markers, and all individual variations and personality traits ignored. When there was the necessity of making a critique of imperialism we see these essentialisms being used in entirely different ways. Ronny Heaslop in E.M. Forster's *A Passage to India* is the essential English colonial: arrogant, self-righteous, pompous and certain that the English are there to do good in India, and even playing God, as Mrs Moore accuses him of doing. Mrs Moore's comment is a critique of the essentialism because she suggests that these are simply roles the British have taken on themselves and played, with no substance. Essentialism here, for Forster, is a façade of justice the English rely on to convey a particular image of themselves to themselves and the colonial subjects. However, in both colonial and postcolonial contexts, essentialisms have also been evoked by nationalists, anti-colonial campaigners and civil rights activists to seek emancipation, rights or legal redress for minoritarian and historically oppressed groups and communities – which is now known in postcolonial studies as strategic essentialism. Within post-colonial feminism essentialisms have figured prominently in the writings of critics who address the First World's attitudes toward 'brown' or 'black' women. Sherene Razack's early work (1995) on Canada notes a crucial distinction in the state's approach to women from Arab and other nations. Razack argues that docile and mild-mannered Indo-Trinidadian women had a greater chance of acquiring asylum and refugee status than the African-Caribbean woman who did not induce the same sense of pity among the whites. Thus two categories were treated with greater pity: the downtrodden Indian woman and the veiled Muslim one, whereas the black woman (who fitted the stereotype of the 'mammy') was often treated as not simply hardy but also a potential criminal. Razack notes how a Muslim woman who expressed fears of the risk of genital mutilation was deemed to be better qualified for asylum than a self-professed feminist from the same Muslim country/culture who had rejected the veil. In other words, these instances, for Razack, exemplify the continuity of imperial frames of reference (pitying the native woman, the preference for the 'gentle' native woman, rescuing the vulnerable native woman) into the contemporary age, as a result of which we see a reinforcement of essentialisms. The new essentialism produces the image of certain cultures (such as Muslim cultures) as embedded in violence and as anti-woman.

ethnicity: The term is often used interchangeably with 'race' to signify a group of people with shared systems of beliefs, cultural practices (language, rituals) and even physical appearance. The emphasis when speaking of ethnicity is on cultural practices. Through the 20th century 'ethnic group' has come to signify numerically lower groups of people in a larger population, also called 'minority'. Thus Bangladeshis in England would be an ethnic group, or minority. Historically, such groups have been at risk from a variety of threats – from the loss of cultural rights and language (captured in Harold Pinter's 1988 play *Mountain Language* about Kurds refused the right to speak in their native tongue) to outright oppression and, in worst case scenarios, extermination (ethnocide). When such groups speak or think about themselves, they assert their *ethnicity*. In postcolonial studies a large body of work by such groups, existing as migrant communities in First World countries, has been extant for some decades now, even as the literature and writings of these groups are being tracked backwards in time (Fisher 2006; Vizram 1986; 2002). Asian American, Black British, Asian British, Chinese American, and Vietnamese American are some of the better known ethnic groups producing a vast body of writing, mostly detailing their hybrid roots and multicultural citizenship. Jhumpa Lahiri, Amy Tan,

Buchi Emecheta, Hanif Kureishi, Zadie Smith, Chimamanda Adichie, and Frank Chin are some of the prominent 'ethnic writers'. There is, however, an argument that the immigrant writers cash in on their appeal as 'different' and market their ethnic identity as well as metamorphose into 'authentic' voices of their communities to produce what Graham Huggan (2001) terms the 'postcolonial exotic'. Others (Lau 2009) have charged the postcolonial, especially the immigrant author, with '**re-orientalizing**', selling their own identities as exotic to the First World reader craving difference.

ethnocide: The term refers to a policy of the extermination of a group or community's culture. In contrast to genocide which is about the extermination of peoples, ethnocide is about cultural practices, territories and belief systems, including language, religion, arts and social modes. This extermination could take many forms with assimilation being the principle mode. The United Nations Declaration on the Rights of Indigenous People (adopted in 2007) uses the word 'ethnocide'. The best example of ethnocide would be of the Native Americans in the USA in the 19th century. The blacks remained a distinct cultural and racial group but the Native Americans were promised equality provided they assimilated and integrated into white culture. Ethnocide in this case therefore meant the loss of a cultural identity altogether – all those features that made the Native American tribes distinct (from the whites but also from each other) were erased. Ethnocide became a mode of imposing so-called equality by rejecting cultural difference.

ethnography (colonial):   Traditionally ethnography is the extended study, through close observation, of a particular social group. The aim of an ethnographic study is to document individual instances of behaviour, ritual or gesture by linking them to the values, norms or patterns of the group as a whole. That is, ethnography is concerned with the systems of meanings of the entire social group that bestow individual acts or gestures with meaning. Colonial ethnography sought to document the rules and norms that gave meaning to individual gestures, speech or behaviour of tribes and ethnic groups in the colony. Studies of villages, aboriginals, tribals or groups during the colonial period were ethnographic in nature (James Prichard 1786–1848; the American LH Morgan 1818–1881). However, as contemporary anthropologists (Clifford Geertz) have noted, colonial ethnographers imposed their own European system of values and norms upon the native practices and derived, as a result, particular kinds of meanings that were often completely different from those of the natives. Thus Geertz and others reject the idea of a neutral colonial ethnography position, arguing instead that the European's values interfere and intervene in interpreting other cultures. Ethnography was about interpretation, and interpretation was not an objective act, as recent work by Geertz, James Clifford and others show. Hence categories such as 'primitive rituals' or 'non-political protest' were European interpretations of native gestures. Thus 'observation', on which ethnography relies (the ethnographer lives with the subject group for extended periods of time), is never neutral. As Jonathan Crary (1992) demonstrates in his study of 19th-century practices of observation and gazing, these actions were mediated by norms of observation that were social and cultural in origin, and thus *not* neutral. In similar fashion the questions that ethnographers asked of the native subjects were those that emerged from the social and cultural concerns of the Europeans. Such questions elicited certain kinds of answers. In other words, postcolonial studies rejects the idea of the scientific objectivity or truth-value of the works in, say, the law texts of Henry Maine (1822–1888) or A.C. Haddon's footage of Torres Strait Islanders (1898). These are texts born out of colonial concerns about control of native subjects, and hence function as instruments of colonial epistemology. Even non-specialists such as travellers and missionaries offered 'expert' ethnographic observations – missionaries often lived in the communities in the colony – that then contributed to the colonial archive on specific tribes or groups. Such ethnographies fed into the larger colonial project of control as well as humanitarian campaigns of societies like the early 19th-century Aborigines Protection Society. Studies of such organizations show how European ideals of civilization and humanitarianism were imposed upon native practices, evaluating them as 'savage', and uniting the globe's distant regions under the aegis of the great humanitarian regime by the moral leader, England (Lester 2000). (See also: **epistemic violence**)

ethnopsychiatry (colonial): The attribution of mental illness and nervous conditions to racial and ethnic identity by European psychiatrists and mental health specialists was a common feature of colonial medicine during the late 19th and early 20th centuries. As late as the 1950s psychoanalytic thinkers like Octave Mannoni, when speaking of the psyches of Europeans and Africans, attributed the colonizing impulse to the English psychological makeup and the dependency complex to the African mental state, thus stereotyping mental states almost exclusively in racial terms. Ethnopsychiatric observations such as these also meant that the diagnosis, such as it was, left the context of the mental illness – such as colonialism, poverty, slavery or oppression – completely out of the ambit. By locating the problem almost entirely in the individual's cultural and genetic structures ethnopsychiatry did away with the necessity of examining environmental factors – the European presence in their lives, the physical threat and violence by the white man – that induced disorders. During his studies as a clinical psychologist and psychiatrist in the French colonial period of Algeria, Frantz Fanon noted (in 'Colonial War and Mental Disorders', in *The Wretched of the Earth*, 1961) that the French psychiatrists simply assumed the innate savagery and violent 'nature' of the black man, and treated him accordingly. Fanon, in his observations of black patients, noted that far from an innate propensity to violence the black man's rage and physical expressions of the same were the consequence of a palpable threat experienced by them due to the presence of the police, the arrests and the racism that characterized every stage of life in colonial Algeria. Further, Fanon proposed that such ethnopsychiatric practices (although Fanon did not himself use the term) did not admit the alienation the black man felt from (i) his land (ii) his people and (iii) his culture due to the colonial presence. Attributing mental conditions to superstition, myths and practices with descriptors like 'the African mind' (monolithic and unified categories themselves), European scientists cleverly shifted the responsibility back to the colonized subject's culture – and damned it as disorder-inducing. A classic postcolonial explication of such ethnopsychiatric representations is that of *Jane Eyre's* Bertha Mason. Of Creole origin, her mental illness is presented as a family condition. Her incarceration in the attic of Rochester's home is kept a secret, and her very presence, as Rochester's wife, prevents him, ostensibly, from marrying the white Jane Eyre. Critics like Gayatri Spivak ('Three Women's Texts and a Critique of Imperialism', 1985) note that Bertha Mason's madness becomes part of her role as the 'fictive Other' to the white woman, Jane Eyre. Bertha Mason has to die so that the two white lovers can marry. By showing Mason as inheriting her madness from her family – and therefore race as well – and not from her English, marital environment, we see Brontë anticipating the ethnopsychiatrist theories of the 20th century. In Florence Marryat's *The Blood of the Vampire* (1897), the vampire, Harriet, is the daughter of a Swiss man and a Jamaican woman, described as 'a fat, flabby half-caste' and a 'sensual, self-loving, crafty and bloodthirsty half-caste'. Harriet becomes a threat to English womanhood itself because in her presence the women seem to lose all life/liveliness and the men are invariably attracted. Her evil nature is traced to her ancestry in yet another instance of ethnopsychiatry so that this hybrid woman, a Creole from the colony, like Bertha Mason before her, unconsciously becomes a threat to English femininity, masculinity and English domesticity. Her very nature and behaviour, temperament and preferences, constitute her as a threat. What is important to note is that in such ethnopsychiatric representations, a certain innately wicked, evil and perverted nature is posited in the case of people from the colonies. Ethnopsychiatric representations such as those of Marryat thus essentialize the native/colonized as 'naturally' prone to vampirism, perversion and sexual deviance or profligacy. This also means that their 'nature' is deemed to be unalterable. (See also: **essentialism**)

Eurocentrism: The term finds its first expression as 'Europe-centric' in the writings of the German Karl Haushofer but was popularized by the economist Samir Amin, who noted that global economic development was determined by Europe's needs, so that raw materials, markets and trade policies all served European interests at the expense of the rest of the world. In the writings of cultural critics such as Edward Said, the term simply signified any practice or ideology that saw Europe as the centre and the world as peripheral. Early Modern cartography and maps of the world by Mercator and others often portrayed Europe at the centre with other nations arranged around it. With colonial empires in the 18th and 19th centuries Eurocentrism gathered strength. Europe began to be seen as the centre of progress, civilization and modernity. It was also the seat of morality. Eurocentrism thus positioned Europe as a model for other nations to emulate, but also as a 'natural' leader for the rest of the world. Eurocentrism is the foundation for the 'white man's burden' ideology where the moral responsibility for the uplift of the rest of the world rests with Europe – this manifest as the great humanitarian regimes of the 19th centuries. Other consequences of Eurocentrism, critiqued in postcolonial studies, were the valorization of European qualities: the colour of the skin to Christianity, its idea of progress (embodied in the Industrial Revolution), and its cultural practices. With Darwinian theories Eurocentrism gained greater currency, with unfavourable comparisons situating other races far below on the evolutionary scale, and European races at the higher end. Anti-colonial struggles were also, occasionally, seen as Eurocentric for the leaders' indebtedness to European thought. Nationalism itself was projected as a European idea and therefore not founded in, say, Asian or African traditions, as the debates between Benedict Anderson (1991, Rev. Ed) and Partha Chatterjee (1986, 1993) famously showed. Postcolonial studies itself has been accused of an implicit Eurocentrism by critics like Arif Dirlik (1997) and Aijaz Ahmad (1992, 1997) who propose that the entire critical field of postcolonialism has been made possible because of migrant academics located in Western universities, trained in Western political and philosophical thought and writing mainly for Western audiences. Since these traditions in politics and philosophy were always complicit with racism, colonialism and imperialism their intellectual legacy in postcolonial studies will always remain Eurocentric, and therefore incapable of (i) being truly faithful to native thought (ii) being a resistant form of thinking.

evangelicalism (colonial):   In Chinua Achebe's *Arrow of God* (1967) Mr Goodcountry declares that he wishes to 'save [the Igbos] from the error [of their religious ways] which was now threatening to ruin them' (1967: 269). The civilizational mission of colonialism was coterminous, and interchangeable, with evangelicalism and proselytizing in Asia and Africa. If the African animist and tribal religious practices were deemed to be primitive and not religion at all, Hinduism in the Indian subcontinent was deemed to be full of superstition and irrational beliefs that prevented the country from progressing even under the British. Alexander Duff declared that 'the intellectual, moral, and spiritual regeneration of the universal mind' was the goal of all colonial evangelical-educational missions. Numerous missionary societies (the Baptist Missionary Society, Society for the Propagation of the Christian Gospel, the Church Missionary Society, among others) were founded in England from the last decades of the 18th century in response to the call of figures like William Carey. Hinduism and Islam were both treated as religions that denied equality to women – a theme that has not disappeared from Western rhetoric if we recall the post-9/11 'project' of saving the Muslim women from the Taliban – and constructed artificial, oppressive categories of caste and other hierarchies. Initially the colonial administrators were unwilling to intervene in the religious matters of the colonies. But this became a more or less accepted function of the administration from the early 19th century in the subcontinent with reforms initiated into women's education, the prohibition of certain religious practices (*sati*), the monitoring and restrictions of pilgrimage and festivals, and the active championing of causes like widow-remarriage. Colonial explorers and administrators like David Livingstone in *Missionary Travels and Researches in South Africa* (1857) explicitly linked evangelical activity to commerce, and Livingstone is believed to have first deployed the phrase 'commerce and Christianity'. Missionary lives and traders are 'mutually dependent', wrote Livingstone.

exile: A condition of being physically distanced from one's motherland is described as an 'exile'. The term includes both forced migrations, say, during wartime, as well as voluntary migration (called expatriation) where people move from one country to another seeking jobs and a better life. Exilic conditions have been one of the oldest forms of displacement in human history, where individuals and groups moved away from places of origin for various reasons – war, oppression, climate change, crop failure, predators, etc. Migrant and immigrant communities carried their physical, psychological and cultural baggage with them and were often instrumental in the transformation of the receiving society. Artists and artisans travelling in the European regions during the 1400–1600 period introduced new forms of mathematics, art, literature and languages and were instrumental, according to Dirk Hoerder (2002), for the European Renaissance. In the post-1500s period Europeans exiled to and migrating to the New World were responsible for the first colonies. Later similar displacement of peoples from Europe into Asia and Africa led to colonialism, even when the Europeans did not settle in India and Africa (unlike in Canada and Australia), but stayed there for extended periods of time. Several of the colonials expressed distress at their state of exile and longed for home. So the exilic foundations of colonialism require some attention. Elizabeth Buettner's study of British families in India, with the children away in England, and complicating the dynamics of 'home' and 'abroad', is one such (2004). Within postcolonial studies exiled writers (as in migrant but also writers forced to live away from their homeland) have attained considerable fame for their reflections on exile, separation from motherland and their native language and their cultural roots. Nuruddin Farah, Derek Walcott, Meena Alexander, Mahmoud Darweesh, Salman Rushdie, Abdulrazzak Gurnah, Monica Ali, Agha Shahid Ali – grouped as writers of the **diaspora** – have all written about their dual legacies – of their motherland and their adopted nation/culture – nostalgia and acculturation. Examining the postcard from his homeland, Kashmir, Agha Shahid Ali captures the pathos of exile when he writes 'the half-inch Himalayas in my hand.../this is the closest/I'll ever be to home' ('Postcard from Kashmir', 1996: 752). Migrancy and dislocation have been excessively praised by people like Rushdie (who spoke eloquently of the migrant's 'historical weightlessness') and critics like Bhabha, and seen as a condition of existence in postcoloniality by Elleke

Boehmer (2006). Debates about the authenticity and inauthenticity of rep-resentations of their homelands and their acculturation have been a part of the exiled writers' fate, where quite often one migrant author accuses another of reinforcing stereotypes that the West wants. (See also: **settler colonialism, diaspora**)

exoticism: The term comes essentially from botany and describes a species from a foreign place and therefore not indigenous. Since the 16th century at least, in Europe, it has come to represent foreignness and alien culture. The exotic is, during the European encounter with the cultures of Africa, Asia and South America, the racial and cultural Other. The exotic was something to be collected and viewed as 'curios' – in the form of museums. Plants, stones, animals – at one point an Indian elephant in England – people (African women, Indian performing artists), textiles, and pottery were taken from various parts of their Empire by European collectors, administrators and treasure hunters, and exhibited. To have seen and brought back items from exotic places was the marker of gentlemanly taste in 18th- and 19th-century Europe. One could desire, acquire and display the exotic, but occasionally also be worried about its utter difference from one's own culture. The exotic was therefore a method of bringing the distant parts of the Empire into com-mon view as spectacle in the museum or the exhibitions (England and Europe hosted these exhibitions from 1870s). Exotic objects that catered to the English/European tastes, literally, included tea, cocoa, coffee, tobacco (this last since the 16th century when it arrived from America), as well as décor such as tapestries, china and carpets. Charles Lamb in his essay on china suggested that the arrival of china in an English household was a marker of its economic-material progress. The exotic was not simply about casting the non-European as the racial and cultural Other but about demon-strating the expansion of European power into distant parts of the world. The exotic was a discourse of borders and boundaries. It lay outside every-day experience and the ordinary (Rousseau and Porter 1990). In Christa Knellwolf's reading, the exotic described both fantasies and real historical responses to cultural difference (2002). The racial and cultural exotic was a reminder of an early, primal stage (Eaton 2006). The quest for the exotic was also manifest in the form of artwork that sought to capture new places and cultural practices for consumption back home. Another form of exoticiza-tion was to cast native practices as strange, fearsome or primitive. The primi-tive was in fact a preferred exotic 'object'. Museums and collections also served the purpose, as Christa Knellwolf has demonstrated, of separating the object from its true setting and placing it in situations where it might be safely observed. The explorers and sportsmen in Asia, Africa and South America in the later decades of the 19th century found that there were no untouched regions in these continents, and hence the exotic was no more. Hunting and the bringing back of animals as trophies by voluntarily entering into jungles and dangerous terrain became a mode of exoticization as well. Occasionally the exotic animal, woman or jewel was also the subject of anxiety. Wilkie Collins' *The Moonstone* was centred around an Indian jewel that, having entered the house of an English family, brings danger to the inmates. Count Dracula has his home in the land beyond the forest (Trans-sylvania) and is a source of threat to English femininity in Bram Stoker's novel. The exotic madwoman Bertha Mason is the obstacle to true English marital bliss in *Jane Eyre*. Postcolonial studies sees exoticization as the stereotyping of the non-European for consumption by the English back home. Hence exoticization was a form of colonial control. Eugenia Jenkins has argued that exoticism was not simply a representation of non-European others: it was a mode of European self-representation in a context of global territorial and economic expansion, and within the circulation of goods, people and ideas (2012). Laura Rosenthal's reading of the European exoticizing discourses proposes that exoticism offered cosmopolitan possibilities for the European individual and society to reinvent the self and the nation (2012).

exploitation colony: In contrast to settler colonialism – whose defining feature was the Europeans settling in the new territory, starting colonies, building cities and even, on occasion, marrying the natives – exploitation colonies were places wherein the Europeans arrived and stayed for periods of time but did so exclusively for the purpose of utilizing the natural resources and local labour. Canada and Australia were settler colonies and the white settlements eventually grew into cities with their own brand of culture. Africa and Asia, including the vast subcontinent of India, were exploitation colonies. Europeans came for trade and resources, and acquired political power in order to facilitate that trading and resource exploitation, but there was no intention of settling in, or merging with the natives. Exploitation colonies served the imperial nation with raw materials for its industries, labour and food products.

exploration (colonial): It is possible to argue that colonialism begins as exploration – both imaginative (in the accounts of fantastic lands in early travelogues) and material (the circulation of goods from distant parts of the world). The narratives of the Early Modern period with its voyages and travels exhibit, according to critics, a 'colonizing imagination' (Singh 1996) and 'proto-Orientalist' concerns (Barbour 2003). The quest for the Northwest passage, the trade routes to the East and the extreme limits of the earth, as well as journeys into the interiors of Africa and South America, may all be grouped under the category 'exploration'. With the discovery of sea routes European trade links with various parts of the world began and flourished. With the discovery of the New World (Columbus) new settlements and colonies were founded in the region. Metaphors of 'virgin lands' and **terra nullius** constructed the new regions in particular ways, mainly as territories waiting to be uncovered, penetrated, examined and eventually owned/dominated. But exploration and its concomitant condition, **discovery**, were also about the people and cultures the Europeans encountered in these regions. It was through exploration and discovery that Europe first acknowledged racial variety and racial difference. Europe also accepted the possibility of different religions. So exploration and discovery need to be seen as contributing to the epistemic empire of Europe: widening its scope of learning across cultures and regions, leading Francis Bacon in *The New Atlantis* to speak of knowledge in terms of space and territory: 'the end of our foundation is the knowledge of causes, and secret motions of things; and enlarging the bounds of the human empire' (1627).

feminism (Islamic): From the 1990s a strand of feminism has emerged from the Islamic nations. This mostly seeks to legally reform Islam, which translates into greater rights and freedoms for women but within the ambit of Islam. Thus, in a departure from traditional (Western) feminisms, Islamic feminism does not abandon its religion, but calls for a gender-sensitive interpretation of Islamic laws (Mojab 2001. Also Cooke 2000). While the West has assumed that Islam is inherently anti-woman, apparently symbolized in the *hijab* and the *purdah*, other kinds of scholarship paint a very different picture. Saba Mahmood has pondered over the politics of feminism (and postcolonial studies) that includes race, class and national differences when discussing gender but has never included religion as a facet of identity-making. Mahmood's argument here is that it is assumed by Western feminism that religious identity is inherently restrictive, anti-individual and anti-agency. Why, asks Mahmood (2000), is the submission to custom or faith in God *not* considered an act of choice and agency on the part of the 'docile agent'? Nivedita Menon (2008) has noted how for Egyptian feminists the veil was a central element of their identity as Muslims *and* as women. They argued, notes Menon, that they chose the veil as a liberatory move and against Western consumerism, and thereby resisted the sexualization and commodification of the woman's body/face. Literature coming out of Pakistan and the Arab region, especially that produced by women, has addressed various gender-particular issues of Islamic society from this vantage point. Assia Djebar, Nawal el Saadawi, and Tehmina Durrani have all pointed to the patriarchal interpretation of Islam in their countries. In works like *The Innocence of the*

The Postcolonial Studies Dictionary, First Edition. Pramod K. Nayar.
© 2015 John Wiley & Sons, Ltd. Published 2015 by John Wiley & Sons, Ltd.

Devil (1994) El Saadawi's women are not only exploited but also become figures of subversion and resistance. What is also significant is that a certain kind of Muslim woman – the one who claims a fear of genetic mutilation and murder by Islamists rather than declares herself a feminist within Islam – receives greater attention from Western feminists and the legal apparatus (for refugees or asylum-seekers). This is so because such women come to embody for the Western the *essential* cultural violence of Islam, and serve the purpose of bringing back the colonial trope of pity-and-rescue. Critics since the 1990s have, however, expressed an anxiety that the migrant commentator or scholar serves as a Native Informant to the First World about all things Muslim (Razack 1995; Khan 2005). (See also: **essentialism, secularism/post-secularism, Native Informant**)

fetish/phobia: In Homi Bhabha's reading of colonial discourse (*The Location of Culture*) he proposes that the white man is deeply divided in his perceptions and responses toward the native/non-European. This **ambivalence** results in what Bhabha terms the 'fetish/phobia' phenomenon. The white man both desires and fears the non-white Other. The native's difference, the exoticism, is at once attractive and frightening/repulsive. This difference is something that needs to be comprehended – and this assimilates difference into the white man's frame. However, this difference is also something to be preserved as difference, as exotic, so that the white man can position himself in contrast to/with the non-white. The white man is afraid of the non-white because of this incomprehensible difference, but is mesmerized by him as well.

filiation/affiliation: Edward Said in *The World, the Text and the Critic* (1983) argued that two forms of belonging are common. The first, through lineage and family lines, which he called 'filiation'. The second, through cultural practices and connections, which he termed 'affiliation'. Said's use of the terms was primarily to see how later critics relate to and correspond with predecessor critics and critical traditions. He argued that the canon of English literature was built up primarily through filiation where predecessor texts are seen as the fount of wisdom that need to be replicated and reproduced in some way or another. Said made the claim that indigenous cultures relate to the culture of the European ruling race through affiliation. When the European culture imposes its hegemony on the subject races the latter begin to abandon their own cultural practices and take to the European ones. They begin to see merit in European assumptions, borrow the wisdom, stereotypes and beliefs of European texts, and start interrogating their own/indigenous cultural practices as, slowly, the European's culture begins to be the background against which the native evolves her/his identity. That is, the native starts finding her/his subjectivity and identity through a connection not with her/his own cultural traditions and customs but with the European ones. This is affiliation – the cultural adaptations and adoptions through which subject societies build connections with the European race.

First World: The concept emerged during the 1960s and the Cold War when the world's nations were clearly divided along ideological lines. It was traditionally used to describe the capitalist bloc nations with the socialist countries of the former Soviet Union being the Second World. The USA, UK, France, the Scandinavian nations, Canada, the Mediterranean countries and Australia are deemed to be the First World whose economy relies on capitalism, and usually has some form of democracy as opposed to the totalitarian socialism of the Second World. Now the term indicates any highly developed nation. The First World is characterized by high income and a high level of industrialization, but also higher social indicators of gender empowerment, equality of opportunities, democratic rights, etc.

Fourth World: A new category after the First, Second and Third World, the Fourth World represents a group of people, or nation, usually within a larger nation. Hence, we can think of the Fourth World as a population without a well-defined territory of its own. The Kurds in Iran-Iraq, the Basques in Spain, and the Romana of Europe are examples. Very often the term is also used to refer to sub-populations, such as tribes, and indigenous populations (also called First Nation people) within a nation-state. Fourth World thus refers to populations that are subsumed into a nation-state although their ancestry, cultural homogeneity and large numbers merit a nation of their own. The movements and cultural revival of indigenous peoples that we see today emerge from this sense of lacking a nation. Crucially, these peoples within a nation-state are seen as second-class citizens even though, arguably, their claims to citizenship and belonging go back further in time than the rest of the nation-state's peoples. The aboriginals of Canada and Australia are cases in point. Their exclusion – or nominal inclusion – in the processes and benefits of the nation-state (in the form of political rights and welfare that accrue from citizenship), means that they remain outside the purview of developmental processes as well. In fact, sociologist of communications technology Manuel Castells, in *End of Millennium* (1998), has termed those segments of populations (working classes, homeless) in First World cities who do not benefit from globalization and technological advances the 'Fourth World'.

geographical morality: The term was first used by the English statesman Edmund Burke during his Warren Hastings impeachment speech (1788) to describe the relativism and hypocrisy that characterized colonial relations and imperial posturing. Burke argued that actions and behaviour considered reprehensible and even cognizable within England were deemed harmless and even desirable when they occurred in the colonies. Burke stated that the 'duties of men in public and private situations are not to be governed by their relations to the Great Governor of the Universe, or by their relations to men, but by climates … parallels not of life but of latitudes'. Thus, corruption that was deemed worthy of imprisonment and public disgrace in England was tolerated and actively encouraged in the East India Company, noted Burke. The geographical morality of the Empire was therefore seen in the different yardsticks by which actions were evaluated in different geographical regions, all bolstered by the claim that the different moral standards of Eastern cultures demanded that English codes be suspended as well when in operation in these places. Burke proposed that such a geographical morality encouraged fraud, corruption, thievery and even murder built on the flawed assumption that such actions were appropriate to the Eastern nations.

geography: Geography was more than just a discipline in the colonial context. The geography of the world was part of the English curriculum through the 19th century, and gave the school child a sense of the globe. But even before the imperial age in Britain, geography as a discipline in schools seems to have exhibited a proto-colonial politics through the way in which it talked about the earth (Cormack 1997. Also Hulme 2008). Paul Carter's work famously argued that 'spatial fantasies' shape, and indicate, a culture's presence (1987). Thus geography books and materials might be read as methods of socialization – of the English school child – into imperial fantasies and the imagining of the extent and power of this *imperium*. In this way, Megan Norcia's work (2010) has shown how the supposed bare recitation of facts in English geography textbooks is more than just that: it places these facts about locations and people in interpretive frames that are drawn from imperialist ideologies. Geographical discourse, in these primers as well as guide books, enabled the Europeans to think of the world's spaces in terms of profits, threats, leisure, emancipatory intervention, conservation, among others. In the 15th and 16th centuries a proto-colonial geography took the form of imaginary lands inhabited by strange creatures. As the travelling voyages of the European nations progressed, more and more of the globe was revealed, and documented. This geographical knowledge included sea routes, distances, winds, people, ports, among others. But mostly, the geography of the world was premised on economic benefits: the world's spaces were thought of and presented in terms of profits to be acquired through colonial expansion into new areas. The slave trade which came in for attention in the late 18th and early 19th centuries from the abolitionists also engendered a humanitarian geography of the world – mapping the regions of the Caribbean, Europe and Africa as aligned in a relationship of suffering, exploitation and profit. In the colonies themselves new forms of geography emerged. Due to the need to study conditions of health and sickness medical geography books were produced as guides to healthy and threatening spaces in the Americas, Africa and India. Tropical medicine, a cognate discipline, emerged aligned with geography during the 19th century, possibly initiated by James's *An Essay on Diseases Incidental to Europeans in Hot Climates* (1768), although a few centuries before this era Shakespearean England had exhibited considerable concerns with disease, infection and porous borders (Harris 1998, 2004). Ports were seen as places of trade and exchange but also as metaphors for invasion (although the pathogen theory of disease didn't exist as yet). English poetry evolved its own geography of the colonial encounter in the form of the returning serviceman figure in Wordsworth, Burns and Coleridge. In postcolonial terms, the tropics were constructed in discourse as unhealthy, profitable, improvable, exotic or threatening – in contrast to the temperate European region.

globe: The globe as a metaphor, as an organizing principle, served to formulate a sense of one's location, but also served as a way of perceiving the world itself (Cosgrove 2001). How Europe located itself on/in this globe was the result of specific cultural, social and political contexts. Shakespeare's plays were staged, as is well known, in The Globe. Cosgrove notes that two discourses, of empire and of humanity, have been central to the Western imagination of the globe, and by extension of the earth and the world (the latter being the social world on the earth's surface). The globe helped the West to fantasize the limits of the empire – with or without geographical accuracy as to the boundaries of the earth – as well as the universality of humans. In the 18th and early 19th centuries the globe was to be united in Enlightenment thought – with universalisms such as humanism and humanitarianism (Lester 2000) evolving as philosophical concepts. The work of geographers like Cosgrove point to the imperial subtexts to scientific texts.

globalization: Since the late 20th century nations have often been subject to economic and political forces that come from beyond their geopolitical borders, from organizations that have no border restrictions. Globalization is the flow of capital, labour and cultural productions across national borders, unifying the world within these flows, although the profits and decision-making processes are very often located in the First World nations. Commentators have argued that globalization is not so new: as early as the Renaissance, Europe had global cultures flourishing within it, in terms of commodities (tapestries, tea, coffee, art) and ideas (Jardine 1996), and trading networks had created 'world systems' (Abu-Lughod 1989; Osterhammel and Petersson 2009). As Abu-Lughod stresses, there are startling similarities between the capitalisms of Asian, Middle Eastern and European empires in their respective heydays and globalization as we know it today. But the pace and extent of globalization have never been so great. Other forms of globalization have also existed in human history, such as that of the humanitarian movement from the late 18th century, where European evangelists and statesmen, physicians and teachers, travelled across the world in order to uplift the savage tribes of Asia and Africa. For postcolonial studies globalization is a version of imperialism. The term has several specific connotations for postcolonial studies. First, it means, simply, the circulation of commodities – entertainment artefacts like film or games, food, fashion, celebrity icons – manufactured by First World companies like Tommy Hilfiger or Coca Cola, in Third World nations. Second, it sees globalization as the continuation of exploitative labour conditions, where First World companies 'outsource' their work to low-paid workers in Asian nations. Third, it implies a serious form of cultural imperialism where local cultures are slowly erased in favour of First World products. Fourth, First World and transnational corporate bodies exploit the natural resources of Third World nations in an extension of older processes of colonialism. Fifth, economic, political and even social policies of nations are determined by treaties, injunctions, rulings and more veiled threats from outside the nation-state. That is, individual national economies are subject to shifts within the global economic system and policy. Finally, globalization for the postcolonial nation is seen as undermining the project of **decolonization**. Where decolonization demands economic, political, linguistic and cultural freedom from the legacies of colonial rule, and greater autonomy of the nation-state and its cultures, globalization imposes a set of global standards, whether in global warming or cultural products. These standards do not respect national borders and in fact erase or erode them. Thus globalization is seen as the antithesis of decolonization. Together, all these might be seen as resulting in the loss of sovereignty of the postcolonial nation. When postcolonial nations claim that globalization is an extension of colonialism into neocolonial forms what they mean is that, while in the earlier era their nations were controlled by European nations, in the present age this same control is exercised by supra-national corporations. There was a global economy even in the earlier age, just as there is one now. However, this new figuration of the empire is seen more as the attribute of the USA than of European nations. Thus the colonial-imperial domination of the world by European nations like Britain, in terms of economy or culture, has been replaced by domination by the USA. Cultural domination also manifests in the form of the global reach and dissemination of American products in food, drink, fashion, entertainment, although local cultures might appropriate these products and resignify them. But globalization also causes international markets to open up for Third World products such as films or artefacts like pottery and masks. Ethnic chic, which is the commodification of, say, Indian food, African masks or Turkish scarves in the West, is read here as a sign of this role. Economists (Gilpin 2000) argue the case, however, for a more nuanced understanding of such a corporate globalization where, for instance, it is only a few nations (USA, Western Europe and Japan) and corporations (Sony, Time Warner) that are actively globalizing in their takeover of markets and resources. (See also: **decolonization, neocolonialism, postcolony**)

hegemony: A term that is deployed extensively in the Marxist writings of Antonio Gramsci and Louis Althusser, it refers to the domination of one ethnic group, nation, class, race or culture by another. In postcolonial studies hegemony refers to the domination of non-Europeans by Europeans. Crucial to the understanding of the term are the modes of hegemonic domination. Hegemony is not simply military conquest and domination by force. Rather, as Gramsci and Althusser treated it, hegemony works more insidiously. The dominant culture constructs myths, belief systems and practices through which the subject culture is presented as inferior and vulnerable. Over a period of time, with accretion and assimilation, the colonized begins to believe this representation, and thus concedes that the European has the moral, ethical and cultural superiority to rule. Once the hegemony has been effectively assimilated then we see the formation of the colonial subject. The colonized individual's very **subjectivity** is forged in the crucible of the white master's language, religion and culture which slowly and assuredly destroys the individual's sense of rootedness in her/his own culture. That is, hegemony is what bestows the identity of 'colonial subject' upon the Asian and African. 'Subjectification' occurs when the non-European concedes the white man's right to rule and govern the non-European's life. Hegemony is thus domination through the *consent* (and not coercion), terms that Gramsci uses, of the dominated. The subject accepts her/his inferiority and ignorance and implicitly gives the European the right to rule. Cultural hegemony is the dominance of the European culture

ABCDEFGHIJKLMNOPQRSTUVWXYZ

The Postcolonial Studies Dictionary, First Edition. Pramod K. Nayar.

over the non-European one, manifest best in the use of English, French, Spanish, Dutch and other European languages as the sign of social mobility, civilized behaviour and progress by the African or the Asian subject. When the native subscribes to (that is, internalizes) European language, historiography, religion, cultural practices, literary representations and even politics, we see colonial hegemony's success because the native now colludes with the colonial structure and therefore is no longer open to the idea of resistance. In Tsitsi Dangarembga's *Nervous Conditions* (1988), Nhamo, having studied in the European mission, returns to his village but finds he cannot be the family's son any more: 'I shall go and live with Babamukuru in the mission. I shall no longer be Jeremiah's son' (48). Dangarembga's novel demonstrates how African family structures are unable to cope with the hegemony of European 'charity' embodied in the mission. In neither of these cases do we see actual force being used by the European but both authors gesture at the more subtle forms of violence that cultural hegemony relies on.

homonationalism: A term coined by Jasbir Puar (2005) to describe national sovereignty as linked to its tolerance (or intolerance) for/of LGBTQ citizens. In a later essay she elaborates her definition as a 'historical shift in the production of nation-states from the insistence on heteronormativity to the increasing inclusion of homonormativity' (2013: 26). Puar pays attention to assemblages and queer connections that are transnational as well. Puar notes that post-9/11 we can discern in nationalist-neoliberal discourses a concomitant condemnation, or anxiety, over alternate sexual identities. Thus, even when the USA (Puar's focus of attention) and its liberals appear to be supportive of Arab, Muslim and other identities there seems to be the supposition that these other cultures are sexist, anti-queer and intolerant. As Puar puts it, this derives from a myth 'of queerness as a white, Christian, secular norm' (27). Puar's work is situated within a larger shift in sexuality and queer cultural studies where national and racial identities are examined in conjunction with sexual identities, especially alternate sexualities, as seen in Gayatri Gopinath's work on South Asian sexualities (2005) and also the work of Martin Manalansan IV (2003).

humanism (European):   Humanism treats the human as the centre of this world. Emerging mainly in the European context during the Renaissance, this 'human' was defined as a rational, coherent, bounded entity, self-aware and possessing the agency to determine his – the gender is crucial here – course of life with rationality being the keystone of his identity. The above inventory of attributes was believed to be common to all humans, and thus Renaissance Europe evolved 'the human' as a generic, universal category. Eighteenth-century debates about human dignity and human rights were founded on this idea of the universal human. For post-colonial studies such an argument about the universal human as a category is open to question. Drawing upon the work of feminist philosophy, contemporary postcolonial thinkers like Fanon have argued that the idea of a universal human with human rights and self-evident dignity evolved, ironically, during the age when Europe was engaged in both the slave trade and imperial conquest. Both of these were the consequence of the European belief that particular races and ethnic groups were less than human, and as such did not require human rights. Blacks, for example, were barely above the animals and were supposedly unaware of themselves as humans. Jews, women, Catholics, gypsies, homosexuals, blacks and Asians have been, critical humanist studies point out, excluded from the very category of the human (Davies 1997). Women were always treated as less-than-human and so 'universal human' actually meant 'universal male'. Imperial conquest and expansion determined an exclusionary rather than inclusionary definition of the human so that slavery and dominance could be put in place in the colony and the plantation. For postcolonial studies alert to this ironic history of European humanism, the category of 'universal human' was a category of differentiation, segregation and ranking where Europeans occupied the top of the human rank and all other races stayed at the lower end. Humanism in such readings is inextricably linked to racial theories of humans, racism itself and imperialism. Certain features, mainly those that Europe has valued over the centuries, were believed to count as irreducible 'human' features, with little regard to other cultures that might have different values for the same features. The high value placed on the autonomy of the individual, a cornerstone of European humanism, does not account, therefore, for Asiatic modes of thinking that see autonomy as less significant than interrelations among individuals. This has been the problem for many of the formerly colonized, for whom freedom has been defined as solely individual, and any observance of custom is seen as restrictive by the West. This valorization of the individual over the community or collective has intensified in the neo-liberal context (Mahmood 2000; Povinelli 2008). All human qualities or features are social constructs, with some being favoured during particular periods in European history, but all presented as 'universal' features toward which the rest of the world needs to strive. In the

20th century, with increasing advances in animal rights studies, technoscience studies, and also technology itself, the category of the human as a self-contained, coherent and autonomous individual has been demolished. Species interconnections and dependence (Haraway 2008) are seen as more crucial to the evolution of the human than autonomy. For postcolonial studies the Haraway argument is an important one because it denies validity to European values or models as the only ones in existence. Further, it demonstrates the close alignment and exclusionary nature of race theories, imperialism, the evolution of disciplines and scientific theories. In the postcolonial era the debates around 'universal human rights' are also centred around the different perceptions of freedom and individual autonomy between Western traditions and, say, Asian or Arab ones.

humanitarianism: Arising as moral position but also as active social-political ethos, humanitarianism in 18th-century Europe bestowed the task of saving, civilizing, conserving the non-European parts of the world on Europeans. Anti-abolitionist campaigns from the 1780s, the social reform movements in the Indian subcontinent from the 1820s and the campaign to protect aboriginals in Australia in the 1820s are examples of this global humanitarian project (Lester 2000). Within England the enactment of poor laws and working class 'improvement' campaigns might be read in the same light. Humanitarianism for postcolonial studies has several problematic aspects. It assumes that Europe was 'chosen' for this humanitarian intervention into the lives, places and cultures of other races, implying a certain moral, social and technological superiority. It also assumes that the rest of the world needed to be brought up to, and brought up on, the system of values that Europe believed all humans and cultures ought to possess. Europe attributed to itself the right to intervene and alter the other cultures. Within colonial writing as well as English literature there are numerous instances of humanitarian projects and figures. St John Rivers in *Jane Eyre* is described as a 'master-spirit' for his determination to go out to India and serve the cause of humanity there. He would probably die in India, speculates Jane. Humanitarianism gave the Englishman an identity (in contemporary postcolonial interpretations), so it was as much about the English as it was about the colony. Querry, the architect in Graham Greene's *A Burnt-out Case*, abandons his fame and his social position in England when he goes out to work for the lepers in the Congo, turning his talents toward a humanitarian mission by building leprosaria for the patients. Debates about human rights that emanate from such humanitarian projects have often attracted criticism from postcolonial nations and the Arab world for eliding cultural differences and imposing and universalizing instead a European model of the human, social order, governance and democracy. Therefore, humanitarian projects could be seen as violent, as modes of imposing a hegemony of thought and action over races that might not even be directly 'subjects' to the European races (as used to be the case under colonialism). Humanitarian intervention in the 20th century has attracted similar controversies, although it is now mainly the USA that, aided by its allies in the EU, engages in such acts. Liberation of Muslim women, preventing so-called conflict (but ignoring genocide in other cases, such as Bosnia and Rwanda), and 'making the world safer for democracy' (a phrase used by Woodrow Wilson to justify the American role in World War I) are interventions that attract criticism because they are seen, not without justification, as being imperial, one-sided and hegemonic. 'Humanitarian imperialism' (Bricmont 2006) and its close adjunct 'military humanism' (Chomsky 1999) are seen less as humanitarian interventions than as modes of acquiring control over territories and their resources by the USA, its allies and powerful business corporations in the guise of 'saving' a segment of society in that region.

hybridity: A term from botany – referring to cross-breeding – hybridity in postcolonial studies refers to the mixing of races (miscegenation) and cultures so that new forms of culture are produced. In the 19th century hybridity was something that frightened the Europeans. The colonials therefore campaigned against miscegenation because they saw the mixing of races as a dilution of their racial attributes. Armed with a strong sense of cultural purity, colonial discourse rejected racial mixing by projecting the other races as inferior, and therefore to be avoided. Hybridity thus was closely aligned with both Social Darwinism and racism because both refused the very idea of cultural-racial mixing (Young 1995). Races had to be preserved in their pure form – an ideological proposition that assumed that there were pure forms of culture, and that some cultures were irreducibly inferior. Colonial fiction of the 19th century, whether Rider Haggard or R.M. Ballantyne, Alice Perrin or Maud Diver, was essentially a genre that propounded the incompatibility of races. While the genre acknowledged the intrinsic attraction of a different culture (the exotic appeal of difference), this difference was to be left alone, not to be mixed with, so that imperial culture remained pure. Racial and cultural mixing was therefore a weakening of the racial dominance. This was the reason why English literature, right from the Early Modern period, was critical of those English who had 'gone native'. We see early examples of this in Philip Massinger's *The Renegado* and Robert Danborne's *A Christian Turned Turk* (Vitkus 2007). Within postcolonial studies, ironically, colonialism itself is seen as enabling the creation of hybrid cultures where the colonized subject adopts European ways of speaking (i.e., adopts the colonial master's language), dressing and eventually thinking as well. Homi Bhabha sees hybridity as an empowering condition where both cultural purity and cultural diversity are rejected. Cultural diversity or difference carries an exotic appeal, while cultural purity assumes that any appropriation of a different cultural register is just contamination. Hybridity thus becomes a means of resisting a unitary identity, emphasizing instead multiplicity and plural identities, existing between cultures (native and colonial master's), in what Bhabha has called the Third Space. Salman Rushdie, Hanif Kureishi and Derek Walcott present hybridity as an empowering condition for some and detrimental to others. While Rushdie laughs at hybrid postcolonials (in the Methwold estate in *Midnight's Children*) who seem to mimic their European masters, in almost all his works he has emphasized cultural mixing. In V.S. Naipaul's *A Bend in the River* (1979) Salim realizes that colonial legacies exist in the domain of language and even thinking in the postcolonial age. Walcott's Corporal Lestrade in *Dream on Monkey Mountain* is rooted in French, English and black cultures. He resents all Africans, and describes them in the language of colonial whites: 'animals, beasts, savages, cannibals, niggers' (216), but is later forced to admit he has African roots as well. Lestrade's conflicted identity is the other side of the empowered hybrid identity that Rushdie and Bhabha praise. For other critics in postcolonialism (Eoyang 2003), however, the hegemonic structures of English can be easily dismantled from *within* by conscious non-native users so that the risk of both, essentializing and exoticism, could be minimized in a language that is clearly foreign to the user. (See also: **transculturation, creolization, mimicry, miscegenation**)

imaginative geography: First used by Edward Said in his *Orientalism*, it refers to the mental construction of spaces and then the construction of cultural and racial difference. Spaces familiar to us are immediately designated as 'ours'. Any unfamiliar space, therefore, is designated as 'theirs'. Said suggests that such imaginative constructions of spatial difference shades into themes of cultural difference. Anybody who occupies a different or unfamiliar territory is believed to be different in terms of mentality, culture or civilization. Imaginative geographies were therefore modes of spatially organizing the world's different cultures, and of course then establishing as 'truth' that this difference was natural because 'they' occupied a different spatial territory. Imaginative geography reads cultural difference into space and spatial difference into cultures. Thus in European travel writing and fiction the space of Africa was always peopled with savages and cannibals – we see this in Defoe's cult text, *Robinson Crusoe*, where Crusoe's first thoughts on arriving as a castaway on the island were anxious ones about cannibals, or in his *Captain Singleton* where walking across Africa the English gold-hunters constantly expect to meet cannibals. In R.L. Stevenson's classic adventure tale *Treasure Island* Hawkins speaks of his childhood's imaginative geographies where 'sometimes the isle was thick with savages, with whom we fought; sometimes full of dangerous animals that hunted us' (unpaginated. Online etext). In Conrad's *Heart of Darkness* Marlow tells us about his childhood fantasies built around and upon maps, where 'blank spaces' seemed 'inviting' and he would 'lose [himself] in all the glories of exploration' (52). The spaces are imagined as empty, predatory

ABCDEFGHIJKLMNOPQRSTUVWXYZ

The Postcolonial Studies Dictionary, First Edition. Pramod K. Nayar.
© 2015 John Wiley & Sons, Ltd. Published 2015 by John Wiley & Sons, Ltd.

and threatening, seductive by the Europeans, who then expect to act out their fantasies and dreams in these empty spaces which are, of course, not really empty. Both Hawkins and Marlow, it must be remembered, then set out to explore these lands of their childhood dreams, in the form of colonial travellers.

imperialism: The term derives from the Roman 'imperium', meaning the 'absolute power of the ruler', and gestures at the total domination of territories and people by the ruler and her/his edicts and institutional structures working in her/his name. While 'colonialism' in postcolonial studies is used to refer to the domination and control of non-European places/people by Europeans settled in that space, imperialism is the principle behind the colonial project. But the term also gestures at the organization of the colony and territories into a profitable economic and political system, with attempts at cultural homogenization as well. The financial, political, social and cultural processes or activities within the Asian or African colony are controlled by European and American (this last in the 20th century) but not necessarily through military presence or takeover of the government. The spectacular feature of the European empires in the 19th and early 20th centuries – and in contrast to the earlier empires in history – was the geographical extent of their territories: often at huge distances from the imperial centre, separated by land and water (earlier empires were usually over contiguous territories). Imperialism's aim is primarily economic domination and regulation of the colony, its resources and wealth, controlled mostly from a distance but through exceptional communication and transport networks (Adas 1990). Thus trading rights, tax treaties or subsidies that the Europeans began with in their 17th-century relations with the subcontinent's kings are early stages of such an imperial control because these were steps toward acquiring monopolistic control over the economy of the Mughal Empire and dominating the European nations' (England was battling French, Dutch and Portuguese for this control) trade relations with the East. Imperialism was the managing of political relations for economic profit in the days of the British Empire through mechanisms such as intervention in succession disputes of local kingdoms, and installing puppet monarchs who would then grant massive trading rights to the English, among others. Imperialism was always about trade and economics, and European capitalism, as V.I. Lenin forcefully argued in his landmark *Imperialism: The Highest Stage of Capitalism* (1917). In the 20th century this imperial behaviour has been the hallmark, according to numerous contemporary thinkers (Hardt and Negri), of the USA. Free trade agreements, import-export embargoes, mining rights (this is especially true in the case of African nations) and treaties for Foreign Direct Investment (FDI) are modes of gaining economic control over the land, people and resources of the Asian/African nation, but without military operations. Organizations like the World Trade Organization (WTO) or the International Monetary Fund (IMF) are now increasingly seen as fulfilling an American, if not a First World, economic imperialist agenda of global control. Recent studies (Waldby and Mitchell 2006; Nayar 2014, 'From Bhopal to Biometrics') have proposed newer forms of imperialism involving Euro-American corporate controls over bodies, tissues and organs of people and populations in Asia, Africa and South America in what these authors call 'tissue economies'.

indentured labour: The term describes a system of labour put into place in the Caribbean, Mauritius and other parts of the European empires after the end of the slave trade around the 1830s. The bulk of indentured labour came from the Indian subcontinent. Workers were hired for low wages for a period of five to seven years. The conditions of transport and work – such as unlimited hours, no time off – in the plantations were horrific. It is significant that in many places the indentured labourers were accommodated in the slave barracks of the previous era. Laws were drafted to ensure the system was not abused. However, laws and policies were manipulated to force the Indians to extend their stay beyond the five years. Indentured labour constituted an early wave of migration (forced) to places like Fiji and Mauritius. In places like the Caribbean the policy was also gendered so that the men would stay for longer periods. Land grants were given from around the 1850s in the hope that the labourers would not return to India. Statistics cited by Robin Cohen tell us that in Mauritius, British Guiana, Natal and Trinidad in the 1830–1920 period there were a minimum of 100,000 labourers, with this figure reaching 450,000 in certain places (2008: 63). Indentured labour according to some commentators marks the evolution of a world system (Cohen 2008). Today it is seen as one more version of slavery, and one of the founding moments of the Indian diaspora in Fiji, Caribbean and South Africa. One of the most detailed literary examinations of the life of the indentured community in the postcolonial canon is Amitav Ghosh's *Ibis* trilogy (two volumes published at the time of writing).

infantilization: Descriptions of the native as 'child-like' date back to the 17th century, at least in English writings on South Asia. Infantilization, as this discourse is called, converts the native from a free subject with agency into a helpless and therefore non-threatening individual. More importantly, infantilization implied a certain kind of power relation between the 'adult' white and the 'child' native. The child-native becomes the responsibility of the white adult, who also therefore has considerable power to chastise, educate, improve and modify the child. The child-native's wishes might be ignored or changed because it is assumed that the child speaks from a position of ignorance. In the case of India the British were even referred to by the natives as 'mai-baap': 'our mother and father'.

kala pani ('Black Water'):   The term is used in two significant ways. First, it refers to one of the most notorious prisons of the colonial era, constructed in the Andaman and Nicobar Islands, south of the Indian subcontinent. The 'Cellular Jail' as it was popularly called, was meant for political prisoners, and was built in the 1890s. Long before this the island was treated as a prison and those rebels of 1857 who were caught were exiled there. From the early decades of the 20th century it housed some of the most celebrated revolutionaries of the Indian freedom movement, including V.D. Savarkar and Barindra Ghosh. The second meaning of the term in postcolonial studies refers to the metaphoric black waters of the Atlantic which indentured Indians (and not just Africans) crossed en route to the Caribbean. The term therefore is irreducibly linked to colonialism and indentured labour. Brinda Mehta's work on Indian women who crossed the Atlantic to go to work as agricultural labour on the plantations (2004) shows how these women constructed their identity, especially in terms of their Indianness and gender. Mehta demonstrates that there was no one Indian identity among these women. *Kala pani* itself was a very crucial concept in this identity-making, since to cross expansive water bodies was associated with contamination, defilement and of course criminality. To voluntarily cross the *kala pani* in the quest for labour and identity by these women might be read, Mehta suggests, as a transgressive act wherein the Indian women opted for a more 'expansive' (Mehta's term) diasporic community over the nuclear Hindu family.

The Postcolonial Studies Dictionary, First Edition. Pramod K. Nayar.
© 2015 John Wiley & Sons, Ltd. Published 2015 by John Wiley & Sons, Ltd.

ABCDEFGHIJ**K**LMNOPQRSTUVWXYZ

lactification: A term popularized by Frantz Fanon in *Black Skin, White Masks*, it refers to the adoption of white ways of being by blacks. Fanon argued that the one thing a black man wants, above all else, is to be white (hence, lactification, from the lactose of milk). To 'become like the whites' is therefore to loss one's racial legacies, whether intellectually or in folk, myth and popular forms like music. It becomes both a metaphor and an analogy for the loss of racial characteristics in the cultural domains. Since 'race' often codes as skin colour, to lose one's race is to lose the colour of one's skin, and become white. Lactification is the result of years of colonial hegemony in the cultural fields. The black man who has assimilated white myths about black inferiority and primitivism begins to shun his own culture. Fanon notes that the blacks begin to speak the European languages as a first step toward abandoning their African roots. Lactification is thus a two-fold process: the slow but certain distanciation of the black/colonized from his/her cultural roots and the move toward Europeanization or Westernization. A more common term in current use is 'deracination'. It has been associated in popular culture with the pop icon Michael Jackson for his increasingly paler skin over the years. Deracination is now often read alongside other colonial/postcolonial processes and effects, such as the making of mimic men. (See also: **mimicry, hybridity**)

liminality: A term that derives from the disciplines of psychology and anthropology (especially in the work of Victor Turner), liminality indicates spaces and conditions of transition, in-between spaces where identities are not fully formed. The terms was theorized in the early stages of postcolonial studies by Homi Bhabha as a space where the colonized is seeking to escape the identity of the colonial subject and move toward the identity of the white man, but has not yet acquired the white man's state/status. 'Liminal' is a term used to capture the uncertainty, instability and disorder of this space as well. For Bhabha the liminal is what resists the hierarchy, upsets the social order. Identity here is not fully formed, and hence is not categorizable. It alters the pre-fixed identities and opens the space up for new ones. In postcolonial studies liminality also gestures at the transitional possibilities of the context, that is, colonial discourse. The term derived from the Latin 'limen', which means 'threshold' and thus carries within it the connotations of 'borders'. For Bhabha the threshold or interstitial space is important because it marks the possibility of cultural hybridity for the colonized. Thus the term is often used in conjunction with other terms, such as 'interstitial' and 'in-between', all suggesting zones of transition and unstable identities. Liminal characters are those who cross borders, whose location is not in this or that space, but in the zones and passages of transition between such spaces. Critics like Edward Said have characterized their own location as liminal, between the country of birth and the country they have adopted and work in, but not abandoning the former and not fully 'at home' in the latter (Said called it a 'median state' with 'half-detachments').

Lusotropicalism: Attributed to Brazilian sociologist Gilberto Freyre, the term refers to Portuguese imperialism and colonization in South America and Africa. The Portuguese were seen as far more humane than the French, Dutch or English when it came to dealings with the colonized subjects. The Portuguese were of course among the earliest of Europeans in Asia and South America, having established trading relations and churches – their Jesuit priests were among the first Christian missionaries in the Indian subcontinent – and having sent out their explorers as early as the 15th century (Vasco da Gama rounded the Cape of Good Hope and found the sea route to India in 1498). Their colonial policy was also marked by a greater adaptability to native conditions, and they had far fewer objections to racial mixing – in terms of liaisons with local women – than their European counterparts. Freyre's argument was that since the Portuguese themselves had been colonized in the past, they proved to be far more humane to their colonized subjects. Pointing to the absence of racist legislation in Africa, Freyre argued that Portuguese colonialism was more about class distinctions than about race.

magical realism: A kind of literary writing where dreams, supernatural elements, and magic are part of the everyday life of a tribe, community and individual. The term itself came from the visual arts, and has been most commonly associated with South American fiction, but is not really a genre as much as a literary style, or way of narration. Ghosts, spirits, supernatural beings and gods appear before and intervene in the lives of people in Ben Okri's fiction (most notably in the form of the *abiku*), for example. Critics see magical realism (or magic realism) as the postcolonial representation of two worldviews, histories, and even ideologies (Slemon 1995; Brenda Cooper 1998). The magical world represents the pre-colonial, pre-capitalist past whereas the everyday represents the colonial present. Thus magical realism is the mixing of opposites, whether in terms of beliefs or politics. The everyday reality of a colonized life is imbued with moments when the pre-colonial past creeps in, or when fantasies and dreams enable an escape from this present. Attempting to negotiate the continued presence of the pre-colonial past and native beliefs with the massively altered present, the postcolonial shows reality itself as breaking down. Authors like Rushdie have argued (2000) that their writing needed to tell stories, however fantastic, but that they as authors were constrained by (Western) notions of what a story should be: an imitation, or mimesis, of reality. A story for Rushdie can be about improbable events; they need not be true. Stories need not obey the laws of the present, or of this universe. In postcolonials like Okri this translates into the appropriation of African myth-making and folklore where gods and commoners in coexistence mix worlds, each operating according

The Postcolonial Studies Dictionary, First Edition. Pramod K. Nayar.

© 2015 John Wiley & Sons, Ltd. Published 2015 by John Wiley & Sons, Ltd.

to different principles. Okri's *The Famished Road* is an excellent example where witches, politicians, spirits, dead people, the undead and the living all seem to appear in Madame Koto's bar. In Gabriel García Marquéz, Maria Vargas Llosa, Thomas King and other postcolonials, magical realism enables an escape from the limits of European norms of writing in terms of linearity or realism. By mixing worlds, timeframes, spaces and human/animal/non-human characters these postcolonial authors call attention to their brand of storytelling, and of the need to develop forms that connect with pre-colonial, folk, tribal and communitarian pasts and worldviews. Since myths and spirits, ghosts and gods are a part of the everyday worldview in most non-European cultures, whether in Africa, Asia or South America, the storytelling that makes use of these aspects captures the postcolonial social-political condition better than the realism of the European novel.

Manichean allegory: Manicheanism was a form of religious thought that rested on the binary between good and evil, light and darkness, in the 3rd century AD. Abdul JanMohamed (1983) used this binarist thought to describe European colonialism and its discourses about race. He argued that colonialism rests on the binary of 'black and white', where the black is always condemned to be secondary, passive and therefore marginal to the discourse. Thus white = modernity, civilization, progress and black = savagery, primitivism and regression according to this allegory. This kind of simplistic, reductive and binaristic stereotyping, according to JanMohamed, is the foundation of all colonial representation and discourse when dealing with Europe and its Others. One term in the binary (black, or non-European) is always deemed to be inferior, and therefore the binary is *not* one of equal and opposite categories but one made up of two elements or categories that are deemed to be inherently unequal. Any postcolonial writer who seeks to address the white audience, or even find a space in the literary canon, would find it impossible to do so because the very structure of the binary – which constructs the categories 'black writer', 'white writer' – rejects the black writer *in toto*. The entire structure of the binary is founded on the assumption that the marginal need not find a space. Further, the allegory takes the simple fact of colour difference and amplifies it, in JanMohamed's reading, into metaphysical and moral difference. It is from within this Manichean allegory of racial, colour, moral and cultural difference that colonizers perceive the colonized. Later critics have argued, however, that the colonial age was not so clearly divided into discrete and identifiable black and white parts. For instance, as Cooper and Stoler (1997) have shown, the centre and periphery were mutually constitutive. The black and brown cultures and territories, not to mention their products and produce were as much a part of the European self-fashioning, whether in terms of their working classes or their aristocracy. Thus the Manichean opposition that JanMohamed proposes, they argue, was not really a valid one. As David Scott puts it: 'it is the colonial regimes ... that drew a sharp dichotomy between the colonizer and the colonized as a function of the requirements of colonial rule ... for scholars of colonialism to deploy such a conception today is only to reproduce a colonial myth' (2008: 395).

masculinity (imperial):   Colonialism and imperialism served to develop models of masculinity for Englishmen. The public school ethos (Tidrick 1990; Bristow 1991) instilled fair play, the sense of justice, devotion to duty, stoicism and 'mateyness' as virtues to be imbibed by future imperialists. Adventure stories instilled the spirit of exploration, discovery, danger and fortitude alongside the implicit assumption of racial and civilizational superiority in comparison with the barbaric racial-cultural Other. Adventure stories also portrayed exploration and subsequent subjugation of natives as a fantasy that could be realized in the colonies. Masculine cultures were built around heroic figures like Robert Clive, General Gordon (Gordon of Sudan) and John Nicholson (the 'hero of Delhi' in the 1857 Indian 'mutiny'), or around explorers like Mungo Park. But English masculinity was also under considerable strain from the social contexts in England – such as the emergence of the 'New Woman' and accompanying demands for equal wages and voting rights. In the colony masculinity found an opportunity to establish itself by positing the effeminate native as a contrast. Sporting activities like hunting were modes of asserting an imperial masculinity by demonstrating the Englishman's control over the Asian/African landscape and fauna, where he, in the role of hunter, also saved the locals from predators. However, despite the overwhelming emphasis on martial and sporting masculinities, variant models made their way into the British imagination due to the colonies. Cross-dressing and homoeroticism in T.E. Lawrence ('Lawrence of Arabia') and E.M. Forster, and even as late as Paul Scott, offered other forms of masculinity and sexuality. (See also: **effeminacy**)

mestizo/a: Related to creolization and transculturation, the term *mestizo* (sometimes in the French written as *métisse*) is used with particular reference to the Spanish and Portuguese colonization of the South American continent. It was originally used as a racial category in the colonial period in South America, which was complicated racially due to the presence of Spanish, Portuguese and black slaves alongside the native Indians. The term itself has both biological and cultural mixing in terms of its contexts and semantic scope, and was used by scientists and biologists in the 19th century to describe the extensive miscegenation occurring in South America. Variant terms for the culturally hybrid generation include *pardo* (Venezuela) and *castas*. In South American postcolonialism the term *mestizo* is used to capture the complicated history of contemporary indigenous identity where the cultural hybridity – European and Native American – is seen as a positive consequence of colonial rule. Gloria Anzaldúa's groundbreaking *Borderlands/La Frontera: The New Mestiza* (1994) used the term to describe a certain categorylessness. Identifying herself as a lesbian, feminist, brown woman (Chicano, she wrote of this new mestiza consciousness as made of contradictions and multiplicities, thus refusing bloodlines and racial purity. She claims that as a mestiza she has no country, no homeland, no race (102–3). The idea of the mestiza has been central to what is now called 'border thinking', of thinking from the border and multilingualism to a whole new epistemology. Border writing, produced by such border thinking, mixes (like the mestiza identity itself) history, personal story, factual accounts, poetry and *testimonio*. A related term in circulation is *mestizaje*. Some critics have argued that, as with Caribbean Creoles, *mestizaje* signifies an acceptable hybridity and identity, although (as Shalini Puri notes in her study of the Caribbean postcolonial, 2004) in the case of Spanish South America the *mestizaje* was the result of actual interracial breeding, whereas in the Caribbean it took the form of social interaction. Two other terms – both from the Spanish colonial period in South America – figure under the category of *mestizaje*: *peninsulares* and *criollos*. *Peninsulares*, as the name indicates, referred to the Spaniards from the Spanish peninsula who had settled (as first-generation colonials) in South America. *Criollos* were Spaniards born in the colonies. These two constituted a hierarchy as well, where the *peninsulares* were mostly administrative and church officers/employees and the *criollos* were landowners. Well below both of these came the *mestizos* or *castas* – mixed-race people.

mimicry: Originally a term used to describe a biological phenomenon in animals where the animal mimics its surroundings in order to hunt or to escape a predator, the term gained currency in critical theory with the work of Homi K. Bhabha (2009). Frantz Fanon had already hinted at this phenomenon well before Bhabha when he spoke of the 'white masks' that 'black skins' wore in his book of the same title. Fanon noted that the aim of the ambitious African was to speak the European tongue like the European himself, and lose all African inflection and accent. Elaborating upon this form of colonial subjection, Bhabha described the reconstruction of natives on the lines of their European masters through an assimilation of European religion, education, literature and cultural practices. Native subjects, argued Bhabha, seeking to be more like the white master, Anglicized and Europeanized themselves. What Bhabha and Fanon are gesturing at is the total domination of the colonized by the colonizer through insidious means. Through their cultural practices and modes such as literature, the white masters convinced the native subjects that they (natives) would be more civilized if they abandoned their native ways and adopted European ones. The result of this mimicry of Western cultural forms and manners by the colonized subjects was the construction of 'mimic men'. The mimicry, the colonized subjects hoped, would gain them some advantage from the Empire. Even during the period of Empire British writers portrayed such pathetic colonized subjects aping the Westerner with not inconsiderable mockery. One of the most unforgettable of such mimic men was Hurree Chunder Mukherjee in Rudyard Kipling's *Kim*. In the postcolonial era writers explored the agonies of mimic men who fitted neither into Western cultures nor their 'native' ones. V.S. Naipaul devoted an entire novel to a study of such 'mimic men' in his novel of that title. Paul Scott in the *Raj Quartet* presented Hari Coomer/Hari Kumar as a mimic man unable to sustain his Englishness in the chaos of India. In Wole Soyinka's *Death and the King's Horseman* Elesin, the king's horseman in Africa, accuses the English Pilkings: 'you stole from me my first-born, sent him to your country so you could turn him into something in your own image' (1984: 205). In Derek Walcott's *Dream on Monkey Mountain* 'Makak' is a native who has even forgotten his real/native name and answers only to 'Makak' or 'monkey'. Lestrade persuades Makak to mimic him, even as he himself mimics the white man's authority. Using the animalizing language of colonialism, Walcott writes of Makak's behaviour: 'everything I say this monkey does do ... I sit down, monkey sit down too' (1970: 223). Such mimic men in postcolonial writing represent the deepest tragedy of the colonized subjects, never at home in their own or the master's culture.

miscegenation: The term originally referred to the sexual union of white and black races. A variant of this theme of interracial union was that of Europeans with Native Americans, of which one of the early stories is that of Pochahontas. There are two points of origin to the European fears of miscegenation. One is the fear of Native Americans and black slaves among the early settlers in America. The second source might be traced to the 19th-century colonial period during which there occurred numerous liaisons and even marriages between white soldiers, administrators and merchants serving in Africa. Colonial administrators believing in the purity of races (and later Social Darwinism) began to worry about the 'contamination' of their ruling race with the blood of the 'primitive' Africans. Accompanying this anxiety of contamination was the fear of the rape of white women by Africans or even the willing sexual intercourse of white women with blacks. The fears around miscegenation were also reinforced due to the prevalent stereotypes of the black male as hypersexed and given to animal passions. In the 1860s in Natal, legislation was therefore introduced to curb black vagrancy because this was seen as a threat to the free movement of the white women in the cities. Administrators in Africa, such as Philip Alexander Bruce, declared that the white woman was always a source of attraction for the oversexed black man. In India the Contagious Diseases Act (1868) was instituted to ensure regular medical examination of the Indian prostitutes who were placed in camps adjacent to Company barracks, while French thinkers on the question were attempting to prepare a graded map of 'hybrid' children based on the degree of pigmentation of their skin (which looks forward to Nazi Germany's obsession with the exact quantum of Jewish or Aryan blood in its citizenry). There was initially some enthusiasm in India about mixed-race progeny, and a separate fund was created for their welfare, as studies of colonial sexual policies and discourses (Ballhatchet 1980) show. In American history the captivity narratives of Mrs Mary Jemison and Mrs Rowlandson heightened the anxiety around the possible kidnap and rape of white women by the natives. *Jane Eyre*, the classic English text, demonstrates the impossibility of such interracial marriages by showing how the Jamaican Creole Bertha Mason is 'unfit' (the novel portrays her as animalesque and mad) to be the very English Rochester's wife. Richard Burton, explorer and geographer in Africa, wrote of his liaisons with African women. In the early 20th century a different version of miscegenation emerges in the writing of African American explorer Matthew Henson (who accompanied Robert Peary to the North Pole) where he admits to sexual relations with the Inuit women of Greenland in the course of their journey. In Anglo-Indian novels (novels written by the British in India) like Maud Diver's *Lilamani* the Englishman Nevil looks forward to having children who would be 'endowed with the best that two great races can give – the spirituality of the East, the power and virility of the West'. Later novels set in colonial India such as E.M. Forster's *A Passage to India* and Paul Scott's *The Raj Quartet* also thematized miscegenation in the form of the rape of the white woman. Even in the 20th century, texts dealing with white-black intimate encounters have attempted to examine the sexual dynamics of race, most notably in Doris Lessing's *The Grass is Singing* (1950). The South African novelist Bessie Head, herself the child of a white South African woman and a black man, and postcolonial critiques of race and racial discourses, especially the work of Robert J.C. Young and Homi Bhabha, have pointed out that attitudes toward miscegenation were never simply condemnatory but were often marked by ambivalence. (See also: **torrid zones**)

multiculturalism: Yasmine Gooneratne's Bharat in *A Change of Skies* says: 'Long before I saw England for the second time ... I knew London ... I knew what muffins tasted like' (1991: 19). Bharat effectively captures the diasporic, multicultural ethos in this statement. He is a person who is at home in both cultures, even if the knowledge of England has come from an inheritance and not always from first-hand experience. He has been accul-tured into England. In postcolonial studies 'multiculturalism' refers to the condition of numerous migrants and diasporic cultures wherein individu-als carry at least two legacies: of their home country and of the country they have adopted. In the age of globalization even the new Empire, as Hardt and Negri have argued, is multicultural. A multicultural society is one where several cultures coexist without losing their distinctive identities (Watson 2002). Multicultural authors like Salman Rushdie write with consummate ease about Renaissance Europe, contemporary London and 20th-century India. Among the postcolonials this multiculturalism could imply either a distance from all cultures – equidistant – or a familiarity with several. Within First World cities like London we see a heightened multicultural-ism, even if it is in the form of street food or the exotic languages we hear. Popular culture – and Bollywood is one of the world's best examples – has always appropriated multicultural features: Bollywood song sequences shot in places as diverse as Switzerland, Amsterdam, Paris, Tokyo and American cities expose the audiences in India to different geographical locations. While this kind of multiculturalism could be read as commodified and ulti-mately just cosmetic, it remains a means of exposing the postcolonial nation to different cultures. In the case of authors like Rohinton Mistry, Timothy Mo, Zadie Smith and Salman Rushdie we see multiculturalism as both a popular mode and a philosophical-political attitude – an attempt to engage with the migrants' battles of acculturation, the nostalgia for 'mother' culture, and a fascination with the new, adopted ones. In such authors multiculturalism approximates to a cosmopolitanism. Multicultural societies, however, also face constant social friction where political battles rage over the cultural rights of ethnic groups and migrants (the right to wear the veil has been at the centre of much acrimonious debate in France and the UK). Whether multiculturalism, especially in the USA, might be read 'postcolonially' for the racial tensions and migration and refugee concerns has also been the subject of political debate (Ong 2003; Sharpe 2008), as has Canada's avowed multiculturalism (Jefferess 2013). (See also: **cosmopolitanism, cultural citizenship**)

national allegory: The argument that postcolonial (or Third World) literature functions as an allegory of the nation was first made by American Marxist critic Fredric Jameson in 1986. Jameson proposed that most post-colonial nations, battling First World cultural imperialism, are speaking of public issues and national concerns even when speaking of the private sphere (of sexuality, family, domesticity) in their literature. Jameson thus sees the treatment of a family crisis in a Third World novel as an allegorical representation of a national crisis, because there is, in his reading, a link between the libidinal and political dimensions of an individual's life. He also makes the point that where Western texts might be political-national allegories unconsciously, those from the postcolonial nations are always conscious and overt. In a critique of American culture, Jameson argues that it has become focused on psychology and private subjectivity whereas the Third World has to remain 'situational and materialist'. In Aijaz Ahmad's (1987) response to Jameson he points out that when there is an attempt to theorize 'third world literature' what is referred to is essentially literature in the 'languages of metropolitan countries' alone, excluding those regional, local languages and dialects. Objecting to Jameson's way of organizing the First World around conditions of production and the Third World around the conditions of experience, Ahmad argues that postcolonial literature gets straitjacketed through this organization. If all postcolonial literature has to do is to respond to its history of colonialism (there being no other history according to the Western scheme of Jameson), and if the only response to this history is nationalist consciousness, then postcolonial writers cannot

The Postcolonial Studies Dictionary, First Edition. Pramod K. Nayar.

narrate anything else. Are all texts that narrate experiences of colonialism 'third world texts'? asks Ahmad. What is also worrying, according to Ahmad, is the implicit suggestion in Jameson that texts which do not speak as national allegories will thereafter not be deemed to be authentic Third World texts. The Jameson-Ahmad debate about the nature of postcolonial texts took on other trajectories elsewhere. Stephen Slemon (1987) called for an entirely different way of treating allegory. Slemon proposes that allegory depends on pre-existing codes (signifying systems) of recognition: thus the colonized subject is 'positioned' within a 'master code or pretext' that comes from the tradition of (colonial/European) representation. There are always preceding signs in which the colonized is interpreted. Colonial discourse might be contested by postcolonial writers through the use of allegory, given the fact that the subjectivity and identity of the colonized and formerly colonized has been constructed within colonial rule. Slemon thus sees allegory as carrying the possibilities of a counter-discourse, where it can serve as an instrument of postcolonial analysis of Europe itself: when the postcolonial writer revisions allegory what s/he does is to reject these prior codes of interpretation, or even, perhaps an entire system of signification by focusing on anti-imperialist figurations. In a later reading of the role of allegory as a postcolonial strategy, Tim Brennan (1995) spoke of a postcolonial nation's 'longing' for an appropriate narrative form. The authenticity debate between Meenakshi Mukherjee and Vikram Chandra (2000–2001) and Rajeswari Sunder Rajan (2001) revolved around the postcolonial author's attempts at offering a sense of 'authenticity' in her/his fiction. Debates about authenticity of representation, whether of the immigrant experience in Monica Ali, Timothy Mo and Hanif Kureishi or of tribal cultures in Ngugi (writing in exile from outside Kenya), continue to haunt postcolonial authors and critics.

nationalism (as discourse):   Simply defined, it means a certain pride in, concern toward and involvement in a geopolitical entity identified as a nation. While some thinkers have emphasized political belonging (citizenship), others see nationalism as an extension of social ordering, ethnic and community formations. Clifford Geertz, for instance, has argued that the new states are driven by two motives: the desire to be recognized as responsible agents and the desire to build a modern state. Geertz proposes that the first, the desire for an identity, is often at odds with the desire to achieve a greater political order and international role (1973). Nationalism is a name for a sense of common belonging, of shared identity – an identity defined in terms of ethnic, racial, geographical or cultural criteria (such as language, territory, race or ethnic group). Individual identities are assumed to be subsumed within/into a national one. This subsuming requires the sense of shared cultural identity. Nationalism, it is argued, originated as an ideal and political idea with the 1770s (the American and French Revolutions) and the founding of the modern state accompanied by older forms of social organization (the feudal, for example). The sense of belonging to a particular cultural, geopolitical and political formation led populations across the world to revolt against what they saw as the illegitimate control of their territory and lives by 'outsiders'. People belonging to a more or less homogenous cultural, ethnic or religious group, or living in contiguous territory, were helped by these cultural practices to imagine themselves as a unified nation (Benedict Anderson 1991). Even though the people of one area might never meet those of another, they would see all of them as 'connected'. Artefacts like maps and museums enable people to see this connection, argued Anderson. There is no 'essence' to the idea of the nation outside these creative and cultural imaginings through artefacts, proposes Anderson. Political sovereignty was a natural extension of this imagining of a unified nation: if as a group we can be unified then we are to be allowed to determine the future of our lives. This sense of belonging was forged, reinforced and disseminated through cultural practices as diverse as popular media, newspapers, literature, speeches and icons. Anderson's arguments came in for serious criticism from Partha Chatterjee (1993), who argued that the nationalism of anti-colonial struggles emerged out of a strong sense of homogeneous cultural identity, of belonging, and that Anderson ignores these cultural specifics in which nationalism as ideology, political project and action emerges. Nationalism emerged in the colonized societies because there was a core domain – the domestic, and often the religious – that was deemed to be uncorrupted by colonial hegemony. But nationalism was also subsumed into what Chatterjee identifies as a statist project. Mass/popular participation, too, gets subsumed under the banner of the nation-state, which in turn, in Chatterjee's reading, is firmly associated with capital. Nationalism revived icons and myths, stories and legends – discourses – from the past to help this imagining, so that these icons became identity-markers for large groups of people, symbols of coherence and cogency. National symbols like flags, songs, buildings and memorials play an important role in this project of unifying people. Nationalism is often merged or identified with the nation-state, the political formation. Anti-colonial struggles that encouraged and thrived on nationalism appropriated folk stories and mythic heroes for the same reason. Literary texts, in local languages especially, addressed regional matters but were also instrumental in developing a sense of the distant spaces of the region, bringing these closer. Nationalism also demanded a certain kind of history-writing whereby it wasn't enough to relive heroic moments and battles; a clear sense of the pre-colonial era which was identified as pure, uncontaminated and authentic (although this was rarely the case with most cultures except the really isolated tribes) was also required. In postcolonial studies nationalism is a significant theme because it is deemed to stand in direct antagonism to colonialism, helping build a sense of belonging, of identity. With globalization and its increasing erosion of the nation-state through global consumer culture, economic intervention by transnational bodies, flow of capital, people and ideas across national borders, nationalism is again at the forefront of debates. It is now assumed that nationalism is not merely a utopian discourse, but is experienced and lived by people in specific ways. Other postcolonial critics note that the nation has to be constantly performed – in the form of narrative articulations of belonging, citizenship, affective attachments, etc. Thus while on the one hand the nation was to be achieved, worked toward by its people, in a process that Homi Bhabha (1990) called a 'pedagogy', on the other people had to be constantly reminded of their state of belonging, identity and unity with the nation. Other tensions of nationalism are also addressed by postcolonial studies (especially by its political theorists). For example, the shift away from universalist ideals of freedom or individual autonomy has been accompanied by the coming together of marginalized groups (**subalterns**) as electoral communities within nations (tribes, ethnic communities – the Dalits in India are examples). Some theorists, like Pheng Cheah, have sought to revive the nation as the space of freedom (this is in contrast to the views of Chatterjee and others who see the nation-state as inherently aligned with capital), where this freedom is primarily written into the popular cultural practices that then lay the foundation for progressive politics. Cheah's argument is that the postcolonial national culture will always be haunted (his book is titled *Spectral Nationality*, 1993) by colonial legacies in the form of the state, even as popular cultural nationalism offers the possibilities of freedom. In such readings, 'nationalism' is the condition of being caught between the evils of the state (the embodiment of one kind of nationalist ideal), with its exclusion, oppression, exploitation and emphasis on capital, and the freedom of popular national cultures beyond the state. More recently writings in sexuality studies posit a '**homonationalism**', where nationalism is measured by its tolerance for/of queer sexualities (Puar 2005).

native: Used as a more or less racialized pejorative by Europeans to describe the non-European races from the 18th century, the term originally meant anybody 'born in a particular land'. In colonial discourse it came to be associated with a position in the racial and civilizational hierarchy – that at the lower end. 'Native' came to signify 'primitive' and non-modern, evaluated in terms of European criteria of progress and modernity, such as, for example, private property. In African and Asian societies the absence of private property laws caused the English – great believers in the right to property – to see them as primitive. 'Native' was therefore coded as civilizationally backward because these cultures did not evolve codes of property ownership. 'Native' was also a term used to dismiss local (non-European) cultural practices, whether this was language, literature, arts or religion. Hence by the late-19th century one of the worst appellations a European could attract was that s/he had 'gone native'. Adopting local ways of dressing, eating or entertainment was also deemed to signify the loss of the European racial-cultural attributes, a dilution of the purity of the Western race – and thus attracted considerable opprobrium.

Native Informant: In *A Critique of Postcolonial Reason* Gayatri Spivak argues that for the Western ethnographer to produce any kind of commentary requires a source that produces the information. Yet this individual providing the information is denied the status of an autonomous, coherent speaker. Thus the Native Informant is at once essential and invisible, providing the 'essential' voice of native culture yet who disappears into the text of the white ethnographer. Retaining her concerns with marginalization undertaken by colonial discourse, Spivak argues a case for the importance of the Native Informant within the colonial project itself. The Native Informant is one who *is* the native voice for a short period but whose voice is simply buried – foreclosed, in Spivak's psychoanalytic language – in the textual apparatus produced by the European as a result of this voice. The Native Informant is therefore complicit in the making of the Western text. But this Native Informant cannot, in a sense, be reclaimed from the text. Spivak is extending an argument made earlier, in her famous, 'Can the Subaltern Speak', and responding to an argument made by Benita Parry that critics like Spivak and Bhabha do not allow the native to speak. Spivak here is seeing in the figure of the Native Informant a later version of the subaltern. If the subaltern did not speak, here the Native Informant does speak, but eventually disappears, leaving some *traces*, into textuality. This is not erasure as much as the occupation by the Native Informant of an impossible space, made invisible – yet the marks of this process of concealment are discernible. When the Native Informant is treated only as the object and source of knowledge for the Western ethnographer, argues Spivak, the latter does not have an ethical relationship to, or hold responsibility for, the former. Even in the postcolonial period, women and men from the Third World would appear to, or remain, Native Informants for First World consumption. Shahnaz Khan (2005), for example, has written about how she finds herself unfortunately complicit in the First World process of rescuing Pakistani women. For the First World, Khan notes, she is the Native Informant. Such a process enables the First World to position East and West as two absolutes, two irrevocably oppositional cultures, and to ignore the transnational nature of capitalism and patriarchy. (See also: **essentialism, feminism (Islamic)**)

nativism: Within postcolonial studies, alongside the rise of cultural nationalism during the anti-colonial struggles, a certain tendency to valorize local, native cultures as a resistance strategy to cultural homogenization by 'Western' or colonial texts arose. Nativism, as this came to be known, called for the preservation and revival of local cultural practices and ways of thinking. It saw within its own traditions the weapons needed to blunt the Westernization of the local populations and cultures. Nativism believes that within folk, minority, tribal and aboriginal texts we can find the uncontaminated conceptual and intellectual apparatuses that will prevent cultural erasure by colonialism. Nativism here is seen as part of the process of **decolonization**, where the formerly colonized seeks to escape the intellectual and cultural confines of the European by returning to vernacular, local, and folk cultures. Thus we see signs of nativism in the writings of Achebe, Tutuola, Paula Gunn Allen, Bhalchandra Nemade and others where the withdrawal from Western forms of thinking and cultural practices is ensured through a return to older forms of speech (especially idiomatic expressions, metaphors and symbolism), music, folk stories and myths. Postcolonial studies has had an uneasy relationship with nativist modes of thought because they are seen as seeking revival of not a plural tradition but a hypothetical 'pure' one, to the exclusion of several other 'minor' traditions even in the pre-colonial era. Nativism is also seen as an essential component of the 'national culture', provided we can see our own pasts as accommodating of difference and dissent. A certain anxiety of 'authenticity' is triggered by nativist forms of thinking because norms of what counts as authentic representations of local culture become matters of dispute. For the detractors of nativism (Ganguly 1997; Paranjape 1997), the assumption that there is a 'pure' tradition, static and unchanging, that can be reclaimed, is itself deeply flawed because no culture is homogenous. Where thinkers like Frantz Fanon warned of the 'pitfalls' of cultural nationalism and national consciousness, nativism, through its revival in the contemporary socio-political fundamentalist movements in numerous postcolonial countries, is seen as a strategy of resistance to globalization.

Negritude: Developed as a concept involving taking pride in African cultures by Aimé Césaire, Léopold Senghor and others, it was central to the anti-colonial struggles in Africa. Just as the 'black consciousness' movement was instrumental in projecting black as 'being' in and of itself and not always in relation to 'white', Negritude enabled the rejection of the colonial's constant undermining of black culture. Finally, it called for a retrieval of older forms of thinking. It was also a strategy to bring together the diversity of African cultures under one umbrella, especially in the USA, where the descendants of slaves and migrants from various parts of Africa united under the sign of 'black' (the Harlem Renaissance was an instance of this unification). Black culture had its own aesthetic and its own philosophy, argued Césaire and others, so the blacks could take pride in their indigenous tradition. As a response to the constant devaluing of African culture as primitive and barbaric, Negritude was instrumental in offering a measure of cultural pride as well as a strategy of resistance that enabled those under colonial rule to turn away from the European culture that had thus far been taken as the 'standard'. Servility and the inferiority complex of the blacks, argued Césaire, could only be removed when they discovered pride in their blackness. As a cultural movement, therefore, it had considerable psychological purchase on the minds of the colonized black: it helped him escape the anxiety over his own servility and brought him closer to the community. It showed the black man that he was not primitive, and this was the start of a process of self-discovery. Postcolonial thinkers like Frantz Fanon admitted that Negritude was instrumental in bringing together diverse and often warring black communities. But Fanon was sceptical, like Césaire, as to whether the blacks could ever go back to a pure African past that was uncontaminated by colonial culture. Fanon also wondered if such a retreat into the past – even if it was glorious – was advisable at all. Fanon saw Negritude as informed by this myth of an older purity of culture and by an **essentialism** that there is one unified and homogenous African culture. In 'West Indians and Africans' (*Toward the African Revolution*, 1967) Fanon wondered whether such a uniform African culture ever existed. For the critics of Negritude such as Fanon, essentialism perpetuated the colonial assumption of the uniform depravity of all blacks, ignoring the vital diversity among black cultures.

neocolonialism: While many nations in Africa, Asia and South America acquired political independence from European nations in the 20th century, economic control over the new nations has continued. Traceable to Kwame Nkrumah from the 1960s, neocolonialism (or neo-colonialism) has several aspects. First, the politically independent nations (former colonies) rarely have economic independence. Their economic policies are usually subject to scrutiny and even pressure by First World nations or supranational organizations (that are essentially controlled by First World nations). Subsidies, Structural Adjustment Programs (SAPs), Foreign Direct Investment, disinvestment, privatization and other policies of these nations are very often determined by powers outside the nation-state. Puppet regimes (that we have seen installed in numerous African nations through the 20th century) are usually an effective way for the First World nations to retain political and economic control over the new nation. Globalization puts particular pressures on the postcolonial nation-state in the domain of economy. Exploitation of the natural resources of the former colonies continues through mining and cheap labour (sweatshops). Economic control is also very often accompanied by cultural imperialism. From the dominance of European languages (especially English) to consumer products to entertainment (Hollywood's empire), cultural imperialism in the age of globalization is the most visible 'face' of neocolonialism. Western models of dressing, eating and social interactions begin to acquire a tenacious hold in the postcolonial nation, even as several local cultural practices and products – from yoga to ethnic art – get commercialized for profit in the Western market, having been first delinked from the postcolonial nation. Neocolonialism is furthered in the former colonies through the role of the elite. Whether in economics or academia, Westernized intellectuals, specialists and cultural intermediaries determine the debates, policies and actions of governments and institutions, and control the flow of ideas. The elite, who might be seen, not without reason, as supportive of globalization, also occupy the places vacated by the former European masters. They become the new ruling classes, and the social hierarchy solidifies, less in terms of race than in terms of class. The new elite, with connections to Western corporate or governance bodies, further the cause of globalization. (See also: **Empire – new figurations of; e-Empire, globalization, cultural imperialism**)

New World: Dating back to around the late 15th and early 16th centuries, and coined by Amerigo Vespucci in 1503, it refers to a whole range of lands and places: the Americas, the Pacific Ocean islands and in some cases Australia (then known as Oceania). Vespucci thereby rectified Columbus' declaration that he had reached the East Indies by demonstrating that it was an entirely *new* world. The New World, in readings such as the Stephen Greenblatt edited volume, *New World Encounters* (1993), was not about European 'epiphany' (as Greenblatt states in his Introduction to the volume). Rather it was the space of encounters of very brutal kinds. The New World has constantly been treated in European narratives as the scene of European triumph. But the above volume, which fits into postcolonial studies as a result of this focus, emphasizes the *other* histories of the New World, with the stories of the natives and their fate at the hands of the Europeans. In addition the New World is the scene of very complicated and complex cultural encounters. The absence of a common language, the difference in symbols and the clear but un-understandable (for the natives) intentions of the Europeans made this encounter extremely fraught. We need, argues Greenblatt, to see four elements in this encounter: the operative cultural understanding of the Europeans, the historical situation in which this understanding is played out, the operative cultural understanding of the natives, and the historical situation in which this understanding is played out. All four elements converge in the course of the encounter.

Occidentalism: Just as the Western world has stereotyped the Asian or African nations/cultures in what Edward Said identified as 'Orientalism', Occidentalism is the portrayal of Western cultures by Asian, African and other cultures. While these representations have abounded in history (James Carrier 1995) contemporary studies (Buruma and Margalit 2006) show how Occidentalism, especially since the 20th century, has taken on the form of a hatred of all things Western. This hatred, born in part of the military, economic and political interventions of the Western, First World developed nations, led by the USA, is also directed at what the non-Western world sees as the unsustainable, greedy and exploitative culture of Westernization, whether in the domain of environment or consumption. Western individualism, which places autonomy and individual interest above society and family, in the eyes of the more collective-bound African and Asian races, seems unacceptably selfish and thus comes in for attack, according to Buruma and Margalit. Very often cultural nationalisms, especially of the extreme variety as seen in Cambodia, called for a complete rejection of Western models of living, agriculture and economy and a return to older, native modes. It could also be argued that the widespread dissemination of Hollywood movies has meant that for many cultures models of Western life are gleaned from these representations, resulting in an Occidentalism.

orality: Notions of literacy have been called into question since Walter Ong's classic study *Orality and Literacy* (1982). Within postcolonial studies, particularly, orality has been at the forefront of considerable debate because

The Postcolonial Studies Dictionary, First Edition. Pramod K. Nayar.
© 2015 John Wiley & Sons, Ltd. Published 2015 by John Wiley & Sons, Ltd.

the Western emphasis on, say, written histories and documentation, had traditionally, under colonialism, rejected songs, ballads and other oral forms of narration. In Africa, Asia and South America there has always been a thriving tradition of oral literature. The slaves taken to the Americas from the 17th century retained their connections with Africa through their songs. The folktale tradition in all these cultures was meant to educate as well as entertain. For postcolonial studies scholars in anthropology, history and literature (Mignolo 2003), the arrival of the European meant that many of these oral traditions were destroyed, or reduced to exotic museumized practices. Oral cultures were deemed to be primitive, traditional and non-modern, whereas written literature or history was deemed to be the mark of civilizational advancement. It is only in the late 20th century that there has been a concerted attempt to evaluate the aesthetic and narrative features of oral cultures. Moreover, these oral cultures had not only aesthetic effects but also political roles to play, raising social consciousness, satirizing the monarch and offering social commentaries. Literary scholars within postcolonial studies show how oral cultures have influenced the writing of fiction in Achebe, Raja Rao and other postcolonial authors. The usage of idiomatic expressions in the register and rhythm of speech in these authors suggests that their oral traditions continue to wield enormous power over them. Other postcolonial authors, like Jean 'Binta' Breeze, retrieved African and Caribbean oral traditions to produce performance poetry and so abrogating, creolizing and reverse colonizing the English language. (See also: **abrogation, hybridity, creolization**)

Orientalism: From the latter half of the 18th century there was a massive European academic and professional interest in the Orient. The Orient's languages, history, literature, religion, law, architecture were studied, documented and commented on. In the case of England's interest in India, the Asiatick Society, established in 1784, and associated with figures like William Jones, was an institutional embodiment of this interest and expertise. 'Orientalists' was the name given to such scholars of the Orient. In 1978 Edward Said published his study of Western attitudes toward the Arab-Asian world, and titled it *Orientalism*. Said identified Orientalism as more than a European academic interest in the Asia-Arab world. Orientalism was an apparatus of representation through which Europe saw the East, and posited this East as the radical racial-cultural Other. Said argued that fiction and fantasies, travelogues and scientific reports all generated a desire for the Orient. This desire was at one level genuinely epistemological, but it was knowledge for the political purpose of domination over the object of inquiry. The Oriental native would be the object that the European would investigate and about which the European would make authoritative pronouncements. The European would therefore be the subject, whose very subjectivity emerged in this process of inquiry. Thus Said made the link between textual knowledge (in the form of the colonial archive) of the Orient produced by the European and the political dominance of the Orient by the Europeans. Orientalism for Said is a systematic process through which the East is studied, researched, administered and 'pronounced upon'. Orientalism produced static images of the Orient, positing it as unchanging, barbaric and occupying the lower end of the civilizational scale. By positing the Orient as unchanging, the European representation ensured that it could be comprehended, that any threat of change would be avoided. Further, Orientalism's repeated emphasis on the barbaric primitivism of the Orient offered the European the justification for his civilizational mission and political dominance over the helpless 'native' of Africa or Asia. Administrators to the East were trained, Said argues, on Orientalist texts so that their very perceptions of the East when they physically arrived there were organized through the texts consumed. Territorial expansion and knowledge of the territories occupied went together here. Said identifies a latent Orientalism that is made up of the fears and anxieties about the East, and a manifest Orientalism which consists of the articulated, expressed opinions of the East. Said's main contribution was to bestow texts with considerable political weight, showing how stereotypes in Western representations of the Arab or the Brahmin produced political effects in terms of policies that then proceeded to dominate, improve or modify these 'types'. Said brought to the forefront the textual component of the imperial project, showing how, even before the political homogenization of the world under European powers, there was a textual empire. Said argued that but for the East there would not have been a Western sense of itself: the West built its identity in contrast with the East, by constantly drawing on this difference (encoded in texts) of 'us and them'. Orientalism was instrumental in producing a series of binaries such as 'East versus West', 'civilized versus barbaric', 'modern versus primitive', 'free versus oppressed', and 'centre versus periphery'. Through these binaries produced in the textual archive of the Empire the West retained its cultural and racial difference from the East. He further proposed that over a period of time even the fictional stereotypes of the racial-cultural Other began to acquire the status of scientific truth, and there was no need to offer explanations and examples for the claims made in these texts. Eventually, the natives of the colonies, forced to read Western texts about themselves, came to believe these stereotypes about themselves, and thus conceded that they were exactly as the West had portrayed them. This meant that, having conceded racial and cultural superiority to the European, the native also consented to being governed by the superior race. Said thus argued that Orientalism and its knowledges were integral to colonial-imperial rule because the texts produced within this structure enabled the European to dominate the native through the latter's consent, that is, without coercion. The native enters the imperial system because s/he accepts the system as benevolent and beneficial and simultaneously concedes, after years of training, that this dominance is essential for the native. Said's reading of the textual and epistemological foundations of imperialism might be said to have inaugurated the field of postcolonial studies and scholars like MacKenzie (1988, 1989), Suleri (1992), Teltscher (2000), Sharpe (1993), and McClintock (1995) extended the Saidian paradigm in their reading of colonial discourse.

Ornamentalism: The term was devised by David Cannadine (2001) in his book of the same title, as a direct echo of Edward Said's *Orientalism*. Cannadine proposes that we cannot separate the history of the Empire from the history of Britain: Britain, in effect, was its Empire. Central to this expansion of the British Empire was an expansion and extension of its social apparatuses, beliefs and attitudes. Cannadine makes a major shift in this argument about imperialism when he suggests that for the British rank, class, social symbols and appurtenances were more crucial than race. Thus the British responded to colonized subjects in terms of their class and rank, while they built social *relations* around these criteria. Class and status determined who the British Empire co-opted into its structures, and how it dealt with its subjects. It was a whole set of class-determined notions (of honour, chivalry, tradition, glory, order) and their symbols (parades, elephants, dress code, processions), or what he calls 'ornamentalism' that constituted imperial relations. Cannadine's contentious argument thus proposes that the native Nizam or tribal chief was 'respectable' enough for the British, arguing that it was the rank and social standing of the native that mattered more than the colour of his skin. Hierarchy was something the British adored, and therefore, they respected the upper echelons of even a brown or black hierarchy. Ornamentalism brought together ranks across races, if Cannadine is to be believed, 'hierarchy made visible ... chivalry and ceremony, monarchy and majesty, were the means by which this vast world was brought together, interconnected, unified' (122).

picturesque (as colonial-imperial aesthetic): In writings and paintings by Europeans, building on their theories of landscape aesthetics of the late 18th century (developed by Uvedale Price, Mark Akenside and William Gilpin), regions like India and South East Asia were represented as offering picture-perfect 'scenes'. Most notably seen in the works of Thomas and William Daniells, William Hodges (who was the draftsman on James Cook's first voyage to Australia), John Glover and others represented the colony and its spaces as mere static sights. Rural scenes, including those of the rural poor, figured prominently in these paintings and literary descriptions. The colonial picturesque was a mode of exoticization where the native world was rendered into visually appealing 'scenes', or by bringing them together into the exhibit that converted the dynamism of the colony into non-threatening, static exotica. The aesthetic would account for the landscape in the natural picturesque or focus on towns and rituals in the civic picturesque (Malcolm Andrews 1994). The former enabled the colonial to represent the colony as more nature than culture, an ancient place of waterfalls, animals (including some predators), and where signs of improvement, industry or modernity were studiously ignored, thus preserving the image of a back-in-time, old-world, rural ideal (Leask 2002). Variety, where the animals, plant life, humans and dwellings appeared in harmony, was the hallmark of the colonial-imperial picturesque. Jill Casid (2005) has proposed that paintings and descriptions such as these constitute a discourse of political and aesthetic control because they position the English traveller-painter as the all-seeing 'I'. Further, by focusing on the colony's

The Postcolonial Studies Dictionary, First Edition. Pramod K. Nayar.
© 2015 John Wiley & Sons, Ltd. Published 2015 by John Wiley & Sons, Ltd.

ABCDEFGHIJKLMNOPQRSTUVWXYZ

ruins as an aesthetic subject, as Hodges did, colonial writers presented a country that physically and culturally had degenerated, and was emptied of its former glory. By presenting the natural landscape as a horticultural or ruined 'idyll' the colonial-imperial picturesque evaded the political problems of peasantry and taxation issues. There are other elements to the colonial-imperial picturesque. Englishmen's plantations and gardens in Jamaica and other places were compared to Italian/European places, even as Europe itself got transplanted into the colony. Transplantation of plants meant the grafting of one colony onto another, or from the New World onto England. It meant a transculturation via aesthetic experiments, of England itself (Casid).

postcolonialism: Initially written with a '-' between 'post' and 'colonialism' as a signifier of chronology, the term was originally meant to convey a historical-material change in the political status of a country: 'after colonialism'. But with the 1980s it became identified with a way of reading and interpretation, a theory and a methodology, that examines the nature of Euro-American nations' conquest, domination and exploitation of countries and cultures in South America, Asia, Africa and regions like Canada and Australia. This domination mode of postcolonial inquiry tracks both historically (the period of European empires) and in the contemporary (**neocolonialism**). Postcolonialism is the academic-cultural component of the condition of postcoloniality. It represents a theoretical approach on the part of the formerly colonized, the subaltern and the historically oppressed, in literary-cultural studies informed by a particular political stance, using the prism of race and the historical context of colonialism, to analyze texts, even as it seeks to produce critical commentary that serves an act of cultural resistance to the domination of Euro-American epistemic and interpretive schemes. Central to postcolonialism's academic project since the 1980s is a study of discourses and rhetoric, involving a re-examination of colonial writings and representations to unravel the racial-racist subtexts, to excavate buried native (non-European) histories and to map the resistance offered to colonialism. Postcolonialism also studies the psychological and cultural impact of colonial rule on the non-European, arguing that the native's subjectivity was itself formed, as Frantz Fanon famously demonstrated, within the violently unstable crucible of colonialism. It seeks to examine the nature of the colonized subject's agency in the face of oppression and dominance. The political position adopted in these interpretations is marked by the commitment to ideas of emancipation, equality and justice. It notes that the Western constructions (in texts, whether literary or scientific) of non-European races were informed by racial ideologies and the larger purpose of dominance over the land, people and cultures of the non-European. Thus, as an academic discipline, it studies the literary, historical, legal, popular 'instruments' (i.e., representational modes) – **colonial discourse**, in other words – of colonial domination, whether in the domain of religion or literature. The term has now come to signify, in the main, cultural productions (film, music, sports, literature) from the formerly colonized nations, and these are themselves assumed to be set in opposition to the colonial's representations of the native. They are also seen as an attempt to carve out (or retrieve) a certain pride and sense of self in one's own history and culture. While given over principally to textual analysis, postcolonialism, especially in its materialist-Marxist version and critiques (Ahmad 1992) and contemporary cultural studies (Mbembe 2001), has called for attention to economic-political contexts of cultural productions both in the colonial and neocolonial eras. Adapting the work of Samir Amin and others from economics, such critiques call for greater historicizing to trace the variant models of colonizations in Asia, Africa and South America. However, besides the former European colonial nations, the USA and its racial history – from slavery to 20th-century migrations and post-9/11 (Koshy 2008) – are also being brought into the ambit. Critics of the term argue that the very nomenclature seems to trap the non-European nation within a European history: that their histories may only be measured in terms of 'pre-colonial', 'colonial' or 'postcolonial'. In terms of its theoretical alignments postcolonialism has been associated with poststructuralism (especially of the Michel Foucault variety, starting with the writings of Edward Said), Marxism (in Fanon, and later in Spivak, the Subaltern Studies group), postmodernism, a mix of psychoanalysis and poststructuralism (Bhabha), and feminism (McClintock). The academic field of postcolonialism has been further organized around issues such as gender (in the work of Clare Midgley, 2007, in history for example), transnationalism and globalization (Dirlik), cosmopolitanism (Appiah, Bhabha) or genres such as travel writing (M.L. Pratt). Periods in history such as the Early Modern/Shakespeare (Greenblatt 1993) or the English Romantics (Fulford 1999; Leask 1993, 2002) have come in for attention for their complicity with the Empire. Scientific discourses, including medical ones, have also been read postcolonially for their contribution to racist thought (Stepan, Arnold, Crosby, Harrison). Material conditions of exploitation engaged in by the contemporary world system (essentially Euro-American corporations) and the crisis of migration in, say, African nations like Sudan and the sub-Saharan regions (as captured poignantly in Dave Eggers' *What is the What*?) have increasingly taken centre-stage in postcolonial studies. This has meant that more materialist critiques are offered, rather than simply the excessive attention to discourse. Uneven structures of development are studied, especially for their role in determining First World/Third World relations. Security discourses that construct migrants, Islam and terrorism in racialized terms and which then work in conjunction with processes of border control and peacekeeping (but also reconfigured notions of citizenship and belonging for Muslims in the USA), have come in for attention from postcolonial scholars as well, especially after 9/11 and the 'war on terror' (Razack 2004; Hartnell 2010). The politics of aid in Third World nations that foreground First World humanitarianism, benevolence and an (alleged) post-racial politics but in fact erase the 'whiteness' of aid (as was the case in colonialism) and treat suffering as localized and outside of global historical conditions that are created/determined by the First World, have been addressed in recent studies (Jefferess 2013).

postcoloniality: The material contexts and conditions – economic, political, geographical, social – of countries in Asia, Africa and South America that acquired political independence from European nations in the course of the 20th century after years of colonial rule are collectively termed 'postcoloniality'. We can map these conditions along several lines. Colonialism's legacies constitute an important aspect of postcoloniality – in terms of the continued relevance, prestige and power of the English (and other former languages of the colonial master). Models of nationalism and governance have also been transmitted to the **postcolony**. Newer forms of exploitation by the First World of the former colonies replicate the colonial era in the age of **neocolonialism** and **globalization**. The continued use of Third World labour in South and South East Asia for serving the industries of First World corporations (sweatshops, as they are called) replicates older forms of labour exploitation approximating, in many cases, to slavery. New economic policies – whether bans on subsidies, loans, aid, free trade agreements – benefit, mostly, the First World businesses and have, as journalists and commentators from the Third World have documented (Shiva), adversely affected the farmer and the small entrepreneur of the postcolony. Migrants from the Third World to the First World continue to face discrimination. Military campaigns and interventions by the USA, its allies and organizations like NATO, in the pursuit of oil, minerals and other natural resources, extend colonial-era exploitation and oppression. Other policies and international 'agreements' (although these are less by agreement than by coercion) on global warming, fossil fuels, human rights, borders are very often one-sided and rarely in the interests of the postcolony. The new figurations of the Empire therefore replicate older ones in far more shadowy and insidious forms. The condition of the postcolony remains, in other words, a different but continuing version of the colony. (See also: **neocolonialism, Empire – new figurations of, globalization**)

postcolony: A term that was first deployed by Achille Mbembe in *On the Postcolony* (2001) to describe the sub-Saharan nation-states of Africa (although the first 'notes', as he calls them, on the 'postcolony' date back to his 1992 essay). Mbembe uses the term to describe certain kinds of nation-states that, having achieved political independence, govern with inherited structures of violence and domination. Thus he draws attention not only to the legacies of colonialism but also to contemporary figurations of these legacies, with respect to Africa (Mbembe, it should be noted, is not referring to all postcolonial nation-states, only the African ones). Mbembe argues that the system of governance and administration established by the European powers in African countries was not only about preparing a civil society, justice, sovereignty or political modernity for the colony. It also established a system of violence built into the very structures of governance. As a result, Mbembe argues, there is no possibility of political sovereignty in the postcolony because governmentality is always already undermined, or at least underwritten, by the legacy of structural violence and the penchant for grand spectacles of authority and power by the ruling class. The political independence of the colony did not mean freedom from the institutional structures – Mbembe's examples are the police station and the military – of the colonial era. Mbembe notes that the postcolony does not really retrieve its history or recover from its colonial past. More importantly, the rise of business regimes – essentially the shift toward privatized 'versions' of state control due to the complicity of business houses with the state or political parties in most postcolonial nations in Asia and Africa – seems to suggest, in Mbembe's reading, the absence of a true political sovereignty or modernity. Clearly, then, the postcolony is a former colony whose present existence is very much informed by structures of violence and systems of thought that are legacies of its colonial past. While historical structures left over from that past, for instance, India's penal code, dating back to the mid-19th century and still one of the cornerstones of the judicial process, might be the most visible of the legacies there are also other kinds, as Mbembe has noted. Cultural traits – for example the dominance of the language (and literature) of the former colonial ruler in the post-independence age – represent another kind of legacy.

postnational: Articulated as a descriptor of the globalized world order by Arjun Appadurai (1996) and others (Habermas 2001), the 'postnational' gestures at a late 20th-century condition where the nation-state has become obsolete. As flows of people, products and finance cut across the borders of the nation-state and there is a palpable increase in the role of transnational corporations and bodies (IMF, WTO, but also NATO and the NGOs) in determining policies, budgets, governments, especially in the 'Third World' or 'Global South', the nation-state loses its sovereignty. Further, there is a greater amount of allegiance to ideas, units and organizations that are beyond national borders (diasporas and their cultural identity would be an example). Even within nation-states the increasing migrant populations produce a shift toward multicultural citizenship and delocalized belonging. Other commentators, like Jeremy Waldron (1995), also emphasize the multicultural belonging of individuals today – a condition that makes it impossible to make a case for a unified or even singular cultural heritage. Yet, despite these flows, Ali Behdad argues, the movement of people and populations is greatly determined, monitored and regulated by the nation-state (2008: 73. Also Sassen 2000). It could also be argued that despite the apparent 'postnational' condition, when it comes to economic benefits and profits the flow is unhesitatingly toward Euro-American nation-states. More importantly, after 9/11 and the 'war on terror', the Western nation-state has focused ever more sharply on the nature of citizenship, the for-eigner, and the immigrant and refugee (Ong 2003; Behdad 2005).

primitivism: Among the many stereotypes of the non-European native in colonial discourse, that of primitivism is one of the oldest. Primitivism first posited the native as located at the lower end of the evolutionary/civilizational scale, with the upper end being occupied by the Europeans. Savages did not merit the same attention, or care, as humanity, and so the discourse of primitivism justified brutal treatment on the part of the Europeans colonials, who claimed that the less-than-human Africans did not feel pain, and so could be made to labour harder. The primitivist dis-course was also connected to temporality, and converted present-day Africa, for instance, into antique cultures, pushed back in time. As such, the natives of Africa or South America were constructed as being closer to Nature, more innocent and authentic. The uncorrupted 'noble savage' was one such myth within the discourse of primitivism, where the 'noble savage' was at once authentic – and therefore to be left undisturbed – but also a challenge to the colonial's civilizational project. The native's languages, religions, and political arrangement were all deemed to be reflective of an ancient past beyond which the African had not progressed (with progress of course measured in European terms). Then, primitivism also constructed the native as politically immature, lacking in systems of governance or regulated private property, and with only a rudimentary economic system. This latter enabled the European to reject all native forms of political and economic organization and install their own instead. 'Modernization' was thus an implicit and later explicit part of this primitivizing discourse wherein colonialism was projected as bringing the ideas of the Enlightenment, political modernity and progress to the savages.

provincializing: A term popularized by Dipesh Chakrabarty's book *Provincializing Europe* (2000), 'provincializing' is the process whereby one sees European history not as a monolith, as seamless and coherent, but as fractured. The term is used to indicate the necessity of seeing European history and history-writing as not universal but local, particular and provincial. Chakrabarty argues that due to Europe's colonial project several parts of Europe, especially the southern regions of Italy, Spain and the Mediterranean region, were themselves Orientalized. We therefore need to resist the idea of a time movement (teleology) of European history as self-contained and self-propelled. Chakrabarty points out that the model of history-writing came from Europe, and relied entirely on this teleological narrative. The history of the rest of the world was also written in this mode with one crucial difference: the colonized were always ancient, ruined, set in the past and primitive whereas Europe was modern and contemporary. 'Progress' in *time* was, in this vision of history, the movement toward the stage Europe had attained. Historical time itself was marked by the absolute difference between West and East, where the West came first and the world later. That is, the colonies had to eventually acquire the current level of 'modernity' enjoyed by Europe. The move from cave-life to settled agrarian society to feudalism to modern industrialized capitalism was seen as the natural model for human progress, and history. Countries such as the colonies of Africa or Asia that did not approximate to this teleology were therefore 'non-modern'. Chakrabarty's major contribution was to show how this model of history, history-writing and progress was by the mid-19th century deemed to be a universal standard, even though in reality it was very provincial, being restricted to Europe alone. He warns us that there were in fact many histories, because cultures took different routes to modernization and political sovereignty. Thus even in Marx Chakrabarty discerns a move toward universalism, and so Marxism retains its **Eurocentrism**. Capital, Chakrabarty argues, develops an archive for itself, incorporating into this archive even those elements that were not part of its history (what Chakrabarty calls History 1). In contrast to, and in antagonism to, this history was life itself (History 2), where the accumulation of capital was not central to the idea of progress. Thus, while Europe's idea of modernization hinged on capital accumulation, this was not a universal feature. It was simply a provincial one. There is a need for Subaltern Histories, to ensure that heterogeneities are preserved, and no attempt is made to bring them into a grand narrative or overarching principle (whether of emancipation, capital or labour). However, as Frederick Cooper argues, despite Chakrabarty's stated aim of provincializing Europe and its key concepts of nation and history, he treats 'post-Enlightenment rationality, bourgeois equality, modernity or liberalism ... not [as] provincial ideologies, but a grid of knowledge and power forcing people to see the nation-state as the only political model' (2008: 406–7).

race: A system of classification of humans where the criteria could be anatomical (i.e., biology), genetic or cultural. However, for a very long time it has rested on biological foundations so that physical appearance and features have taken centre-stage in any racial typology. Postcolonialism as a mode of interpretation tracks race and its cognates, racial difference and racism, as an organizing principle of literary texts and history-writing but, more than anything else, of colonialism. Colonialism was the domination of one set of races by another – with the dominant race being European. Colonialism emerges as a result of European thinking about racial difference in particular ways where the 'other' races were inferior, primitive, vulnerable, child-like, treacherous and incapable of governing themselves. This racial binary was deemed to be absolute and extended, in colonial **Manicheanism**, into moral, cultural and social fields so that the racially different other was the opposite of the European self. The European self could only emerge by retaining this alterity of the racial Other. Race theory was integral to scientific thought as well (Bolt 1971) and this 'naturalized' racial difference by casting it in biological terms. Social Darwinism, which arose in the late 19th century, was heavily influenced by race theory. However, as later postcolonial critics noted (Bhabha), the racial binary of white/non-white was always an ambivalent one because on the one hand the non-white race was deemed to be completely primitive and savage while on the other it was (i) idealized as the 'noble savage' and (ii) deemed to be improvable. Race theory was responsible for the generation of endless stereotypes, where these stereotypes then perpetuated themselves and

The Postcolonial Studies Dictionary, First Edition. Pramod K. Nayar.
© 2015 John Wiley & Sons, Ltd. Published 2015 by John Wiley & Sons, Ltd.

ABCDEFGHIJKLMNOPQRSTUVWXYZ

furthered race theory in a kind of vicious colonial cycle. This meant, simply, that the occurrence of the stereotype of the cannibal African or the treacherous Brahmin in a literary text would simply *reflect* a 'known fact' even though it was the discursive operation (textual representation) of the racial type that converted a myth into a scientific or natural 'fact'. For postcolonial studies it is the discursive construction of race that comes in for attention, given the field's emphasis on textuality and the link of knowledge with power. Thus Cornel West (2002) and others working within Critical Race Theory or Critical Race Studies note the links between race theory manifest as discourses or literary-cultural representations and economics or politics. Critical Race Theory has moved beyond the study of the European/non-European race binary to address concerns of **aboriginals** and First Nation peoples. Chicano/a thinkers like Gloria Anzaldúa have added one more dimension to the field by examining the nature of mixed-race people, or *mestizaje*. Also constituting an important component of contemporary studies of race is Black Feminism, founded on the assumption that the black woman's experiences are radically different from those of the white woman, and that the black woman is doubly marginalized, as a black and as a woman. The links between nationalisms, anti-colonial struggles and sexuality have also been studied (see Parker *et al.* 1992 for an early volume). Queer postcolonial studies examines the work of writers like Suniti Namjoshi, Cherrie Moraga, Shyam Selvadurai and the contexts in which ethnicity and race intersect with sexuality. The heteronormative remains the most dominant mode in diasporic cultures as well (Takagi 1996). In an early statement that initiated the forging of a relationship of queers across races, Gloria Anzaldúa declared: 'as a lesbian, I have no race, my own people disclaim me: but I am all races because there is the queer of me in all races' (1994: 102–3).

refugee: Two of the best known of contemporary postcolonial authors, Mohsin Hamid (*The Reluctant Fundamentalist*, 2007) and Kamila Shamsie (*Burnt Shadows*, 2009) have refugees in pivotal roles in their work, and give some credibility to Aihwa Ong's (2003) assertion that for the 20th century the refugee is the ultimate ethical figure. For postcolonial studies, the refugee is a figure that emerges with the massive dislocations of the modern era. Genocide, ethnicide, wars, economic hardships, and denial of cultural rights all produce the refugee. The refugee is also a test case for humanitarian aid and citizenship norms as more and more countries seek to tighten controls on asylum applicants and citizenship rights of refugees and migrants. Ong

(2003) proposes that in the case of the USA the attempt to assimilate various ethnic groups into standard American categories manifested as the 'moral politics of poor relief'. Thus, reforms targeting the working classes or the poor aligned poverty, welfare and morality in order to determine categories of 'deserving citizenship' and 'undeserving' ones. Different kinds of ethnic groups among the refugees are perceived and treated differently. The refugee is also constructed as a category in opposition to the 'citizen'. The social contexts of receiving societies and their values determine how the refugee can be redesignated, if at all, as 'citizen'. Ong notes that economic value, hygiene, health and moral worthiness – the legacy of an earlier era with far more racialized attitudes – continue to be factors in determining this process of redesignation. The refugee in the globalized age is akin to the native of the colonial period where the native was evaluated for qualifying as a 'good' or 'bad' subject, and had to demonstrate how s/he qualified as the former. Today the refugee needs to subscribe to the First World's (i.e, receiving society's) values of family, health, language (tests for the refugee's English or European language skills) and cultural beliefs. Can the refugee retain her/his native beliefs – which had led, in many cases, to the persecutions back home – in any part of the world, or does the shift from 'refugee' to 'citizen' status demand a quiet toning down, or even abandonment, of these beliefs? The dissident immigrant in Hamid and Shamsie also gives us the obverse of the helpless and disempowered refugee, especially in the wake of 9/11 (Harleen Singh 2012).

re-orientalism: A term first deployed by Lisa Lau (2007) to describe the orientalizing of the Orient by the Orientals themselves in the postcolonial age. The term has some affinity with the arguments of Graham Huggan in *The Postcolonial Exotic*, and draws upon earlier concepts like 'ethno-Orientalism', 'self-Orientalism', among others. 'Orientalism', as Edward Said theorized it, was the imaginative construction of the Orient as fixed, primitive, non-modern, etc. It was the essentializing and stereotyping of the East by the Occident because the Westerner had the power to represent the non-European culturally different Other from the outside. The Oriental was the silent, passive recipient of European knowledge and construction of the Orient. However, as Lau argues, this stereotyping and orientalizing is not the privilege or obsession of the Occident/West. Orientalizing is now performed by the Orientals themselves, especially by diasporic Oriental authors from the South Asian region. Whereas in colonialism the outsider-European represented the Oriental, in 're-orientalism' the power of representation is in the hands of somebody who is at once insider and outsider – being a diasporic member of the Orient. Unlike the European these diasporic authors are not entirely alien to the cultures they represent (hence 'insiders'), and their identities are drawn from their Oriental ancestry and affiliations. By virtue of their location at the centre of literary and cultural production (Euro-America) – as well as their consumption of these stereotypes and texts – the diasporic Oriental authors are able to make pronouncements about their community, ethnic group and culture. Further, their pronouncements and commentary are consumed as authentic and authoritative. The identities of South Asia, Lau argues, are being crafted by diasporic South Asian writers residing in the West, and these identities very often build on exoticisms and difference from the West. Thus re-orientalism partakes of the same tendencies as colonial orientalism in that it, too, thrives on stereotyping, exoticization and emphasis of cultural difference of the 'East' from the 'West', which then begin to be seen as definitive and 'insider' accounts of the Eastern culture. The popularity of Khaled Hosseini, Marjane Satrapi and the numerous South Asian women authors, such as Kamila Shamsie or Tehmina Durrani, might be at least partly attributed to this re-orientalizing. Re-orientalizing might also be read as instantiating a certain anxiety on the part of the diasporic author, an anxiety to demonstrate authentic 'Indian' or 'Sri Lankan' identity. Meenakshi Mukherjee (2000), arguing for the 'anxiety of Indianness', points to the diasporic author's insistence on drawing upon Indian epics and traditions in order to demonstrate her/his authenticity. This might be seen as an instance of re-orientalism where the 'authenticity question' is answered (in diasporic authors) by returning to the very stereotypes the West has always perpetuated and sought.

representation (colonial): In the purely linguistic sense, it is the presentation of an empirical reality in language, through a system of signs. In critical theory, in which postcolonial theory finds its origins as well, representation has meant more than just this. Representation constructs the subject because identities are constructed within discourses. Discourses and their representational modes, whether in science (biomedical representations of, say, healthy individuals or populations), economics (representations of labouring and economically productive people) or literature (good and bad characters who approximate to 'types' of humans) are based on prior notions of race, gender, ethnicity, sexual orientation and morality. In turn, representations influence the way the individual or group is perceived along these lines of race, gender or ethnicity. Therefore representations are not neutral, and are informed by the power relations between the one being represented and the one doing the representation. Forms of representation are themselves founded on prior aesthetic and political ideology. Stereotypes are a form of representation in which it is assumed that a set of core features of a group can be captured and stabilized in the form of a portrait or description (verbal representation). Representation here is about power: the power to depict, define and eventually dominate the object represented. As these stereotypical representations circulate, for example in **colonial discourse**, about the martial Pathan, the primitive Aboriginal, or the just Englishman, our perceptions of these people, and of reality itself, is mediated by them. Representations construct reality for us to perceive and respond in certain ways. For postcolonial studies colonial discourse and its texts have been instrumental in defining the 'true' nature of the colony and the colonial subject for the white races. European writing from Columbus to the 19th century forever constructed the **Carib** as cannibal, with or without any empirical evidence. The identity of the Carib as cannibal was 'fixed'. For the native, too, these representations by 'authoritative' ethnographic or scientific **texts** – in scientific and ethnographic discourses the representations were believed, till the late-1980s, to be objective and neutral – acquire the sanctity of truth. Over time these representations function as truth, and the viewer/reader stops paying attention to the *forms* of representation because these are seen only as a true reflection of reality. Also, representation was always linked to questions of power. The representation of the Hindu widow as vulnerable enabled the white man to posit himself as her rescuer and benevolent protector. Therefore the representation led to the construction not only of the native woman but also of the Englishman, and the eventual establishment of a particular relationship: helpless native woman protected by powerful white man. The system of colonial relations itself was therefore dependent on particular forms of representation. Within postcolonial studies and critical theory much attention is paid to the strategies of representation because these are seen as political, even when disguised as aesthetic modes in literature or painting. Much of postcolonial literature has been devoted to undoing the representations of native cultures within colonial texts because it is argued that the power, authority and right to represent one's own culture is a marker of sovereignty, a sovereignty denied by the colonial regime. Debates about authentic and inauthentic representations of tribes and cultures, in both colonial and postcolonial texts, are essentially debates about the right to represent as well as an assertion of the belief that representations are not simply signs but construct identities and relations.

Requerimiento: A legal document of 1513 from the Spanish colonies in South America, it is an excellent example of the discursive construction of hegemony and racialized relations. The document stipulated that the natives accept Spanish rule and that they convert to Christianity. Interestingly, the document was read out aloud to any group of natives that the advancing Spaniards encountered, not unlike the Miranda. If any group refused to accept the provisions of the *Requerimiento*, so the document stated, the Spaniards were free to declare war on them. That is, the natives had to submit to the provisions of the document voluntarily, or the Spanish could legally – if this document be considered legal at all – evict them or wage war against them. From the postcolonial perspective, it was the Spanish who invented this legal framework with no native inputs, and it was up to the Spanish to execute the provisions of the document as well: the entire process constructed a cycle of legality that is in and of itself illegal. When the natives failed to comply with provisions listed in the document that they did not understand, the Europeans 'legitimately' waged war against them until they complied.

reverse colonization: Jamaican-English poet Louise Bennett's poem 'Colonization in Reverse' spoke of the flow of immigrants of all races into England as a process of 'reverse colonization'. They arrive in England 'Be the hundred, be de tousan' 'An turn history upside dung!' Then the speaker wonders about how the English who 'face war an brave de worse' will 'stan/ Colonizin in reverse'. Reverse colonization as a process was anticipated in the writings of several English poets. Thus William Wordsworth in Book VII of *The Prelude* spoke of London as a multicultural city:

> The Swede, the Russian; from the genial south,
> The Frenchman and the Spaniard; from remote
> America, the Hunter-Indian; Moors,
> Malays, Lascars, the Tartar and Chinese,
> And Negro Ladies in white muslin gowns.

In a Victorian England obsessed with hygiene and purity, Arthur Conan Doyle wrote in *A Study in Scarlet* of London as a 'cesspool' into which all the idlers, leftovers and no-good returnees of the Empire were 'drained'. Reverse colonization is also, according to some critics (Arata 1990), the key theme of Bram Stoker's 1897 novel *Dracula*, where England is to be 'invaded' by the East European vampire. Today, reverse colonization is an accepted condition where England (and other European nations, but mainly England, the headquarters of one of the world's largest empires until about the mid-20th century) has become irreducibly multicultural. Reverse colonization does carry a certain pejorative connotation because it not only recalls a history of European colonization but also suggests that modern-day migration and cultural mixing is as violent as the more traditional forms of colonial conquest. Writers like Louise Bennett, Timothy Mo, Hanif Kureishi, and Zadie Smith examine an England that is multicultural, although they do not quite see it as any kind of *colonization* at all. It is possible to argue that England's reverse colonization and multicultural populations have also forced some white authors to come to grips with their nation's problematic history. Thus Adam Foulds, a new novelist-poet, in *The Broken Word* (2008), a narrative poem about the Kenyan Mau-Mau uprising, evaluates the effects of colonial violence upon white people. Foulds suggests in the transformation of Tom into a violent killer of black people how the colony brought out the worst in the otherwise gentle and caring English public schoolboy.

secularism/post-secularism: Secularism, in nation-states like India, is a political concept and state policy which calls for the state to recognize citizens of all religions, without favouritism or prejudice toward any. It has been, at least in India, one of the foundational principles of the newly independent nation right from the 1950s. However, communal violence and periodic eruptions of discontent over policy and social conditions – which includes questions of majoritarianism, 'minority appeasement', among others – have often rendered secularism a problematic concept for cultural commentators and political scientists. Linkages of secularism with nationalism in postcolonial societies like India and Sri Lanka have also produced their own share of controversies about belonging and religious affiliation (Gyan Pandey's well-known 1999 essay was titled 'Can a Muslim be an Indian?'). Early commentators, such as Ashis Nandy, argue that the anger and fanaticism in believers is the effect of a sense of defeat and impotence due to modernity, the nation-state and secularism (1990). Post-secularism, often traced in first use to Jürgen Habermas, refers to a resurgence (but perhaps is a mere persistence) of religious beliefs and rituals in the late 20th century. Habermas argues that the term can only be applied to affluent societies in the modern age where people's religious ties have declined. With greater 'functional differentiation of social subsystems' (Habermas' phrase, 2008), religious institutions lose their control over domains like law, politics, education and public welfare, and stay restricted to religious matters. Habermas points to the missionary expansion, fundamentalist radicalization and the political exploitation (his term is 'instrumentalization')

The Postcolonial Studies Dictionary, First Edition. Pramod K. Nayar.
© 2015 John Wiley & Sons, Ltd. Published 2015 by John Wiley & Sons, Ltd.

of the potential for violence in all religions. He suggests, however, that this interpretation of the world's events as indicative of a 'post-secular' condition lies in the fact that (i) there is a broad perception that these global conflicts hinge on religious strife, (ii) religion is gaining influence in private and public spheres, (iii) there is increased migration from societies with traditional cultural backgrounds so that receiving societies become plural in terms of faiths and cultures. Commentators like Saba Mahmood have argued that debates about secularism have only been cast within the language of the nation-state and within binaries like 'free speech' versus blasphemy (2009). Others, like Bruce Robbins (2013), are more conscious of the history of the concept and conclude that the West cannot easily identify with secularism either and that the West was never 'constitutively secular', just as the non-West has never been 'constitutively religious'. (Robbins also notes, following Frederick Cooper, that during the colonial period the secularists in the West were a beleaguered lot.) Some postcolonial texts explore ways of thinking about other possibilities within secularism that, according to Manav Ratti (2013), would find 'inspiring features' in religion devoid of the violence that attaches itself to religious beliefs and principles. Ratti, therefore, seeks to undo the binary of secularism *versus* religion. This might involve, over a period of time, the use of the dominant signifiers and ethical principles from religion which then need to be 'secularized' within the present material and historical contexts.

settler colonialism: In the case of Canada, Australia and the northern American continent, Europeans arrived from various places in Europe with the clear intention of remaining in the new place. Settler colonialism is the term used to distinguish this form of colonial occupation from the mode followed in, say, India. The latter is called 'colony of occupation', where the Europeans spent some time for economic and political reasons, dominated the natives, but did not intend the colony to become their permanent home. Settler colonialism is now seen as an extremely violent invasion, usually accompanied by the massacre and complete extermination of the local inhabitants, such as the aboriginals and the Native Americans – and this genocide-**ethnocide** is one of the central features of the settler colony. If in colonies of occupation the Europeans worked with existing systems (trade, law, markets, even cultures), in the case of settler colonies, they sought to erase all native cultures, even as they made use of the natives as labour. The settlers very often carried political, cultural and historical baggage from Europe. In fact, the early settlers would replicate the structures and political order from their home country, and were even supported in this by their home country. Later, the settlers, after a generation or two, would seek to move away from this legacy (the settling of the United States is an example) and evolve their own distinct culture in the new land. Settler colonialism entailed, in several cases, some adaption of the local culture as well. In the case of Australia, settled as a penal colony, two key elements constitute its identity – the displacement of the Aboriginals and the punishment of large numbers of British and Irish people, mainly from the poorer classes, for supposed crimes against the wealthier classes in England. Thus, unlike Canada or the Americas, the colony was not seen as an extension, or 'completion', of England but rather as a space of deviance and contradictions (Hodge and Mishra 1990). Recent studies have linked the lives of settlers and the sheer boredom of their lives in the vast expanses of the Australian outback with the modernist movement (Saikat Majumdar 2013).

situated knowledge: Feminist theory from the 1980s argued that knowledge proceeds from the experiences of individuals, where experiences shape perceptions of the world. 'Standpoint epistemology', as Sandra Harding, Donna Haraway and others have termed it, lays emphasis on the subject position of the observing individual. These thinkers also insist that **subalterns** possess forms of knowledge due to their subordinated position, but that this knowledge has been ignored. Only the knowledge created by a class of people – the scientists – is treated as 'objective' and acceptable *as* knowledge. They thus make the link between power and knowledge explicit. The 'situation' of an individual in terms of race, class and gender determines the kind of knowledge they have access to or might possess. Situated knowledge means giving centrality to the experiences of people within a system. Knowledge here is practice-based. Thus experiments in the deployment of new technology would entail asking the women users of the technology how they perceive the device/process. This also means that the end-users of any technology or process, by virtue of having to deal with this in their everyday lives, are perhaps best qualified to speak about them. Contexts, therefore, are integral to knowledge in this view. How a community uses a particular idea or process or device determines what kind of knowledge they would possess about, say, architecture or gardening or farming. Fields of work divide communities not only in terms of the work they do but also in terms of the knowledge that comes out of this work. Communities of users generate their own knowledge, and this localized, embodied and particular knowledge might not fit in with the theorizing done by science. Situated knowledge therefore rejects the transcendental, all-seeing and objective mode of knowledge-production that science has developed for itself. The theory of situated knowledge has been invoked in postcolonial contexts mainly to speak of alternative systems of learning and in critiques of development. It has also found resonance in theories of education – such as Henry Giroux's – where multicultural class-rooms are seen as vital to the dissemination of ways of knowing, of cultural differences in perception that revitalize texts and open up new ways of inter-pretation. Instead of an authoritarian, top-down system of disseminating 'true' knowledge without accounting for the audience/recipients and their experiences, this emphasis on situated knowledge pays more attention to how different communities respond to history, for example, how people of different races and ethnicities see the 'heroism' of Columbus or the evolu-tion of humanism (both were Eurocentric). What they bring to the reading is their own experience of racism and national identity and this produces a certain form of knowledge about historical figures and events.

slavery: This is not a feature restricted to colonial societies – slavery has existed in societies around the world since antiquity. For postcolonial pur-poses, however, it is the modern world's subjugation and exploitation of certain races that attracts attention. From the early 16th century Dutch, French and English trading companies seeking to establish plantations and colonies in the 'New World' but also in Asia and Africa required labour to clear forests, cut roads, build residences and to farm. They found this labour in Africa. The Middle Passage is the name given to the slaving voyages that transported Africans from various places in Africa to the Caribbean, Americas and other regions. Postcolonial studies shows how the entire European economy of the 1550–1800 period relied on slave labour (David Brion Davis 1966, 1999; Finkelman 1999). Slaves were also part of the colo-nial's household, in the form of servants and cooks, nannies and maids. In other cases, the black woman was the mistress of the landlord or overseer, and very often the plantation was overrun by mixed progeny. Slavery had legal apparatuses to justify and smoothen its functioning – so the trade in slaves was often systematized. Slaves could be classified as 'property': they could be bought and sold. Versions of slavery continued to exist in parts of the British Empire even after the trade in slaves was banned. These took the form of indentured labour, ostensibly wherein the individuals volunteered to go into the system as labour. Slavery of course hinged upon the discourse of racial difference, where the black was deemed to be inferior, inhuman and animal-like, and therefore could only be property with no agency, dignity or rights of his/her own. When abolitionists campaigned for the end of the slave trade (in English literature this constituted a large volume of poetry, by Hannah More, Robert Southey, Helen Maria Williams, and others, in the 1780–1830 period), they depicted racial difference in a different way: showing the Europeans how innocent, impressionable and vulnerable the black man/woman was. Contemporary postcolonial fiction, by David Dabydeen, Caryl Phillips and numerous others, examines the institution of slavery but also its legacies. Derek Walcott treats the entire Atlantic – the site of the Middle Passage – as embodying the history of slaves ('The Sea is History'). Paul Gilroy's work *The Black Atlantic* argued that Western civilization, especially after 1600, was possible through the white race's extensive engagements with the black races, thus arguing that transculturation was a part of the white race's culture already.

stereotyping: Ever since Edward Said's *Orientalism*, stereotyping – the depiction of a set of characteristics that are then taken as the 'essential' features of an entire group or community – has been seen as a key element in European colonial writings about the non-European races. Stereotyping, closely aligned with **essentialism**, 'fixes' and 'freezes' a community with a set of attributes. Every individual is then deemed to possess the characteristics attributed to the group, so much so that it becomes enough to merely mention the stereotype – the black athlete, the treacherous Brahmin, the cannibal African/Caribbean, etc. – with no need of a further explanation. The stereotype is unchanging, and thus becomes an easily understood feature of the colonial subject. As Peter Hulme puts it (1992), a stereotype is a self-fulfilling prophecy. Thus if a tribe is stereotyped as 'martial' it follows that any tribe expressing a distrust of the colonial would immediately be classified as 'martial'. Stereotyping was also a useful literary and representational strategy for depicting any racial-cultural Other. Thus, in the context of the black races, black women were routinely depicted as mammies and matriarchs, the faithful nanny or a sexual object, and the 'family' as a structurewas depicted as meaning very little to black culture. Other stereotypes that have been influential in European writings include the 'noble savage' (Fulford 2006) or the suffering black slave in abolitionist writings (Ferguson 1992; D. Lee 2002). Daniel Defoe inaugurated the stereotype of the docile, native in the character of Friday, even as he constructed the stereotype of the enterprising white colonial male in Robinson Crusoe. Stereotypes reflect the values of the culture from which they emerge. Stereotyping not only fixes the Other as unchanging, it also enables the establishment of a power relation where this Other is seen as vulnerable, childish, effeminate and therefore incapable of taking care of him-/herself, and thus justifies, within discourse, the domination by the 'superior' European. In this way stereotyping serves an important political function – of power relations and domination. The difference between races in such stereotyping is seen as preordained and natural, although in reality the difference is the effect of years of discourses. In an influential postcolonial reading of the colonial stereotype Homi Bhabha (2009) argued that for the white races the native had to be 'fixed' as unchanging for comprehension but also had to be treated as carrying the *potential* for change. Stereotyping produced the colonial subject, argues Bhabha. This latter was essential for the success of the colonial mission of civilizing the native along European lines. This was the ambivalence of the colonial stereotype which, according to Bhabha, was not only about the native but about the European as well. The latter understood themselves only in terms of their difference from the native – a difference they had portrayed as irreducible and insurmountable. Stereotypes are an index of anxieties over change: colonials needed a constant, and this was the unchanging stereotype of the native. In postcolonial theorizing, cultural stereotypes have come in for sustained attention after Said and Stuart Hall. In postcolonial writing the colonial stereotype comes in for considerable reversal. In Coetzee's *Foe*, for instance, rather than the confident and enterprising white colonial Crusoe, we see a bumbling, weak and perhaps slightly deranged 'Cruso' who, in sharp contrast to his literary predecessor, cannot build anything practical (he builds terraces, which have no practical use on the island) and refuses to keep an account of his stay on the island. Instead of the dynamic white adventurer, Coetzee gives us a female castaway, Susan Barton, who slowly acquires control over the story (being told, in the novel, to an author Daniel Defoe) about the island and Cruso himself. Finally, unlike the reformed cannibal-slave, Friday, in Defoe's original text, Coetzee leaves it ambiguous as to whether Friday is incapable of speech or whether his silence is a mode of resistance itself. Another example of a postcolonial reversal of the stereotype is seen in Derek Walcott's play *Pantomime*. Again a reworking of the Crusoe-Friday story, here the black Jackson 'plays' (there is a play within the play) Crusoe and the dissolute Englishman Harry Trewe becomes Friday. Through the play, it is the black man who issues instructions and 'teaches' Trewe how to run his hotel.

strategic essentialism: A concept made famous by Gayatri Spivak in her writings on subalternity, strategic essentialism extends the traditional colonial concept of essentializing and stereotyping of the native/non-European subject. Essentialism is the compiling of a set of characteristics as the defining features of a race/group/culture. These characteristics are assumed to be common to all members of that group, in other words, it homogenizes everything and everybody, without variation, under the sign 'Indian', 'feminine' or 'Asian American'. In postcolonial studies essentialism and its close associate, stereotyping, has come in for criticism because essentialism is seen as serving the needs of the colonial ruler by fixing the native's culture and behaviour as unchanging, whether inferior, savage, vulnerable or treacherous. Postcolonial studies argued that such essentialisms were constructions in colonial discourse that enabled the Europeans to craft identities for the subjects which, over time, were assimilated by the subjects themselves so that they saw their inferiority and savagery as 'natural' to their culture or community. However, in Spivak's arguments, some amount of essentializing by the natives, not as universal but specific to their contexts and immediate needs, serves a crucial purpose when battling European essentialisms. This she termed 'strategic', and situated it as a response, as resistance, with a political purpose, to European discourses. Spivak's argument about strategic essentialism as a response to colonial essentialisms is in fact simply the acknowledgement of a process central to any and all anti-colonial movements. Reverting to folk heroes and traditions as essential to their cultures (Africa), to Hindu gods and goddesses as 'Indian' (and not just Hindu) by Indian nationalists like Bal Gangadhar Tilak, or Gandhi's turn to an 'Indian spiritualism' as a response to the presumed 'materialism' of the West are all instances where strategic essentialism specific to a local culture and context was deployed as a means of unifying the various segments of the population in the anti-colonial struggle. Such a strategic essentialism might be read as a means of resisting incorporation into the colonial master's discourse because it offers an entirely different 'essence' of the native culture from that constructed by the European. Spivak sees this form of essentializing useful in that it furthers the interests of particular communities, especially historically oppressed or marginalized ones, when they make claims as a homogenous community with shared needs and aspirations out of necessity and for a political purpose. To argue for 'women's rights' rather than break up the category of the 'woman' along racial, cultural, ethnic and class lines, in other words, serves the immediate political purpose of demanding rights as a *whole* unit. In the 18th century, Felicity Nussbaum notes, race was a 'portable' category where Africans, Asians, and Native Americans were all interchangeable in the eyes of the European (2009). They were all, in other words, essentialized as 'black', the racial-cultural Other to the white European.

However, during civil rights and other human rights movements, the category of 'black' was revived as a uniform category to describe American-born blacks (the descendants of slaves in the USA) as well as black migrants from the Caribbean or even Africa itself, aligned with other racial minorities such as Asians, in order to campaign for equality across races. Here strategic essentialism works to further a political interest, of civil rights, for all those historically denied rights, whether Asian or black.

subaltern: Originally a British military term to describe a junior officer in the army, it was first popularized as a critical concept by the Italian Marxist Antonio Gramsci to describe those *classes* of people with little political and cultural power – possessing 'the general attribute of subordination' (Guha 1982: vii) – and who were dominated by elite classes such as the bourgeois. During the 1990s in critical theory and related fields such as history/historiography and literary/cultural studies it served as a catch-all term referring to disenfranchised segments of populations, classes, races, cultures and genders. Gramsci's argument was that the history of a nation is almost always seen as the history of the elite classes and the subalterns are erased from this history as though they have no identity, beliefs or, if they do, these are politically insignificant. They do not have the right to represent themselves. Gramsci suggested that subaltern classes were as complicated as the elites and it was only the structure of political and economic power that kept them out of the nation's histories and representations. Such an argument appealed to critics working with colonial histories and postcolonial contexts. Within postcolonialism's reading of colonial histories of South Asia, Africa and South America, the subaltern might be defined as the racial, cultural, gendered and ethnic subordinate of the white colonial, the product of colonial hegemonic practices and discourses. Postcolonialism's interest in post-independent nations' subalterns focuses on structures of power (the parliament, the judiciary, the market) and forms of discourse (education, religion, popular culture, publishing) that exclude the experiences, life stories, belief systems and knowledge production of particular groups of people (such as tribals or aborigines) from the discourse of the nation. Postcolonialism sees development, economics, political and cultural practices even in post-independent societies as disenfranchising large sections of the people. The colonized was seen as the subaltern race because it was unable to find a space in the European writing of, say, African or Indian history. When Alexander Dow, Robert Orme or James Mill wrote histories of India they did not refer to native sources or structures of thinking, or they dismissed these as irrelevant. The colonized subject was forever condemned to be represented by and spoken for by the colonizer. This politics of representation was also the hallmark of nationalist historians who rejected the contributions of, say, tribals, aborigines and local groups toward the anti-colonial struggle, and focused instead on the so-called heroism or sacrifices of a few members of the elite classes. A group of historians seeking to remedy this bias in history-writing formed themselves into the Subaltern Studies Collective, headed by Ranajit Guha, and produced a series of studies of South Asia wherein they focused on marginal groups and their contributions to history. These paid attention to belief systems – including folklore, superstitions, myths – of the marginalized. Subaltern Studies, seeking a 'history from below', proposed that tribal, aboriginal and local forms of resistance – including voodoo, rumour, ghosts stories and religion – should be deemed to be political because for too long the political had been defined in particular ways only and had rejected alternate forms of expression of dissent or anger. Shahid Amin, for example, argued (*Subaltern Studies III*, 1984) that it was rumours of Gandhi's miracle-work that enabled a popularization of nationalist ideals from leaders of the anti-colonial struggle. The tribal or the peasant is seen merely as a member of a crowd, and rarely as a thinking, reasoning being with political acuity. Peasant rebellions, for example, that do not figure in nationalist accounts of the country's anti-colonial struggles, or if they do, get absorbed into national frames at the expense of local immediacy and context, represent the subaltern contribution to the freedom movement – and this is what the Subaltern Studies project seeks to document. In Ireland the United Irishmen's rebellion of the early 19th century was directed, eventually, at rights for Catholics after Ireland was united with Britain. Whether this kind of rebellion constitutes an anti-colonial struggle (Irish Catholics versus Britain) is a moot point, if we retain the Subaltern Studies group's objection to traditional Western interpretations of 'rebellion'. Further, this group of historians proposed that Subaltern Studies needs to resurrect alternative knowledge traditions, since traditional and official histories, both colonial and nationalist, had ignored ways of knowledge-production and reasoning by classifying these as non-knowledge. Thus, in colonialism, alternate, non-Western forms of knowledge in language, science and medicine were systematically marginalized. Gayatri Spivak argued that one cannot escape essentializing the subaltern, or even retrieve a pure subaltern consciousness, even as we claim to let the subaltern speak for herself. How one defines a subaltern is itself, she proposed, an act of elitism. Spivak argued that subalterns were themselves divided, uneven and heterogeneous and to imply a uniform category of 'the subaltern' was to homogenize them. Further, subalterns always remain the subjects of others' representations, lacking a voice in which to articulate themselves. Institutions of discourse such as colonial historiography work by excluding certain kinds of voices and articulations. That is, subalternity is constituted within particular *discourses* such as nationalism, class and patriarchy wherein some groups, individuals, languages and forms of thought are deemed to be 'subordinate'. Eventually these discourses that become ossified as official begin to take on the aspect of a self-evident and natural truth that reinforces the subordination of particular segments of society. There has been since the late 1990s a shift in the focus of Subaltern Studies, from a quest to identify subaltern groups and communities to the discourses and apparatuses within which subalterns are made, as Gyan Prakash (1994) pointed out. A textual rather than empirical emphasis has been increasingly visible in the later volumes of the Subaltern Studies series as a result. Within postcolonial studies, despite the attempt of critics like Bhabha to assign a greater role for the subaltern – Bhabha argued that the subaltern would become a part of the independent nation once decolonization was complete – material realities have ensured they remain dominated. Yet, as Sumit Sarkar famously pointed out (1997), the categories of 'subaltern' and 'autonomy' were themselves essentialized in Subaltern Studies. He was referring to Partha Chatterjee's appropriation of Marx's ideas of community, which referred to pre-capitalist social formations. Chatterjee, by applying these to Bengal peasant life of the 1920s, decontextualized the very specific nature of 'community'). The nature of subalternity has always been disputed. For instance, whether the subalterns are conscious of their oppression and that this then leads them to revolt is a moot point. José Rabasa (2005), pursuing this line of thought, proposes that 'the ability to understand and articulate historico-political conditions of oppression is already a sign that one is no longer a subaltern' (374). But then, 'the question is … whether the language one uses to articulate these conditions must correspond to Euro-American theory, whereby all nativistic discourses would signal a condition of subalternity' (374). Rabasa calls for attention to processes of subalternization rather than to assume that subalterns exist as social groups. Despite such criticism, Subaltern Studies as a project and as a methodological tool in unravelling histories of oppression and resistance continues to resonate with social sciences and humanities disciplines, especially in literary analyses of postcolonial texts (Williams 2006) and in analyses of revolutions, social dissent and the new capitalist formations (Chibber 2013), and has been used to examine entire subnationalisms and ethnic identity movements, such as that of Native Americans (Rifkin 2005).

subjectivity (of Europeans, colonial period):   In Western thought, the individual is a self-conscious, autonomous and bounded entity, whose awareness of its separation from the world is very clear. The roots of this view of the Self might be traced to European Enlightenment thinking, the rise of psychological theories from the late 18th century and the emergence of psychoanalysis in the late 19th and early 20th. But with poststructuralism the dominant notion in critical theory has been that an individual's sense of self is constructed within discourses. An individual comes to an awareness of her/himself because s/he is acted upon by ideology and discourse, made to believe in certain beliefs, trained to possess certain desires and fear other things. That is, a subject is the sum total of numerous discourses that circulate in the world. In the case of the colonial subject, psychoanalysts like Octave Mannoni proposed a European psyche that was already prone to dominance. This suggested a self prior to the colonial experience. Psychoanalytic models of the psyche, however, also offered a qualifier to this view in the works of Sigmund Freud. The self was deemed to be constituted by a conscious component and an unconscious one, with the latter being full of primitive, uncivilized and savage desires and fears. With theories of colonialism such as Mannoni's the African and Asian were seen as representing the uncivilized model of the psyche. The work of Frantz Fanon, Homi Bhabha and others suggests a different model to the European's subjectivity. A European subject is fully formed within the context of colonial rule. Dominating the non-European Other, asserting himself in the colonial, and engaged in particular discourses (of benevolent paternalism and protectionism toward the native, of 'fair' rule, of Christian progress, etc.) the European comes to an awareness of himself primarily as a member of the ruling race. In the 1830s–1920s period the writings of Thomas Hughes (*Tom Brown's Schooldays*), R.M. Ballantyne (*The Fur Traders, The Coral Island*) and Baden Powell-Scott (*Scouting for Boys*) presented English boys reading the adventure novels and other genres, and brought up to believe in discourses of sacrifice for the Empire, hard work for the Empire, imperial masculinity, and taking care of the vulnerable, idiotic native. The English public schooling system instilled notions of imperial/white responsibility as well. If education is a key site where the self is made, then the English schoolboy's self begins to be shaped through the internalization of such discourses and beliefs about his role in the Empire. European women, functioning as Memsahibs in the colony, were able to find new selves in the role. As Kumari Jayawardene (1985), Phillippa Levine (2004) and other commentators have argued, the Englishwoman having grown up within Victorian ideals of domesticity and femininity found the colony a relatively free space for the assertion of their female agency. Enabled by the Empire to dominate natives, both male and female, the European woman managed to overcome some of the disadvantages of her class and gender background from back home. Being a part of the imperial structure gave her a marginal agency. European male subjectivity was also formed in particular ways in the colony. Take the character of Kurtz in *Heart of Darkness* or Kim in *Kim*. Kurtz discovers his true nature only within the African jungle. His propensity for violence, dominance and governance are revealed to him within the African space, where he is free to do exactly what he wants as the white man. In his case, clearly, the unconscious component of the European psyche, with its violence and dark desires, finds an outlet when in Africa. Colonialism thus calls out to the savage buried beneath the veneer of civilization even in the European. Kim, despite being much younger than the venerable lama, is able to assert himself as a master spy, a resourceful traveller, and an accomplished actor within the context of the Great Game and the Empire. The European boy heals maps, navigates the streets of Lahore and traverses the enemy territories in the Himalayas with consummate ease, suggesting that unhindered physical mobility through the spaces of the colony is the marker of European identity (Mohanram 1999). Kim comes to know him-self through these acts in the colony. The colonial furnishes the European man the context within which the self can be moulded. Thus we now see colonial subjectivity as emerging, for most Britons, within the context of the Empire, where the self is trained to dominate, control, govern and comes to believe in its role in guarding and governing the Other. With new thinking on materiality (the work of Barad 2007, Braidotti 2010 and others) the emphasis in studies of subjectivity has shifted away from the 1990s poststructuralist paradigm of discursive constructions to address matters of embodiment, biopolitics, affect and ontology. These are considered as emerging from experience, material effects and connections across bodies, environment and objects (often clustered under 'the new materialism'; Coole and Frost 2010). Postcolonial scholars and practitioners in fields like psychiatry, sociology and psychoanalysis are attempting, as part of this 'return' to the material movement, to reinstate lived experience as a key component of identity-formation. Fazwia Fazal-Khan and Kalpana Seshadri-Crooks argue that we need to get away from what they identify as the 'pre-occupation' of postcolonial studies (linguistic, rhetorical and symbolic analyzes) and return to more charged political and economic questions (2000). Debjani Ganguly therefore looks at the caste system in India (2005) and Farhad Dalal seeks to account for social and emotional elements of lifeworlds that are constitutive of identity (2002). Judith Butler calls for a return to questions of vulnerability and shared precarity that brings home to us the intersubjective nature of all subjectivity (2004). These shifts, while accounting for the discursive constructions of categories and identities, emphasize the corporeal nature of subjectivity, for instance, and show that this corporeality and its vulnerability might be a form of universalism.

subjectivity (of natives, colonial period):   The colonial subject finds her/himself to be, over a period of time under colonial rule, untethered from the cultural and psychological moorings of her/his subjectivity when colonialism destroys native cultures, rejects native belief systems and systematically undermines the artefacts, practices and ideas that inform the ethos in which the native used to be embedded. Frantz Fanon's critique of colonialism points to this effect, where native cultural practices are rejected as pagan and primitive, the landscape is transformed through European boundaries or buildings, structures of administration and the law, and the native begins to find her/his world changed inside out. Further, with Western education, the native begins to see himself through the texts produced by the West. As such, the images of the self that the native possesses begin to be Western images. Internalizing these images, the native starts to see her/himself as inferior, primitive, vulnerable, child-like and incompetent. The native's subjectivity is the effect of a sustained subject-position within colonialism. Judith Walsh's work on Bengali women's magazines has demonstrated how advice columns in such periodicals constructed models of femininity for the Bengali women, some of which were meant to thwart Westernization that was seen as invasive and evil (2004). Later commentators such as Partha Chatterjee have, however, proposed that within the domain of domesticity the English colonial influence was minimal, and Bengali women therefore might have retained their native/Bengali/Indian subjectivities. In Krupabai Sathianathan's fiction we see female subjectivity (and male) being constructed within two specific contexts: Christian conversion of the Hindu native and colonialism. The colonized native learns to think, behave, and even dress according to the models provided by the

European teacher, priest, judge and policeman. We see this even in the photographs of the well-groomed native students – with the Bible and school books in their hands – published in Christian periodicals like *India's Women* and *Juvenile Missionary Herald* of the 19th and early 20th centuries. Later commentators like Partha Chatterjee (*The Nation and its Fragments*) have proposed that colonial subjects found ways of escaping colonial subjectivity. Nandy, looking at the psychological devices of colonialism, argued that the colonized was treated as infantile/childish and effeminate/emasculated so that the colonial master was, in contrast, masculine and adult. In Nandy's reading cultural resistance to this form of colonial subjectivity appears in 19th-century India in the form of a valorization of androgyny and the feminine and, in Gandhi, of non-violence as an equally powerful weapon against the hypermasculine Empire. In the domestic realm, with an assertion of the spiritual-religious, for example, the colonized in India managed to retain their native sense of self untouched by the colonial system.

sublime (as colonial aesthetic):   Theories of the sublime entered Europe in the 17th century through the translations of Longinus' *On the Sublime*. Edmund Burke's famous 1757 tract codified principles of aesthetics with regard to the 'beautiful' and the 'sublime', even as commentators and aestheticians like Mark Akenside, Uvedale Price, William Gilpin and philosophers such as Immanuel Kant theorized the picturesque and other aesthetic modes. In colonial writings, the sublime was the aesthetic of danger in non-European spaces. It was characterized by boundarilessness, vastness and an unnameable-uncontrollable nature. From the Burkean concepts, we see deployed an imagery of furious oceans, endless horizons, and unidentifiable forests as sources of fear and awe. Magnificent mountains or vast deserts also inspired the sense of the sublime. We see in the descriptions of the wide and threatening ocean in Coleridge's 'Ryme of the Ancient Mariner' ('water, water everywhere' and the sounds of the ice in the sea) examples of a sublime Other space which is not-England, not-Europe. In travel writings set in Africa and Asia there are accounts of large waterfalls and forests that appear threatening. There were also accounts of the border-less, unmapped subcontinent which, to the British, seemed uncontrollable and which therefore demanded mapping and boundary-marking. The sublime landscape of the colony was one that demanded the European overcome and overwhelm the land, and possess it through maps, exploration and control. Fencing in forests, constructing borders and preparing documents of ownership were forms of imposing such control. The sublime therefore was the aesthetic of control in the colonial context, a kind of imperial sublime. In Charlotte Dacre's *Zofloya* (1806) the European Victoria meets her black friend and eventually her lover, Zofloya, in the wilds of the Apennine mountains. The interracial liaison is set in the sublimity of the mountains and results in the destruction of Victoria's self, family, and eventually her life. The sublime was an aesthetic where the European male overcame obstacles, both natural and manmade, and triumphed. Thus feminist readings of the sublime (Yaeger 1989) depict it as a masculine aesthetic serving to retain the *status quo* of gender roles and relations in terms of the male conquest of the feminine landscape.

syncretism: The term has its roots in religious studies to describe the mixing of two distinct traditions (in thought or rituals) to generate a third. A more common term in usage is '**hybridity**', which has been sometimes criticized for its pejorative origins and meanings – about individuals of mixed racial ancestry, seen as embodying the sins and evils of both and thus not to be trusted – in 19th-century colonial lexicon (Young 1995). Syncretism is instead seen as a more positive merging of distinct ideas and beliefs so as to transcend the problems of either individual strand. Immigrant cultures in First World countries are often seen/described as syncretic because they are located at the intersection of both their adopted countries/cultures and their 'original' ones. Even nationalist discourses in anti-colonial struggles or civil rights campaigns have been syncretic in Third World nations. For example, ideas of equality or democracy, 'self-rule' and emancipation in anti-colonial struggles of a Gandhi or a social reformer like B.R. Ambedkar in India (who campaigned for the rights of the so-called 'untouchable' castes) came from their reading and assimilation of Western thinkers as diverse as John Ruskin and John Dewey. Combining these ideas with their own traditions and reading of Indian texts, whether scriptural (Gandhi) or radical (Ambedkar), these activist thinkers evolved their own ideas of freedom and rights. Frantz Fanon in Algeria appropriated Marx, existentialism (briefly) and psychoanalysis to forge theories of black subjectivity in *Black Skin, White Masks* and other writings. Such a syncretism, importantly, erases the centre (imperial) and periphery (colony) distinction and distance. Studies in history (Hall 2002; Burton 1998; Fisher 2006) reveal the extent of syncretism among Asian, African and other people from the peripheries of the Empire into late 19th- and early 20th-century England. Such studies reveal how the dominant ideologies of empire and race were often not entirely hegemonic and native intellectuals and thinkers were very often able to appropriate all sorts of ideas to produce complex views of their own. Syncretism thus enabled the colonial subject to escape colonial subjecthood itself. Contemporary theories of multicultural citizenship (Kymlicka 1995) in the age of globalization are increasingly premised on an individual or community's ability to forge a merger between two traditions.

terra incognita: The term was first used in the 2nd century to describe, or rather hypothesize, lands beyond the known world. Australia was deemed to be one such region, called 'terra Australis incognita' in the early map of Mercator, *Theatrum Orbis Terrarum* (1570). The trope of 'unknown lands' begins to disappear from the mid-19th century with much of the globe being explored and mapped. The 'terra incognita' idea was a crucial theme for Early Modern Europe because by positing the unknown it offered the inspiration for knowing, in the form of quests, about the hypothetical new lands. But, as Graham Burnett has demonstrated in his *Masters of All They Surveyed* (2000), images of the interior of Guiana (later British Guiana) and even the European quest for the mythic city of El Dorado were driven by the idea of the 'unknown land', or at least an unmapped land, which they could then 'discover', map and dominate. As Burnett argues, landmarks indicated not only the European passage through unfamiliar regions but also the limits of the *terra incognita*, ensuring these places would never be called 'incognita' again. Myths, notes Burnett, were important modes of marking the significance of these 'unknown' lands as well. Other commentators (such as Paul Carter 1987) have proposed that the idea of the *terra incognita* offered obstacles to the imperial surveyor and administrator because these represented untamed, unknown and therefore potentially dangerous places in sharp contrast to the organized, domesticated and mapped colonial spaces. For postcolonial studies the trope, along with that of the *terra nullius*, is a politically loaded one. It is a preliminary moment to colonialism, a way of imagining distant places before setting out to discover

The Postcolonial Studies Dictionary, First Edition. Pramod K. Nayar.
© 2015 John Wiley & Sons, Ltd. Published 2015 by John Wiley & Sons, Ltd.

and dominate them, especially in the travel documents compiled by Richard Hakluyt (16th century), Samuel Purchas (early 17th century), and the writings of Walter Raleigh and others. It was the place of unknown wealth (the mythic kingdom in the legend of Prester John, for example, in Early Modern Europe). *Terra incognita* is therefore less the 'unknown land' than the 'land waiting to be discovered by the European'.

terra nullius: Derived from Latin, it literally means 'land that belongs to no one'. The term comes from the *Papal Bull Terra Nullius* issued by Pope Urban II in 1095, at the beginning of the Crusades. The *Bull* allowed Europeans princes and kings to 'discover' or claim any land occupied by non-Christian peoples in any part of the then known and to-be-known world. In 1452 this policy was extended by Pope Nicholas V. The term signifies possession and ownership of territory by distinguishing between Christians who are entitled to own land and barbarians/non-Christians who are not. This *Bull* led to what came to be known as the *Doctrine of Discovery*, and was one of the inspirational ideas (and ideologies) behind Columbus' expedition in 1492. It could also be treated as the driving motif behind the 'frontier thesis' and the Westward expansion of the 19th century in North America: since the Native Americans were living in a 'state of nature' they could not be deemed to own the land – an attitude exemplified in Thomas Jefferson's attitude toward the natives (Curtin 2005: 134. Also Buell 2005). Eighteenth-century articulations of the colonial discourse of *terra nullius* with regard to other parts of the world might be seen in James Cook who, arriving at Botany Bay in the 1770s, chose to see the land as 'empty'. When Cook, for example, pronounced that Australia was in 'a pure state of nature' with not 'one inch of Cultivated Land in the Whole Country' he was putting in place the idea of a *terra nullius*: what the natives did was not cultivation, it was all 'natural'. The term came into regular use and controversy from the 1820s when Australia began to be populated by the white convicts from England (the first convict ships arrived at Botany Bay, a name given by Joseph Banks, in 1788). Cook the explorer and Banks informed the British Parliament that the Aborigines had no legal right to the land since they did not cultivate it, and so could be made to conform to English laws. The lands were therefore treated as belonging to no one by the English through their denial of rights of ownership to the indigenous tribes. Having established that the lands were *terra nullius* – literally and metaphorically 'emptying' the land of its original inhabitants who were suddenly transformed into tenants and interlopers on the lands they had occupied and cultivated for centuries – the English then claimed the lands for themselves. English law became Australian law, under which the natives owned no land. Indeed the very idea of 'discovery' and settlement was a manifestation of the *terra nullius* idea. The country had been inhabited and settled for, literally, thousands of years before the Europeans arrived to 'discover' and 'settle' it. Thus, ignoring the signs of human intervention in the land, the European could declare the land 'empty' and ready for the Europeans to cultivate. That is, European discourses denied the native presence and activities on the land and then their ownership. *Terra nullius* is not only, therefore, a legal idea within colonial discourse, it is also a cultural project. The rejection of native cultural practices on the land, whether in agriculture or music or art, enabled the colonial to claim that the land was devoid of memories, cultural heritage, history and therefore civilization itself. *Terra nullius* was a cultural ideal of 'pure nature', almost as though the indigenous people had had nothing to do with it. European civilization was, in such a cultural politics, the first real intervention in that country. The trope of the *terra nullius* was, in fact, not restricted to European constructions of Australia and other regions. Zionist writings on Palestine also often spoke of the place as being without people or without the 'proper' features of a nation-state (Stein 2008: 328).

testimonio: A term popularized by John Beverley (1992) and George Yudice (1991) to describe narratives by genocide survivors of Guatemala, but first used by Elie Wiesel to describe narratives of concentration camp survivors, it is now a standard genre-marker for any kind of testimonial writing by victims of and witnesses to catastrophe and violence. The *testimonio* differs generically from the autobiography in that the autobiography is usually the life story of a successful individual who seeks to present her/ his life as an exemplar, while the *testimonio* is about the social order's obstacles to an individual's success or even society's torture of the individual for her/his ethnic, class, gender and caste identity. *Testimonios* have emerged from South Africa's apartheid era, the Partition of the Indian subcontinent, the Holocaust – which remains one of the key 'contributors' to the genre – genocidal regimes and cultures of Bosnia, Rwanda, and other places. *Testimonios*, often treated as testimonial literature, are usually first-person accounts of the sufferings of the individual, or of human rights violations, while several of them speak of communitarian suffering as well. They have the feel of oral literature since they are meant to be experiential and not always reflective accounts of the individual. These texts are therefore socially and politically significant and often become evidentiary texts for human rights campaigns in various parts of the world. Accompanied by graphic depictions of suffering, nervous breakdowns and sometimes impregnable silence, *testimonios* exhibit what Michael Rothberg calls 'traumatic realism' (2000). These texts are now seen in graphic novel format as well. Studies of the genre examine the first-person narrative mode, the encoding of trauma (Felman and Laub 1992), the tensions of primary and secondary witnessing – where the narrator is not necessarily the one who experienced the horrific events (LaCapra 1999; Nayar 2006) – and the reception of these texts in classrooms (Felman and Laub) and society itself. It has been argued that *testimonios* now represent an alternate history of a nation or society (Hartman 2001; Payne 2008), and that societies/cultures now understand themselves through these alternate 'stories' of exclusion, oppression and suffering. Contemporary studies examine the circulation of these texts as instances of globalization (Whitlock 2007). It is also argued that a 'narrative society' (Nayar 2012, *Writing Wrongs*) first defends the production of such narratives and, second, calls for greater ethical response (in terms of reading practices but also through law, social change and reform) to such narratives. *Testimonio* narratives are now a key genre in postcolonial literary canons. In the 20th century *I, Rigoberta Menchu* was one of the first such *testimonio* narratives. Menchu summarized the project of testimonial literature when she wrote: 'This is my testimony. I didn't learn it from a book and I didn't learn it alone. I'd like to stress that it's not only *my* life, it's also the testimony of my people'. Dalit writing from India (Bama's *Karukku*, Sharankumar Limbale's *The Outcast*), and survivor accounts from Rwanda are other instances. Second-generation *testimonios*, such as Art Spiegelman's graphic memoir *Maus* (in two parts, 1986 and 1991), incorporate and retell first-generation survivor accounts.

text/textuality (colonial):   Textuality, as in textual *representation* – literary, for instance, but also scientific or philosophical – has been treated in postcolonial studies in the wake of Edward Said as a key instrument in the construction of the racial-cultural Other. Said, writing in the poststructuralist vein, demonstrated how texts that only claimed to represent the 'real' actually constructed this reality in particular ways. Likewise Homi Bhabha's critique of the text stems from a deep distrust of the tradition of Western writing where the text is deemed to mimetically represent, or reflect, the real. He sees a link between historicism and realism where the 'linear order and coherence' of history is to be seen in the 'real' of literature. Bhabha proposes a greater alertness to the forms of textuality because, as he argues, texts mediate and produce reality, even as they claim that the real was always 'out there'. Drawing upon Saussurean linguistics and poststructuralism, Bhabha calls attention to literature not simply as a mimetic representation of the real, but as something that produces the real in certain ways. Traditional views of literature, says Bhabha, simply assume categories of the 'universal' which are made available, unmediated, within literary texts. In fact, it is the fictional text that produces the universal. In the case of colonial writings and representations of the colonial subject (the non-European/native) we have to be aware that meanings are produced in institutions and processes, of which literature is also one. It was in English literature's representations of African savages, Caribbean cannibals, and Asian thugs that these 'types' became 'real' for English readers. Texts naturalize stereotypes and establish meanings of terms like 'universal'. In colonial texts, difference – of races – are also, similarly 'naturalized' so that the text is seen as simply reflecting the real world of 'barbaric' native and 'advanced' Westerner when in fact the colonial text is what constructs these categories in the first place. The colonial text, in Bhabha's reading, is an instrument of organization, categorization and mediation of racial difference whereby the meaning of this difference (barbaric versus advanced, for example) is produced within the rhetoric of a literary text. It is when texts deny their own fictionality – by suggesting that they simply represent the real – that we need to be alert, because fictionality is what produces the real for the reader. Tim Brennan uses the term 'image-function' to describe the 'rules of perception' that organized information produced by the West about the 'rest' and which then enabled the European colonial nation to construct a certain idea of the periphery (2008).

Third World: Attributed to economist and politician Alfred Sauvy writing in the early 1950s, the term (now increasingly used between quotation marks to signify its problematic semantic scope) is used to collectively describe nations in Asia, Africa and South America. The First World, in this classification, is the capitalist nations of the USA and Europe. The Second World consists of communist nations, the former Soviet Union and others. The term is now derided in postcolonial studies because it obviously positions the Asian and African nations as later nations, with capitalist and socialist-communist countries coming First and Second respectively in the world's hierarchies. For postcolonial studies the 'Third World' is one more signifier, and stereotype, from the legacy of colonial discourse. 'Third World' is a signifier of poverty, disease, corruption, nepotism, primitivism and despotism and the category 'Third World women' evokes images of oppressed women. Likewise, in the age of global capitalism we hear of 'Third World labour' – sweatshops in South East Asian nations – that conjures up images of unending suffering and exploitation. Increasingly the term 'Third World' has been replaced by the 'Global South' or 'developing nation'. Thus the term has very definite economic foundations, but also social ones.

torrid zones: The equatorial regions of Africa, Arabia, and Asia but also South America where the temperatures are high, vegetation is thick and green, and where there is greater humidity. 'Torrid zones' is also the title of Felicity Nussbaum's (1995) book that examined this colonial stereotype. These regions, right from the travelogues of the 17th century, were also represented as 'torrid' in another sense. The inhabitants of these regions were deemed to have greater sexual appetites, body 'heat', tempers and a greater capacity for sheer indolence. Francis Bacon famously described the 'spirit of fornication' as a 'little foule, ugly Aethiope'. John Ovington, writing of India in the 1680s, said the Indians spent afternoons indoors and that they seldom 'went to sleep without a wench in their arms'. Attributing these qualities of character to the temperatures and humid climate, colonial discourse established a link between geography, climate and morals. 'Pornotropics' is a term used in postcolonial studies (McClintock 1995) to describe the 'torrid zones' of colonial discourse, although other writers had earlier pointed to the sexualizing of the colonized subject (see, for instance Carolyn Cooper 1993). It captures the dual nature of the term: 'tropics' referring to the geographical organizational concept of the globe, and 'trope' as a figure of speech in literary and cultural texts. The 'hot-blooded' Arab and Indian in colonial fiction embody the pornotropics of colonial writing. It was the zone of sexual aberration, excesses, and anomaly. Polygyny and lasciviousness were built into the very moral fibre of the African, according to this sexualized racial discourse of the pornotropics. McClintock also suggests that the pornotropics had another dimension and political purpose. The white men projected themselves as saviours of the black women who had been, according to the white man, enslaved by the black men. Thus women became the 'boundary marker' for the imperial project, making the native woman the 'object' of white men's attention. Details of native life were eroticized and often cast, Carolyn Cooper noted in the case of European travel writing, as fantasies of conquest that then fed into the voyeuristic fantasies of the armchair travellers back in Europe.

Mimi Sheller's work on the Caribbean and its representations in European colonial writings has shown how black bodies and slave sexuality generated an interest in questions of black (and European) morality, violation and sexual relations. Even the horror at violations and miscegenation between races enabled a certain shocked pleasure at the sights and accounts of black bodies (Sheller 2003; Levine 2013). But 'torrid zones' or 'porno-tropics' were also used as metaphors and descriptors for the risks the European undertook when s/he entered the tropics: of being tempted by the easily available pleasures of the flesh in these 'heated' environments. When Roxana, in Daniel Defoe's novel of the same name (1724), dances in a *Turkish* costume a certain amount of erotic fantasy is grafted onto the European woman's body, because the European woman's entire 'seductive' dance is consumed as a version of the highly erotic Oriental's. Stories of Arab seraglios and harems, of houris and the imprisoned native woman, of the 'mysterious' spaces of the Alhambra, were hugely popular fare in the 19th century, and contributed to the construction of the 'porno-tropics' (Saglia 1995). As late as the 20th century we have Adela Quested in E.M. Forster's *A Passage to India* claiming that Dr Aziz molested her in the caves, but Forster's account clearly implies that Adela's interpretation of Aziz might be the result of her own 'heated' sensibility – sensuality? sexual arousal? – in the proximity of the young Muslim man within the heated environs of the caves. This suggestion is reinforced in an indirect way when, during the trial of Aziz, Adela's attention, even in the midst of the traumatic proceedings, is focused on the sweaty body of the *punkah*-boy in the court-room. The writings of Richard Burton about his sexual exploits and experiences in the Arab world, and his translations of the *Kamasutra* and other erotic works from the Orient, further contributed to the view of the hypersexualized Orient. In the postcolonial era we have works like Doris Lessing's *The Grass is Singing* that revisit the torrid zone trope, with the white woman attracted to the African male in the heat and dust of an African farm, or Ruth Prawer Jhabvala's *Heat and Dust* (1975), which has a similar theme in the context of princely (pre-Independence) India. (See also: **miscegenation**)

transculturation: Mary Louise Pratt's *Imperial Eyes* (1992), a pioneer study of travel writing, popularized the term (originally used by sociologist Fernando Ortiz in the 1970s) to describe zones of encounter between European discoverers, scientists, conquerors, travellers and native/indigenous cultures where, according to Pratt, both sides appropriated practices and beliefs from the other culture. While Pratt accepts that such zones of cultural encounter – which she famously terms 'contact zones' – often demonstrate unequal, unjust and asymmetrical power relations between Europeans and indigenous peoples, she also suggests that there is often considerable exchange and mutual learning that occurs therein. Every age in European history has had such transcultural processes. Thus Lisa Jardine and Dirk Hoerder have shown how the European Renaissance was partly driven by the arrival and circulation of Arab, Indian and other artists in Florence and other places. The quintessential English novel arose, Srinivas Aravamudan (2005) has argued, out of translation of and transculturation with European and other traditions. New work on the Renaissance (Singh 2009), Enlightenment (Carey and Festa 2009), Romanticism (Fulford 1999; 2006) and Victorianism (McBratney 2010) has unravelled the non-European, multiracial and multicultural bases of European thought, literature and culture. Europe's concern with Native Americans, Turks (Vitkus 2007), Chinese (Porter 2002; Markley 2006), Arabs and Indians (Leask 1993; 2005) modulated, or occasionally intensified, as the acquisition of not only artefacts and commodities but also habits and cultural practices took place. The imperial fiction of Rider Haggard and Alice Perrin, among others, is now seen as embodying this transcultural condition that grew out of colonialism. The concept of transculturation has enabled such readings to point to resistances, assimilation and hybridization of European colonial cultures. Transculturation shows how European concepts of racial and cultural purity were always undermined by on-the-ground practices of cultural adaptation and appropriation, by both Europeans and natives. Further, it suggests that the centre-periphery model of colonial empires (the European centre versus the indigenous – Asian, African – periphery) is not tenable because there was a constant inflow of the periphery in the form of goods, ideas and people into the centre. While this flow was not equal or mutually favourable in economic terms or in terms of political power, it did have considerable cultural impact. Thus Michael Fisher and Rozina Visram have documented the presence of Asians in Britain since the 1600s, while Catherine Hall, Antoinette Burton and others have examined the enormous presence of Indians, Arabs and others from the peripheries of the Empire in metropolitan London in the 19th century. Transculturation could very well be considered a new model of the colonial encounter. It rejects the earlier model of domination-subordination in favour of a more nuanced understanding where European domination of indigenous cultures was accompanied by cultural adaptation from/of the local and the indigenous. But transculturation also produced interesting hybrids of the colonial subjects. Fernando Ortiz (in Otto 2008) proposed that it takes five stages: antagonism (where the colonized subject seeks to resist colonial culture), compromise (a slow mixing of races/cultures), adjustment (mainly mimicry by the mixed-race, miscegenated Creoles), self-assertion (the creoles wish to assert their own distinct identity as a unique race) and integration (Cortiz argues that we have not reached this stage yet). (See also: **miscegenation, hybridity, creolization, mimicry**)

transnationalism: A term increasingly used to describe the economic and social linkages involving the free flow of goods, finance, people, ideas and cultural practices across nation-states in the globalized age, it has special resonance for literary studies and particularly within postcolonial studies. Postcolonial studies, or more accurately postcolonial methodologies of reading, have since the mid-1990s tracked the cross-border and cross-cultural connections of English and other European nations. Volumes like *A Companion to the Global Renaissance* demonstrate how something thus far identified as a uniquely European phenomenon was in fact the effect of a series of such linkages, economic, cultural-artistic and ideational. Studies of the 18th century in English literature, similarly, demonstrate how the quintessential 'English' genre, the novel, itself arose through an assimilation and adaptation of numerous European genres (Aravamudan 2005). English identity, it appears, was forged through its transnational connections. Lisa Jardine (1996) has mapped the flow of goods across European nations in the Early Modern period. David Porter (1999; 2002) and Elizabeth Chang (2010) note the arrival and widespread taste for Chinoiserie from the early 18th century, while tea became an English drink sometime in the late 17th and the English taste for fabrics like muslin was established from the early 17th. Historians like Linda Colley (1992), Catherine Hall (2002) and Antoinette Burton (1998) have noted that the sense of English identity was constructed through an engagement with the peripheries of its Empire in Africa and South Asia. These studies suggest that England's and Europe's transnational relations were central to how England perceived itself. Transnational concerns are also visible in the form of England's interest in other races. The campaign against slavery foregrounded the African races, Islam and Turkey were always a European obsession (Vitkus 2007) while even the most English of poets, such as the Romantics, had an abiding interest in Native Americans (Fulford 2006), Jews (Scrivener 2011) and even other European cultures, from Poland to Russia (Maclean 2012). With the accelerating globalization of the late 20th century, transnationalism has also come to be manifest as the humanitarian work of non-governmental organizations (a version of the global humanitarian regimes in Europe from the early 19th century as studied by Alan Lester) but also through the increased hybridity and flexi-identities of authors like Rushdie, Pico Iyer, Monica Ali, Kamila Shamsie and Vikram Seth. Moving across cultures from 'Third World' to 'First' these authors are at home in both, i.e., they are cosmopolitan, and works like Shamsie's *Burnt Shadows* (moving from Japan to Pakistan, Afghanistan and the USA) demonstrate a transnational belonging. In writers from formerly colonized nations, the transnational is a form of belonging that resists both the nativist 'return-to-roots' model or the simple diasporic binary in favour of a multi-locational identity. Beyond literary studies commentators on con-temporary biomedicine and science are speaking of global 'tissue economies' that enmesh bodies, organs, DNA in global circuits of trade (both legal and illegal) and research banks (Waldby and Mitchell 2006). In a sense such transnational linkages premised on bodies continue to racially exploit Third World bodies through (illegal) organ harvesting (Nayar, 'From Bhopal to Biometrics') but also human trafficking and the differential biovalues placed on bodies (such as the injured in Bhopal's tragedy for which a meagre compensation was paid by Union Carbide-Dow Chemicals).

tricontinentalism: In lieu of 'Third World' as a spatio-political category to describe the formerly colonized nations and developing countries, Robert Young coined the term 'tricontinentalism' in his *Postcolonialism: An Historical Introduction* (2001). Young argues that Asia, Africa and South America were 'triangulated' into a global alliance in the form of a 'Tricontinental' at the Conference of the Organization of Solidarity of the Peoples of Africa, Asia and Latin America, which took place in Havana in 1966. The alliance was forged as part of a movement against imperialism and in support of a more equitable global society. For Young the new counter-knowledge and politics emerging from this alliance is a resistance to Eurocentrism. Others date tricontinentalism to the Bandung Conference of 1955, which brought together Asian and African nations to attempt to create new political and cultural alliances, as well as the Non-Aligned Movement (Adesokan 2011).

tropicality: A term used by Nancy Stepan (2001) and David Arnold (2005) to describe the imaginative and textual construction of the tropics as a geographical zone in English/European colonial writings but also as a metaphor for the Other to Europe. Romantic poetry, paintings, natural history and medical writings located the tropics as the contrast to temperate Europe. Like Said's theorization of Orientalism, Arnold sees 'tropicality' as a mechanism of Othering Asia and its various regions. Nancy Stepan uses it to examine how European writings in medicine, natural history and the human sciences such as anthropology constructed the tropics as not just a geographical space but as a space distinctive from Europe. Tropicality therefore is the use of 'devices' like cartography, surveying, medical histories, aesthetics, anthropology and literature to map the colony as the space of cultural and racial difference. It exoticized the tropics, since exoticism was the cornerstone of discourses of difference. Thus tropical medicine showed how the English constitutions could not survive in the humid, cholera-and-malaria-ridden tropics. Works like James Lind's *An Essay on Diseases Incidental to Europeans in Hot Climates* (1768) and John Clark's *Observations on Diseases in Long Voyages to Hot Countries* (1773) were early texts that constructed the tropics as spaces of medical difference. The tropics were the exact opposite of the temperate England, not just in terms of climate and vegetation but also in terms of culture and modernization. There is a variation on Arnold's theme of tropicality in contemporary revisionist readings that detect in English literary texts a fear of the 'tropicalization' of England itself wherein tropical diseases, plants and fruits seemed to be invading the home nation. Alan Bewell's work (1999) on the English Romantic poets demonstrates how their poetry is full of images of the tropicalization and hence pathologization of England. The diseased sailor, traveller (of which Coleridge's Ancient Mariner is an example) who returns home to England after a sojourn in the tropics, is thus possibly carrying infectious diseases that would then 'tropicalize' England itself. We can see the anxiety over such a tropicalization take the form of a fear of **miscegenation**, or the mixing of races, in the colonial fiction of Rider Haggard, Maud Diver and others. The tropics' invasion of England in the form of tropical women might be seen in the character of Bertha Mason in *Jane Eyre*, where 'pure' English womanhood, marriage and family are under threat due to the presence of the Jamaican Creole woman.

universalism: A key term in the rise of European humanism and Enlightenment, 'universalism' is the belief in the commonality of certain human features and attributes. Universalism sees particular behaviour and cultural traits as not specific to locality, ethnic identity, community or even nation. Literature in particular has been seen as the vehicle through which such universals – of suffering, happiness, virtue – could be disseminated. Stories of the 'human spirit' in heroic tales were deemed to be universal because they transcended country or culture. Universalism reaches its climax in the 20th century with the UN Declaration of Human Rights (1948) and the worldwide campaigns for women's freedoms, children's rights and animal liberation. Such universalisms, as postcolonial thinkers from Asia, the Middle East and other regions have argued, ignore the fact of the different forms of experience of women in, say, the Middle East or interior Africa. To speak of 'women's experiences' as universal is to ignore the African or Indian woman's experience of puberty, motherhood, marriage or widowhood. Feminist studies from the mid-1980s (Mohanty 2003; Razack 1995) have shown how Western feminism uses the white woman as a model for theorizing women's sexuality and identity when clearly the African woman's experience of sexuality is very different from that of the Euro-American. Within literary studies the universalism of English literature has come into question by scholars like Gauri Vishwanathan (1989) who demonstrate how English values and political beliefs were deemed to be universally applicable, indeed necessary, and were therefore instilled into Indian students through textbooks, pedagogy and literary texts. Universalism in

The Postcolonial Studies Dictionary, First Edition. Pramod K. Nayar.
© 2015 John Wiley & Sons, Ltd. Published 2015 by John Wiley & Sons, Ltd.

ABCDEFGHIJKLMNOPQRSTUVWXYZ

postcolonial studies becomes, therefore, a mode of imposing one worldview – the Christian, white, capitalist, European – upon the colonial subjects. Universalism ignores cultural difference in favour of a standardizing homogeneity where there can only be one cultural dominant – the European one. When, for example, Western (European and American) literature is taught to African or Indian students, its models of individual development and individualism (most notably in the *Bildungsroman* genre of Goethe, Henry Adams, Henry Fielding) are touted as 'universal'. For the African or Asian with traditionally strong filial, familial and communitarian links and affective relations, this literature either ignores his/her belief systems entirely or presents them as negative/inimical to the individual's growth. Over a period of time the African or Asian student begins to believe that individualism rather than communitarianism is the model to be adopted. In the African fiction of Flora Nwapa, Tsitsi Dangarembga and others the insistence on community and familial relations is therefore a direct postcolonial response to the (universal) individualism that European colonialism had brought into the mindset of the Africans. From another domain, the models of modernity that colonialism brought into Africa and Asia – emphasizing clock-time, rationalization of space, professionalization of work – as 'universal' did not quite fit into the cultural practices of these societies. In the age of globalization, universalism seems to take on a different guise, with Western fashion, entertainment, work-practices and consumption patterns – from the pizza to the famous open-floor office plan – becoming the 'standard' in Asian and African nations. European modernity's evacuation of religion from political-public life also did not fit into the colonized region's sense of the public, as Gandhi demonstrated in his anti-colonial struggle. Contemporary debates around secularism/ post-secularism (Mahmood 2000; 2009) have addressed the West's universalization of a certain kind of secularism as the sole guarantor of rights and a just nation-state.

vernacular: Etymologically, this means the 'language of slaves' (from 'verna' in Etruscan, meaning 'slave'). Eventually it came to mean 'the language of natives'. The term has acquired a measure of opprobrium and linguists often prefer 'dialect' as a substitute. There are numerous dimensions to the present and past use of the term. During colonial rule the native languages were often derisively labelled 'vernaculars'. The European languages became the dominant ones in law, trade and politics although the colonials had to take recourse to native languages, translators and interpreters in order to engage with the subject races. Native elites accepted the colonial master's language as a means of social mobility into the new structures of power and for the entrenchment of their social authority. They became the new empowered class of professionals as a result, with considerable prestige associated with their knowledge of English, a phenomenon that persists even today (Chandran 2006; Canagarajah 2005). Those studying English literature, belonging to particular elite groups, can suffer from what Spivak termed an 'alienating cultural indoctrination ... out of step with the historical moment', but English literature also offers a base from which a critique may be launched (2001 [1993]: 56). The denuding of status for native languages resulted in a slow erosion of the value of native knowledge-systems as well (Spivak in the same essay notes that the goal of teaching literature is epistemic, the transformation of ways in which objects of knowledge are constructed). In the postcolonial context Ngugi's arguments about English (1999) might be seen in this framework of the tension between a fledgling nation-state seeking pride in its native cultures

The Postcolonial Studies Dictionary, First Edition. Pramod K. Nayar.
© 2015 John Wiley & Sons, Ltd. Published 2015 by John Wiley & Sons, Ltd.

ABCDEFGHIJKLMNOPQRSTU**V**WXYZ

and languages in a bid to escape the tyranny of English (the colonial master's language) and the continued dominance of European languages because these are the languages of a global economy. Debates about mother-tongue/ vernacular versus English/European languages abound in Asia, Africa and South America. The debates revolve around two positions in postcolonial cultures. Those defending the vernacular see the native languages as endangered, and this threatens the loss of distinctive cultural identities for ethnic and minority groups (Phillipson 1992). Hence Minority Language Rights (MLR) campaigns have sprouted in the above continents, arguing that the insistence on English-language education continues the colonial policy of alienating the people from their own language cultures (Ramanathan 2004). On the other hand there is the very obvious reason for choosing, among the middle and working classes especially, English and European languages because these represent the languages of employment, trade and therefore social mobility. Postcolonial nations have seen a resurgence of linguistic fundamentalism, mother-tongue pride campaigns and 'local language only' activism even as English continues to hold sway as the language of commerce (especially big business in the globalized world), science and most of higher or professional education. But in several countries the debate about native/vernacular languages has also acquired an additional dimension, and this has to do with the dominance of any one native language as a sort of 'national language' (Hindi in India and Sinhala in Sri Lanka are two instances) so that other language speakers feel the need to contest this linguistic dominance (numerous states in India have rebelled against Hindi and the Tamils in Sri Lanka have similarly protested against the statutory nature of Sinhala, although this 'statutory' is often merely symbolic). In the globalized era postcolonials and migrants have evolved their own brands of English, thereby marking a symbolic overturning of the hegemony of English as they culturally appropriate for their own purposes the language of the former master. Postcolonial societies are now witness to campaigns for the preservation of fast-disappearing languages: in India, the People's Linguistic Survey of India and the *Bhasha* movement are of significance in this regard. (See also: **abrogation, chutneyfication**)

whiteness/white studies: Also referred to as 'critical white studies', the interdisciplinary field owes its origins to both white and non-white scholars from the early 20th century. The focus of the field is to examine the ways in which 'white' as a category came to be constructed within discourses – whether literature or science. Kim Hall, studying the European Renaissance in her *Things of Darkness* (1995), argued that the meaning of 'fair' as indicative of both skin/complexion as well as a moral quality developed due to the regular contact with the Africans arriving and passing through England. Whiteness was constructed through 'tropes of blackness'. Race studies contributed to whiteness studies by unravelling the semiotics of racial categories and representation in scientific discourse (see Nancy Stepan, Christian Bolt, among others). In such discourses, especially after Darwinian theories, certain races were deemed to be more biologically advanced than others, although there was no concrete evidence for this claim. Theodore Allen's detailed study, *The Invention of the White Race* (1997), focused on the USA where, he argued, race and class went together as a form of social ordering as America built itself through the late 17th and 18th centuries. Whiteness studies also sought to understand how hierarchies of whiteness – for example Eastern Europeans or Irish or Australians as white variants – were constructed. The Irish immigrants to the USA, as Noel Ignatiev argued in his *How the Irish became White* (1995), sought to become American whites by erasing their nationality, so as to fit into the New World. Part of this 'whitening', Ignatiev proposed, involved behaving like American whites, and treating the black races as inferior. In other words, in order to be accepted as the 'as-white-as-us'

ABCDEFGHIJKLMNOPQRSTUVWXYZ

The Postcolonial Studies Dictionary, First Edition. Pramod K. Nayar.
© 2015 John Wiley & Sons, Ltd. Published 2015 by John Wiley & Sons, Ltd.

by the Americans, the Irish migrants adopted an identical racial discourse toward the blacks. A criticism made of whiteness studies is that it forces the whites to admit to the 'guilt' of being white, in sharp contrast to, say, black studies, which tells the black race to be proud of being black. But this criticism aside, the significance of whiteness studies lies in its emphasis that racial differences were not ever natural but socially constructed.

World Literature: Johann Wolfgang von Goethe in the late 18th and early 19th centuries used the term *weltliteratur*. Anthologies of World Literature appeared in the 20th century and theoretical commentaries on the domain made their appearance in the work of Franco Moretti (2000), David Damrosch (2003; 2009), and Christopher Prendergast (2004). World Literature in the 20th century might be read as part of the processes of globalization and the making of a 'world system' (Immanuel Wallerstein's term). Translated texts play a major role in the domain of World Literature. Reading them requires, Damrosch argues in *How to Read World Literature* (2009), a reading across time, an understanding of the different literary assumptions of different cultures (including what different cultures mean by 'literature'), reading across cultures, and an awareness of the biases and choices of translators. Thus, for instance, when reading epics, we need not, argues Damrosch, immerse ourselves in a sea of 'antiquarian details' (his term) nor assimilate the text into our own time so that we assume it should give us the same pleasure as a contemporary TV soap opera. Rewritings, borrowings and echoes increase the pleasure of both the ancient and the contemporary texts, argues Damrosch. Another way of thinking about World Literature is to see it as a system of circulation and reception (Moretti opens his 2000 essay by noting that Goethe was reading a Chinese novel when he formulated the idea of a 'world literature') of texts. Moretti argues that world literature is 'one and unequal' because there is one world literary system of inter-related literatures but this system is unequal. A target literature might borrow from a source literature, but the latter frequently only ignores the former. Cultures on the periphery of the world literary system develop genres and styles as a result of the 'compromise' (Moretti's term) between *western/foreign form*, *local materials* and *local form*. Moretti proposes a 'distant reading' that allows one to focus on units that are larger than texts, such as genres and systems (rather than themes and tropes). We should not think, says Moretti, like Damrosch, of looking for only source-borrowing patterns but seek variations as well (indeed Moretti sees the system of World Literature as a system of *variations*).

worlding: First used by Gayatri Spivak in 'Three Women's Texts and a Critique of Imperialism' (1985), the term refers to the processes through which the colony is brought into the geopolitical and cultural map of the world. The world is deemed to pre-exist the colony, but more importantly, the colony can enter the geopolitical and cultural map only through its assimilation into European maps and narratives. Take for instance the very idea of the 'New World'. The Native Americans who had lived on the land for centuries become a part of the European imagination and maps when Columbus stakes his nation's claims to it. Colonization becomes a method of appropriating the natives' land into the European fold. Spivak proposes a further mode, however. Over a period of colonization the native also experiences his/her space – the one s/he is born into and lives in – as imperial space. This is so because the native has to experience his/her own culture and space through the imperial laws, literature, cultural practices and political conditions. 'Native space', as such, does not exist because it has been 'worlded' into a colony. Worlding must therefore be understood as an imaginative, cultural, but also very material, experience of the Asian or African space as imperial space, by both the European and the native, but as something which *erases* its processes of textual and imaginative construction of the 'Third World'. It marks the conversion of the native's space into something radically different due to the architectural, spatial, political and cultural alterations effected upon it by the colonial ruler. Further, inscribed into such a European discourse – maps, histories, literature, ceremonial practices – the native's space can now only be 'seen' as a part of the European world picture. Spivak's argument clearly gestures at the Eurocentric constructions of Asian, African and other colonial spaces.

References

Abu-Lughod, J. *Before European Hegemony: The World System, AD 1250–1350*. New York: Oxford University Press, 1989.

Achebe, C. *Arrow of God*. New York: John Day, 1967.

Adas, M. *Machines and the Measure of Man: Science, Technology and Ideologies of Western Dominance*. Delhi: Oxford University Press, 1990.

Adesokan, A. *Postcolonial Artists and Global Aesthetics*. Indiana University Press, 2011.

Agarwal, B. 'The Gender and Environment Debate: Lessons from India', *Feminist Studies* 18.1 (1992).

Ahmad, A. 'Jameson's Rhetoric of Otherness and the "National Allegory"', *Social Text* 17 (1987): 3–25.

Ahmad, A. *In Theory: Classes, Nations, Literature*. New York: Verso, 1992.

Ahmad, A. 'The Politics of Literary Postcoloniality'. In P. Mongia (ed.), *Contemporary Postcolonial Theory: A Reader*. Delhi: Oxford University Press, 1997, pp. 276–293.

Ali, A.S. 'Postcard from Kashmir'. In J. Thieme (ed.), *The Arnold Anthology of Post-colonial Literatures in English*. London: Arnold, 1996, pp. 752.

Ali, M. *Brick Lane*. 2001. London: Doubleday, 2003.

Allender, T. 'Surrendering a Colonial Domain: Educating North India, 1854–1890', *History of Education* 36.1 (2007): 45–63.

Amin, S. 'Gandhi as Mahatma: Gorakhpur District, Eastern University Press, 1921-2', *Subaltern Studies III*. Delhi: Oxford University Press, 1984.

Anderson, A. *The Powers of Distance: Cosmopolitanism and the Cultivation of Detachment*. Princeton, NJ: Princeton University Press, 2001.

Anderson, B. *Imagined Communities: Reflections on the Origins and Spread of Nationalism*. London and New York: Verso, 1991. Rev. ed.

The Postcolonial Studies Dictionary, First Edition. Pramod K. Nayar.
© 2015 John Wiley & Sons, Ltd. Published 2015 by John Wiley & Sons, Ltd.

Andrews, M. 'The Metropolitan Picturesque'. In Stephen Copley and Peter Garside (eds), *The Politics of the Picturesque: Literature, Landscape and Aesthetics since 1770*. Cambridge: Cambridge University Press, 1994, pp. 282–298.

Anzaldúa, G. *Borderlands/La Frontera: The New Mestiza*. 1987. San Francisco: Spinsters/Aunt Lute, 1994.

Appadurai, A. *Modernity at Large: Cultural Dimensions of Globalization*. Minneapolis and London: University of Minnesota Press, 1996.

Appiah, K.A. *In My Father's House: Africa in the Philosophy of Culture*. London: Methuen, 1992.

Appiah, K.A. *Cosmopolitanism: Ethics in a World of Strangers*. London: Penguin, 2006.

Arata, S.D. 'The Occidental Tourist: *Dracula* and the Anxiety of Reverse Colonization', *Victorian Studies* 33.4 (1990): 621–645.

Aravamudan, S. 'Fiction/Translation/Transnation: The Secret History of the Eighteenth-century Novel'. In P.R. Backscheider and C. Ingrassia (eds), *A Companion to the Eighteenth-Century English Novel and Culture*. Malden: Blackwell, 2005, pp. 48–74.

Arnold, D. *Colonizing the Body: State Medicine and Epidemic Disease in Nineteenth-century India*. Berkeley and London: University of California Press, 1993.

Arnold, D. *The Tropics and the Travelling Gaze: India, Landscape, and Science 1800–1856*. New Delhi: Permanent Black, 2005.

Asad, T. (ed.), *Anthropology and the Colonial Encounter*. London and Ithaca, NY: Cornell University Press, 1973.

Ashcroft, B., Griffiths, G. and Tiffin, H. *The Empire Writes Back: Theory and Practice in Post-colonial Literatures*. London and New York: Routledge, 1989.

Atwood, M. and Pachter, C. *The Journals of Susanna Moodie*. 1970. Boston and New York: Houghton Mifflin, 1990.

Bacon, F. *The New Atlantis*. In *The Works of Francis Bacon*. Ed. J Spedding, R.L. Ellis, D.D. Heath. Vol. V. Boston. Brown and Taggard, 1862, pp. 347–414.

Ballhatchet, K. *Race, Sex and Class under the Raj Imperial Attitudes and Policies and their Critics 1703–1905*. London: Weidenfeld and Nicolson, 1980.

Banerjee, S. *Becoming Imperial Citizens: Indians in the Late-Victorian Empire*. Durham and London: Duke University Press, 2010.

Bank, A. 'Of "Native Skulls" and "Noble Caucasians": Phrenology in Colonial South Africa', *Journal of Southern African Studies* 22.3 (1996): 387–403.

Barad, K. *Meeting the Universe Halfway: Quantum Physics and the Entanglements of Matter and Meaning*. Durham and London: Duke University Press, 2007.

Barbour, R. *Before Orientalism: London's Theatre of the East 1576–1626*. Cambridge: Cambridge University Press, 2003.

Barker, F, Hulme, P. and Iverson, M. (eds). *Cannibalism and the Colonial World*. New York: Cambridge University Press, 1998.

Barringer, T.J. (ed.), *Colonialism and the Object: Empire, Material Culture and the Museum*. London and New York: Routledge, 1998.

Bayly, C.A. *Empire and Information: Intelligence Gathering and Social Communication in India, 1780–1870*. Cambridge: Cambridge University Press, 1999.

Behdad, A. 'Nation and Immigration', *Portal Journal of Multidisciplinary International Studies* 2.2 (2005): 1–16.

Behdad, A. 'On Globalization, Again!' In A. Loomba *et al.* (eds), *Postcolonial Studies and Beyond*. Ranikhet: Permanent Black, 2008, pp. 62–79.

Beverley, J. '"Through All Things Modern": Second Thoughts on *Testimonio*', *boundary 2* 18.2 (1991): 1–21.

Beverley, J. 'The Margin at the Center: On *Testimonio* (Testimonial Narrative)'. In S. Smith and J. Watson (eds), *De/Colonizing the Subject: The Politics of Gender in Women's Autobiography*, Minneapolis: University of Minnesota Press, 1992, pp. 91–114.

Bewell, A. *Romanticism and Colonial Disease*. Baltimore, Maryland: Johns Hopkins University Press, 1999.

Bhabha, H.K. 'Of Mimicry and Man: The Ambivalence of Colonial Discourse'. *The Location of Culture*. London and New York: Routledge, 2009, pp. 121–131.

Bhabha, H.K. 'Signs Taken for Wonders: Questions of Ambivalence and Authority Under a Tree Outside Delhi, May 1817'. *The Location of Culture*. London and New York: Routledge, 2009, pp. 145–174.

Bhabha, H.K. 'Sly Civility'. *The Location of Culture*. 1994. London and New York: Routledge, 2009, pp. 132–144.

Bishop, A.J. 'Western Mathematics: The Secret Weapon of Cultural Imperialism', *Race and Class* 32.2 (1990): 51–65.

Boehmer, E. *Colonial and Postcolonial Literatures: Migrant Metaphors*. 1995. Oxford: Oxford University Press, 2006.

Bollen, K and Ingelbein, R. 'An Intertext that Counts? *Dracula*, *The Woman in White*, and Victorian Imaginations of the Foreign Other', *English Studies* 90.4 (2009): 403–420.

Bolt, C. *Victorian Attitudes to Race*. London: Routledge and Kegan Paul, 1971.

Boyd-Barrett, O. 'Media Imperialism Reformulated'. In D. Thussu (ed.), *Electronic Empires: Global Media and Local Resistance*. London: Arnold, 1998, pp. 157–176.

Braidotti, R. 'The Politics of "Life Itself" and New Ways of Dying'. In D. Coole and S. Frost (eds), *New Materialisms: Ontology, Agency, and Politics*. Durham and London: Duke University Press, 2010, pp. 201–220.

Braidotti, R. *The Posthuman*. Cambridge: Polity, 2013.

Brantlinger, P. 'Victorians and Africans: The Genealogy of the Myth of the Dark Continent', *Critical Inquiry* 12.1 (1985): 166–203.

Brantlinger, P. *Rule of Darkness: British Literature and Imperialism, 1830–1914.* Ithaca, NY: Cornell University Press, 1988.

Brathwaite, E.K. *The Development of the Creole Society in Jamaica 1770–1820.* Oxford: Clarendon, 1971.

Brennan, T. 'The National Longing for Form'. In H. K. Bhabha (ed.), *Nation and Narration*. London and New York: Routledge, 1995, pp. 44–70.

Brennan, T. 'The Economic Image-Function of the Periphery'. In A. Loomba *et al.* (eds), *Beyond Postcolonial Studies*. Ranikhet: Permanent Black, 2008, pp. 101–122.

Bricmont, J. *Humanitarian Imperialism: Using Human Rights to Sell War*. Monthly Review Press, 2006.

Bristow, J. *Empire Boys: Adventures in a Man's World*. London: HarperCollins, 1991.

Buell, L. *The Future of Environmental Criticism: Environmental Crisis and the Literary Imagination*. Malden, MA: Wiley-Blackwell, 2005.

Buettner, E. *Empire Families: Britons and Late Imperial India*. Oxford: Oxford University Press, 2004.

Burbank, J and Cooper, F. *Empires in World History: Power and the Politics of Difference*. Princeton, NJ: Princeton University Press, 2010.

Burnett, G. *Masters of All They Surveyed: Exploration, Geography and a British El Dorado*. Chicago: University of Chicago Press, 2000.

Burton, A. *At the Heart of the Empire: Indians and the Colonial Encounter in Late Victorian Britain*. Berkeley: University of California Press, 1998.

Buruma, I and Margalit, A. *Occidentalism: The West in the Eyes of Its Enemies*. New York: Penguin, 2006.

Butler, J. *Precarious Lives: The Powers of Mourning and Violence*. London: Verso, 2004.

Campbell, M.B. 'Anthropometamorphosis: John Bulwer's Monsters of Cosmetology and the Science of Culture'. In J.J Cohen (ed.), *Monster Theory: Reading Culture*. Minneapolis and London: University of Minnesota Press, 1996.

Canagarajah, A.S. 'Dilemmas in Planning English/Vernacular Relations in Post-colonial Communities', *Journal of Sociolinguistics* 9.3 (2005): 418–447.

Cannadine, D. *Ornamentalism: How the British Saw their Empire*. London: Penguin, 2001.

Carey, D and L. Festa. *The Postcolonial Enlightenment: Eighteenth-Century Colonialism and Postcolonial Theory*. Oxford: Oxford University Press, 2009.

Carrier, J. (ed.) *Occidentalism: Images of the West*. Oxford: Clarendon, 1995.

Carter, P. *The Road to Botany Bay: An Essay in Spatial History*. London: Faber, 1987.

Casid, J.H. *Sowing Empire: Landscape and Colonization*. Minneapolis: University of Minnesota Press, 2005.

Chakrabarty, D. 'Postcoloniality and the Artifice of History: Who Speaks for "Indian" Pasts?'. In Padmini Mongia (ed.), *Contemporary Postcolonial Theory: A Reader*. Delhi: Oxford University Press, 1997, pp. 223–248.

Chakrabarty, D. *Provincializing Europe: Postcolonial Thought and Historical Difference*. Delhi: Oxford University Press, 2000.

Chakrabarty, D. 'Postcolonial Studies and the Challenge of Climate Change', *New Literary History* 43.1 (2012): 1–18.

Chandra, V. 'The Cult of Authenticity', *Boston Review* 1 February 2000. http://bostonreview.net/vikram-chandra-the-cult-of-authenticity/. 4 September 2014.

Chandran, K.N. 'On English from India: Prepositions to Post-Positions', *Cambridge Quarterly* 35.2 (2006): 151–168.

Chang, E.H. *Britain's Chinese Eye: Literature, Empire,* and *Aesthetics in Nineteenth-century Britain*. Stanford: Stanford University Press, 2010.

Chatterjee, P. *Nationalist Thought and the Colonial World: A Derivative Discourse. The Partha Chatterjee Omnibus*. New Delhi: Oxford University Press, 1999. (First published 1986).

Chatterjee, P. *The Nation and Its Fragments: Colonial and Postcolonial Histories. The Partha Chatterjee Omnibus*. New Delhi: Oxford University Press, 1999. (First published 1993).

Cheah, P. *Spectral Nationality: Passages of Freedom from Kant to Postcolonial Literatures of Liberation*. New York: Columbia University Press, 1993.

Chi, J. and Kuckles. *Bran Nue Dae*. In H. Gilbert (ed.), *Postcolonial Plays*. London and New York: Routledge, 2001, pp. 324–347.

Chibber, V. *Postcolonial Theory and the Specter of Capital*. London: Verso, 2013.

Chomsky, N. *New Military Humanism*. Monroe, ME: Common Courage, 1999.

Clifford, J. *The Predicament of Culture: Twentieth-Century Ethnography, Literature and Art*. 1988.

Clifford, J. *Routes: Travel and Translation in the Late Twentieth Century*. Cambridge, MA: Harvard University Press, 1997.

Coetzee, J.M. *Foe*. New Delhi: Penguin, 1988.

Cohen, J.J. (ed.). *Monster Theory: Reading Culture*. Minneapolis and London: University of Minnesota Press, 1996.

Cohen, R. *Global Diasporas: An Introduction*. Oxford: Routledge, 2008.

Cohn, B.S. *Colonialism and Its Forms of Knowledge: The British in India*. 1996. New Delhi: Oxford University Press, 1997.

Colley, L. *Britons: Forging the Nation, 1701–1837*. New Haven: Yale University Press, 1992.

Colley, L. *Captives: Britain, Empire, and the World, 1600–1850*. New York: Anchor, 2004.

Collins, W. *The Moonstone*. Ed. Anthea Trodd. Oxford: Oxford University Press, 1982.

Comaroff, J and Comaroff, J.L. 'Naturing the Nation: Aliens, Apocalypse and the Postcolonial State', *Journal of Southern African Studies* 27.3 (2001): 621–651.

Conrad, J. *Heart of Darkness*. In Conrad, *Youth, Heart of Darkness, The End of the Tether*. London: Dent, 1974, pp. 43–162.

Cooke, M. 'Women, Religion, and the Postcolonial Arab World', *Cultural Critique* 45 (2000): 150–184.

Coole, D. and Frost, S. (eds). *New Materialisms: Ontology, Agency, and Politics*. Durham and London: Duke University Press, 2010.

Cooper, B. *Magical Realism in West African Fiction: Seeing with a Third Eye*. London and New York: Routledge, 1998.

Cooper, C. *Noises in the Blood: Orality, Gender and the 'Vulgar' body of Jamaican Popular Culture*. Durham, NC: Duke University Press, 1993.

Cooper, F. 'Postcolonal Studies and the Study of History'. In A. Loomba *et al.* (eds), *Postcolonial Studies and Beyond*. Ranikhet: Permanent Black, 2008, pp. 401–422.

Cooper, F. and Stoler, L.A. 'Between the Metropole and Colony: Rethinking a Research Agenda'. In Cooper and Stoler (eds), *Tensions of Empire: Colonial Cultures in a Bourgeois World*. Berkeley: University of California Press, 1997, pp. 1–56.

Cooppan, V. 'The Ruins of Empire: The National and Global Politics of America's Return to Rome'. In A. Loomba *et al.* (eds), *Postcolonial Studies and Beyond*. Ranikhet: Permanent Black, 2008, pp. 80–100.

Cormack, L.B. *Charting an Empire: Geography at the English Universities, 1580–1620*. Chicago, IL: Chicago University Press, 1997.

Cosgrove, D. *Apollo's Eye: A Cartographic Genealogy of the Earth in the Western Imagination*. Baltimore and London: Johns Hopkins University Press, 2001.

Crary, J. *Techniques of the Observer: On Vision and Modernity in the Nineteenth Century*. Cambridge, MA: MIT, 1992.

Curtin, D.W. *Environmental Ethics for a Postcolonial World*. Rowman and Littlefield, 2005.

Dabydeen, D. *Hogarth's Blacks: Images of Blacks in Eighteenth Century English Art*. Manchester: Manchester University Press, 1985.

Dalal, F. *Race, Colour and the Processes of Racialization: New Perspectives from Group Analysis, Psychoanalysis and Sociology*. Hove and NY: Brunner-Routledge, 2002.

Damrosch, D. *What is World Literature?* Princeton, NJ: Princeton University Press, 2003.

Damrosch, D. *How to Read World Literature*. Cambridge, MA: Wiley-Blackwell, 2009.

Dangarembga, T. *Nervous Conditions*. London: The Women's Press, 1988.

Das, K. 'An Introduction'. In J. Thieme (ed.), *The Arnold Anthology of Post-colonial Literatures in English*. London: Arnold, 1996, p. 717.

Davies, T. *Humanism*. London: Routledge, 1997.

Davis, C. 'Histories of Publishing under Apartheid: Oxford University Press in South Africa', *Journal of Southern African Studies* 37.1 (2011): 79–98.

Davis, D.B. *The Problem of Slavery in Western Culture*. Ithaca, NY: Cornell University Press, 1966.

Davis, D.B. *The Problem of Slavery in the Age of Revolution, 1770–1823*. Oxford: Oxford University Press, 1999.

DeLoughrey, E.M. 'The Myth of Island Isolates: Ecosystem Ecologies in the Nuclear Pacific', *Cultural Geographies* 20.2 (2012): 167–184.

DeLoughrey, E.M. 'Satellite Planetarity and the Ends of the Earth', *Public Culture* 26.2 (2014).

Derrida, J. *On Cosmopolitanism and Forgiveness*. London: Routledge, 2001.

Derrida, J. with Anne Dufourmantelle. *Of Hospitality*. Stanford, CA: Stanford University Press, 2000.

Dirks, N.B. *Castes of Mind: Colonialism and the Making of Modern India*. New Delhi: Permanent Black, 2003.

Dirlik, A. 'The Postcolonial Aura: Third World Criticism in the Age of Global Capitalism'. In P. Mongia (ed.), *Contemporary Postcolonial Theory: A Reader*. Delhi: Oxford University Press, 1997, pp. 294–320.

Dirlik, A. 'Literature/Identity: Transnationalism, Narrative and Representation', *Review of Education, Pedagogy and Cultural Studies* 24 (2002): 209–234.

Dobson, A. *Green Political Thought*, 3rd edn. London: Routledge, 2000.

Dobson, A. *Citizenship and the Environment*. Oxford: Oxford University Press, 2003.

Eaton, N. 'Nostalgia for the Exotic: Creating an Imperial Art in London, 1750–1793', *Eighteenth-Century Studies* 39.2 (2006): 227–250.

Edney, M. *Mapping an Empire: The Geographical Construction of British India, 1765–1843*. Chicago: Chicago University Press, 1997.

El Saadawi, N. *The Innocence of the Devil*. Trans. Sherif Hetata. Berkeley: University of California Press, 1994.

Eoyang, E.C. 'English as a Postcolonial Tool', *English Today* 19.4 (2003): 23–29.

Esty, J. 'The Colonial *Bildungsroman*: The Story of an African Farm and the Ghost of Goethe', *Victorian Studies* 49.3 (2007): 407–430.

Fanon, F. *Black Skin, White Masks*. 1956. Trans. C.L. Markmann. London: Pluto, 2008. Rept. of 1986 edn.

Fanon, F. *Toward the African Revolution*. Trans. H. Chevalier. New York: Grove, 1967.

Fazal-Khan, F. and Seshadri-Crooks, K. 'At the Margins of Postcolonial Studies'. In F. Fazal-Khan and K. Seshadri-Crooks (eds), *The Pre-occupation of Postcolonial Studies*. Durham and London: Duke University Press, 2000, pp. 3–34.

Felman, S. and Laub, D. *Testimony: Crisis of Witnessing in Literature, Psychoanalysis and History*. London: Routledge, 1992.

Ferguson, M. *Subject to Others: British Women Writers and Colonial Slavery 1670–1834*. London: Routledge, 1992.

Finkelman, P. and Miller, J.C. (eds). *Macmillan Encyclopedia of World Slavery*. New York: Macmillan, 1998.

Fisher, M. *Counterflows to Colonialism: Indian Travellers and Settlers in Britain, 1600–1857*. Hyderabad: Orient BlackSwan, 2006.

Forster, E.M. *A Passage to India*. Harmondsworth: Penguin, 1970.

Fulford, T. 'Romanticizing the Empire: The Naval Heroes of Southey, Coleridge, Austen and Marryat', *Modern Language Quarterly* 60.2 (1999): 161–196.

Fulford, T. *Romantic Indians: Native Americans, British Literature, and Transatlantic Culture 1756–1830*. Oxford: Oxford University Press, 2006.

Gamal, A. 'The Global and the Postcolonial in Postmigratory Literature', *Journal of Postcolonial Writing* 49.5 (2012): 596–608.

Gandhi, L. *Affective Communities: Anticolonial Thought and the Politics of Friendship*. Delhi: Permanent Black, 2006.

Ganguly, D. 'G.N. Devy: The Nativist as Postcolonial Critic'. In M. Paranjape (ed.), *Nativism: Essays in Criticism*. New Delhi: Sahitya Akademi, 1997, pp. 129–152.

Ganguly, D. *Caste, Colonialism and Counter-Modernity: Notes on a Postcolonial Hermeneutics of Caste*. London and New York: Routledge, 2005.

Geertz, C. 'The Integrative Revolution: Primordial Sentiments and Civil Politics in the New States'. In C. Geertz (ed.), *The Interpretation of Cultures*. New York: Basic Books, 1973, pp. 255–310.

Geertz, C. *Local Knowledge: Further Essays in Interpretive Anthropology*. 1983.

Gellner, E. *Nations and Nationalism: New Perspectives on the Past*. Oxford: Blackwell, 2006.

Gilbert, S.F. 'The Genome in Its Ecological Context: Philosophical Perspectives on Interspecies Epigenesis', *Annals of the New York Academy of Sciences* 981 (2002): 202–218.

Gilpin, R. *The Challenge of Global Capitalism: The World Economy in the Twenty-First Century*. Princeton, NJ: Princeton University Press, 2000.

Goodlad, L. 'Cosmopolitanism's Actually Existing Beyond: Toward a Victorian Geopolitical Aesthetic', *Victorian Literature and Culture* 38 (2010): 399–411.

Gooneratne, Y. *A Change of Skies*. Sydney: Pan-Picador, 1991.

Gopinath, G. *Impossible Desires: South Asian Public Cultures*. Durham and London: Duke University Press, 2005.

Gorsevski, E. 'Wangari Maathai's Emplaced Rhetoric: Green Global Peacebuilding', *Environmental Communication* 6.3 (2012): 290–307.

Greenblatt, S. (ed.), *New World Encounters*. Berkeley: University of California Press, 1993.

Guest, K. (ed.). *Eating their Words: Cannibalism and the Boundaries of Cultural Identity*. Albany: State University of New York Press, 2001.

Guha, R. 'Some Aspects of the Historiography of Colonial India'. In R. Guha (ed.), *Subaltern Studies I: Writings on South Asian History and Society*. New Delhi: Oxford University Press, 1982, pp. 1–8.

Guha, R. 'Chandra's Death'. In R. Guha (ed.), *Subaltern Studies I: Writings on South Asian History and Society*. New Delhi: Oxford University Press, 1987, pp. 135–165.

Guha, R. and Martinez-Alier, J. *Varieties of Environmentalism: Essays North and South*. Delhi: Oxford University Press, 1998.

Habermas, J. *The Postnational Constellation: Political Essays*. Trans. and Ed. Max Pinsky. Cambridge: Polity, 2001.

Habermas, J. 'Notes on Post-Secular Society', *NPQ* 25.4 (2008): 17–29.

Hall, C. *Civilizing Subjects: Metropole and Colony in the English Imagination 1830–1867*. Chicago: University of Chicago Press, 2002.

Hall, K.F. *Things of Darkness: Economies of Race and Gender in Early Modern England*. Ithaca NY: Cornell University Press, 1995.

Haraway, D.J. *When Species Meet*. Minneapolis: University of Minnesota Press, 2008.

Hardt, M. and Negri, A. *Empire*. Cambridge, MA: Harvard University Press, 2000.

Hartman, S. *Lose Your Mother: A Journey Along the Atlantic Slave Route*. 2007. New Delhi: Navayana, 2011.

Harris, J.G. *Foreign Bodies and the Body Politic: Discourses of Social Pathology in Early Modern England*. Cambridge: Cambridge University Press, 1998.

Harris, J.G. *Sick Economies: Drama, Mercantilism, and Disease in Shakespeare's England*. Philadelphia: University of Pennsylvania Press, 2004.

Harrison, M. *Climate and Constitutions: Health, Race, Environment and British Imperialism in India, 1600–1850*. Delhi: Oxford University Press, 1999.

Hartman, G. 'Witnessing Video Testimony'. Interview, *The Yale Journal of Criticism* 14.1 (2001): 217–232.

Hartnell, A. 'Moving through America: Race, Place and Resistance in Mohsin Hamid's *The Reluctant Fundamentalist*', *Journal of Postcolonial Writing* 46.3–4 (2010): 336–348.

Hirschkind, C and Mahmood, S. 'Feminism, the Taliban and Politics of Counter-Insurgency', *Anthropological Quarterly* 75.2 (2002): 339–354.

Hodge, B. and Mishra, V. *Dark Side of the Dream: Australian Literature and the Postcolonial Mind*. North Sydney: Allen and Unwin, 1990.

Hoerder, D. *Cultures in Contact: World Migrations in the Second Millennium*. Durham and London: Duke University Press, 2002.

Huggan, G. *The Postcolonial Exotic: Marketing the Margins*. London and New York: Routledge. 2001.

Hulme, P. *Colonial Encounters: Europe and the Native Caribbean, 1492–1797*. 1986. London: Routledge, 1992.

Hulme, P. 'Beyond the Straits: Postcolonial Allegories of the Globe'. In A. Loomba et al. (eds), *Postcolonial Studies and Beyond*. Ranikhet: Permanent Black, 2008, pp. 41–61.

Hyam, R. *Empire and Sexuality: The British Experience*. Manchester and New York: Manchester University Press, 1990.

Jameson, F. 'Third-World Literature in the Era of Multinational Capitalism', *Social Text* 15 (1986): 65–88.

JanMohamed, A. *Manichean Aesthetics: The Politics of Literature in Colonial Africa.* 1983.

Janu, C.K. *Mother Forest: The Unfinished Story of C. K. Janu.* Written by Bhaskaran. Translated by N. Ravi Shanker. New Delhi: Kali for Women, 2004.

Jardine, L. *Wordly Goods: A New History of the Renaissance.* New York and London: WW Norton, 1996.

Jayawardene, K. *The White Woman's Other Burden – Western Women and South Asia during British Rule.* New York: Routledge, 1995.

Jefferess, D. 'Benevolence, Global Citizenship and Post-racial Politics', *Topia* 25 (2013): 77–95.

Jenkins, E.Z. 'Introduction: Exoticism, Cosmopolitanism, and Fiction's Aesthetics of Diversity', *Eighteenth-Century Fiction* 25.1 (2012): 1–7.

Johansen, E. 'Imagining the Global and the Rural: Rural Cosmopolitanism in Sharon Butala's *The Garden of Eden* and Amitav Ghosh's *The Hungry Tide*'. *Postcolonial Text* 4.3 (2008). http://journals.sfu.ca/pocol/index.php/pct/article/view/821/631. 5 September 2014.

Keneally, T. *The Chant of Jimmie Blacksmith.* Victoria: Penguin, 1973.

Khan, S. 'Refiguring the Native Informant: Positionality in the Global Age', *Signs* 30.4 (2005): 2017–2035.

Kilgour, M. *From Communion to Cannibalism: An Anatomy of Metaphors of Incorporation.* Princeton, NJ: Princeton University Press, 1990.

King, T. 'The One about Coyote Going West'. In J. Thieme (ed.), *The Arnold Anthology of Post-Colonial Literatures in English.* London: Arnold, 1996, pp. 420–428.

Knapp, J. 'Elizabethan Tobacco', *Representations* 21 (1988): 26–66.

Knellwolf, C. 'The Exotic Frontier of the Imperial Imagination', *Eighteenth-Century Life* 26.3 (2002): 10–30.

Koller, C. 'The Recruitment of Colonial Troops in Africa and Asia and their Deployment During the First World War', *Immigrants and Minorities* 26.1–2 (2008): 111–133.

Kowaleski-Wallace, B. 'Tea, Gender, and Domesticity in Eighteenth-Century England', *Studies in Eighteenth-Century Culture* 23 (1994): 131–145.

Kumar, A. 'A Bang and a Whimper: A Conversation with Hanif Kureishi', *Transition* 10.4 (2001): 114–131.

Kureishi, H. *The Buddha of Suburbia.* New York: Viking, 1990.

Kureishi, H. 'In Charge of His Own Definitions: Conversation with Sandip Roy'. *Trikone* 16.3 (2001): 6.

Kymlicka, W. *Multicultural Citizenship: A Liberal Theory of Minority Rights.* New York: Oxford University Press, 1995.

LaCapra, D. 'Trauma, Absence, Loss', *Critical Inquiry* 25 (1999): 696–727.

Lal, V. 'North American Hindus, the Sense of History, and the Politics of Internet Diasporism'. In R.C. Lee and S-L. C. Wong (eds), *Asian America.Net: Ethnicity, Nationalism, and Cyberspace.* New York and London: Routledge, 2003, pp. 98–138.

Lau, L. 'Re-Orientalism: The Perpetration and Development of Orientalism by Orientals', *Modern Asian Studies* 43 (2009): 571–590.

Leask, N. *English Romantic Writers and the East: Anxieties of Empire*. Cambridge: Cambridge University Press, 1993.

Leask, N. *Curiosity and the Aesthetics of Travel Writing, 1770–1840: 'From An Antique Land'*. New York: Oxford University Press, 2002.

Leask, N. '"Wandering through Eblis": Absorption and Containment in Romantic Exoticism'. In T. Fulford and P.J. Kitson (eds), *Romanticism and Colonialism: Writing and Empire, 1780–1830*. 1998. Cambridge: Cambridge University Press, 2005.

Lee, C.H. (ed.). *Western Visions of the Far East in a Transpacific Age, 1522–1657*. London: Ashgate, 2012.

Lee, D. *Slavery and the Romantic Imagination*. Philadelphia: University of Pennsylvania Press, 2002.

Lester, A. 'Obtaining the "Due Observance of Justice": The Geographies of Global Humanitarianism', *Environment and Planning D* 20.3 (2000): 277–293.

Levine, P. *Gender and Empire*. Oxford: Oxford University Press, 2004.

Levine, P. 'Naked Truths: Bodies, Knowledge, and the Erotics of Colonial Power', *Journal of British Studies* 52.1 (2013): 5–25.

Lingis, A. 'Animal Body. Inhuman Face'. In C. Wolfe (ed.), *Zoontologia: The Question of the Animal*. Minneapolis and London: University of Minnesota Press, 2003, pp. 165–182.

Linklater, A. *Owning the Earth: The Transforming History of Land Ownership*. London: Bloomsbury, 2014.

Luo, S-P. 'The Way of Words: Vernacular Cosmopolitanism in Amitav Ghosh's *Sea of Poppies*', *Journal of Commonwealth Literature* 48.3 (2013): 377–392.

MacKenzie, J.M. *The Empire of Nature: Hunting, Conservation and British Imperialism*. Manchester: Manchester University Press, 1988.

MacKenzie, J.M. (ed.). *Imperialism and Popular Culture*. Manchester: Manchester University Press, 1989.

Mahmood, S. 'Feminist Theory, Embodiment, and the Docile Agent: Some Reflections on the Egyptian Islamic Revival', *Cultural Anthropology* 16.2 (2000): 202–236.

Mahmood, S. *Politics of Piety: The Islamic Revival and the Feminist Subject*. Princeton, NJ: Princeton University Press, 2005.

Mahmood, S. 'Religious Reason and Secular Affect: An Incommensurable Divide?' *Critical Inquiry* 35 (2009): 836–862.

Majumdar, S. *Prose of the World: Modernism and the Banality of Empire*. New York: Columbia University Press, 2013.

Mallot, J.E. '"A Land Outside Space, an Expanse without Distances": Amitav Ghosh, Kamila Shamsie and the Maps of Memory', *Literature Interpretation Theory* 18.3 (2007): 261–284.

Manalansan IV, M. *Global Divas: Gay Filipinos in the Diaspora*. Durham and London: Duke University Press, 2003.

Mannoni, O. *Prospero and Caliban: The Psychology of Colonization*. Trans. Pamela Powesland. London: Methuen, 1964.

Margulis, L. *Symbiosis in Cell Evolution*. San Francisco: W.H. Freeman, 1981.

Margulis, L. 'Symbiosis and the Origin of Protists'. In L. Margulis, C. Matthews and A. Haselton (eds), *Environmental Pollution: Effects of the Origin and Evolution of Life on Planet Earth*. Cambridge, MA: MIT, 2000.

Markley, R. *The Far East and the English Imagination, 1600–1730*. New York: Cambridge University Press, 2006.

Mbembe, A. *On the Postcolony*. Berkeley: University of California Press, 2001.

McBratney, J. 'Reluctant Cosmopolitanism in Dickens's *Great Expectations*', *Victorian Literature and Culture* 38 (2010): 529–546.

McClintock, A. *Imperial Leather: Race, Gender, and Sexuality in the Colonial Contest*. London and New York: Routledge, 1995.

McLaughlin, J. *Writing the Urban Jungle: Reading Empire in London from Doyle to Eliot*. Charlottesville and London: University Press of Virginia, 2000.

McLean, T. *The Other East and Nineteenth-century British Literature: Imagining Poland and the Russian Empire*. Basingstoke: Palgrave Macmillan, 2012.

McManus, A-M. 'Sentimental Terror Narratives', *Journal of Middle East Women's Studies* 9.2 (2013): 80–107.

Mehta, B. *Diasporic (Dis)locations: Indo-Caribbean Women Writers Negotiate the Kala Pani*. Jamaica: University of West Indies Press, 2004.

Menon, N. 'Between the Burqa and the Beauty Parlor? Globalization, Cultural Nationalism, and Feminist Politics'. In A. Loomba *et al.* (eds), *Postcolonial Studies and Beyond*. Ranikhet: Permanent Black, 2008, pp. 206–225.

Metcalf, T.R. *An Imperial Vision: Indian Architecture and Britain's Raj*. Berkeley: University of California Press, 1989.

Midgley, C. *Feminism and Empire*. London: Routledge, 2007.

Mignolo, W.D. *The Darker Side of the Renaissance: Literacy, Territoriality, and Colonization*. 1995. Michigan: University of Michigan Press, 2003.

Miller, T. *Cultural Citizenship: Cosmopolitanism, Consumerism, and Television in a Neoliberal Age*. Temple University Press, 2008.

Mirzoeff, N. 'Visualizing the Anthropocene', *Public Culture* 26.2 (2014).

Mohanram, R. *Black Bodies: Women, Colonialism, and Space*. Minneapolis: University of Minnesota Press, 1999.

Mohanty, C.T. 'Under Western Eyes: Feminist Scholarship and Colonial Discourses'. In Mohanty, *Feminism Without Borders: Decolonizing Theory, Practicing Solidarity*. New Delhi: Zubaan, 2003, pp. 17–42.

Mojab, S. 'Theorizing the Politics of "Islamic Feminism"', *Feminist Review* 69 (2001): 124–146.

Moorehouse, M.M. 'Black Soldiers in the White Military', *Afroeuropa* 4.2 (2010).

Moretti, F. 'Conjectures on World Literature', *New Left Review* 1 (2000), http://newleftreview.org?II/1/franco-morett-conjectures-on-world-literature. 25 August 2014.

Mukherjee, B. *Jasmine*. New York: Fawcett Crest, 1989.

Mukherjee, M. *The Perishable Empire: Essays on Indian Writing in English*. New Delhi: Oxford University Press, 2000.

Naipaul, V.S. *A House for Mr Biswas*. New York: McGraw-Hill, 1961.

Naipaul, V.S. *The Mimic Men*. London: Andre Deutsch, 1967.

Nandy, A. 'The Politics of Secularism and the Recovery of Religious Tolerance'. In V. Das (ed.), *Mirrors of Violence: Communities, Riots and Survivors in South Asia*. Delhi: Oxford University Press, 1990, pp. 69–93.

Naregal, V. *Language Politics, Elites, and the Public Sphere: Western India under Colonialism*. Hyderabad: Orient Black Swan, 2001.

Narayan. *Kocharethi*. Trans. C. Thankamma. New Delhi: Oxford University Press, 2011.

Nayar, P.K. 'Bama's *Karukku*: Dalit Autobiography as *Testimonio*', *Journal of Commonwealth Literature* 41.2 (2006): 83–100.

Nayar, P.K. *Postcolonialism: A Guide for the Perplexed*. New York and London: Continuum-Bloomsbury, 2010.

Nayar, P.K. 'The Vernacularization of Online Protests: A Case Study from India'. In R. Kothari and R. Snell (eds), *Chutneyfying English: The Phenomenon of Hinglish*. New Delhi: Penguin, 2011, pp. 71–81.

Nayar, P.K. 'Beyond the Colonial Subject: Mobility, Cosmopolitanism and Self-fashioning in Sarat Chandra Das' *A Journey To Lhasa And Central Tibet*', *New Zealand Journal of Asian Studies* 14.2 (2012): 1–16.

Nayar, P.K. *Writing Wrongs: The Cultural Construction of Human Rights in India*. New Delhi: Routledge, 2012.

Nayar, P.K. 'Mobility, Migrant Mnemonics and Memory Citizenship: Saidiya Hartman's *Lose Your Mother*', *Nordic Journal of English Studies* 12.2 (2013): 81–101.

Nayar, P.K. 'From Bhopal to Biometrics: Biological Citizenship in the Age of Globalization'. In S. Slovic, S. Rangarajan and V. Sarweswaran (eds), *Ecoambiguity, Community and Development: Toward a Politicized Ecocriticism*. Lanham, MD: Lexington, 2014, pp. 85–98.

Nayar, P.K. 'The Body of Abu Ghraib', *Seminar* March 2014. http://www.india-seminar.com/semframe.html.

Nayar, P.K. 'Abu Ghraib@10: The Empire of the Senseless', *The Four Quarters Magazine* April 2014. http://tfqmagazine,corg/issue/april-issue-2014/pramod-k-nayar/.

Nayar, P.K. 'Brand Bollywood Care'. Forthcoming in PD. Marshall and S. Redmond (eds), *A Companion to Celebrity Studies*. Malden, MA: Wiley-Blackwell.

Ngugi Wa Thiong' O. 'On the Abolition of the English Department'. In B. Ashcroft, G. Griffiths and H. Tiffin (eds), *The Post-colonial Studies Reader*. London and New York: Routledge, 1999, pp. 438–442.

Nixon, R. 'Slow Violence, Gender, and the Environmentalism of the Poor' *Journal of Commonwealth and Postcolonial Studies* 13.2-14.1 (2006–2007): 14–37.

Norcia, M.A. *X Marks the Spot: Women Writers Map the Empire for British Children, 1790–1895*. Athens: Ohio University Press, 2010.

Nussbaum, F.A. *Torrid Zones: Maternity, Sexuality, and Empire in Eighteenth-century English Narratives*. Baltimore and London: Johns Hopkins University Press, 1995.

Nussbaum, F.A. 'Between "Oriental" and "Blacks So Called", 1688–1788'. In D. Carey and L. Festa (eds), *The Postcolonial Enlightenment: Eighteenth-Century Colonialism and Postcolonial Theory*. Oxford: Oxford University Press, 2009.

Okri, B. *The Famished Road*. New York: Doubleday, 1991.

Ong, A. *Buddha in Hiding: Refugees, Citizenship, and the New America*. Berkeley and London: University of California Press, 2003.

Orsini, F. *The Hindi Public Sphere 1920–1940: Language and Literature in the Age of Nationalism*. New Delhi: Oxford University Press, 2002.

Orsini, F. *Print and Pleasure: Popular Literature and Entertaining Fictions in Colonial North India*. New Delhi: Permanent Black, 2009.

Osterhammel, J and Petersson, N.P. *Globalization: A Short History*. Princeton, NJ: Princeton University Press, 2009.

Otto, M. 'The Caribbean'. In John McLeod (ed.), *The Routledge Companion to Postcolonial Studies*. London: Routledge, 2008, pp. 95–107.

Paley, R. 'eEmpires', *Cultural Critique* 57 (2004): 111–150.

Pandey, G. 'Can a Muslim be an Indian?' *Comparative Studies in Society and History* 41.4 (1999): 608–629.

Parajuli, P. 'Beyond Capitalized Nature: Ecological Ethnicity as an Arena of Conflict in the Regime of Globalization', *Cultural Geographies* 5 (1998): 186–217.

Paranjape, M. 'Beyond Nativism: Towards a Contemporary Indian Tradition in Criticism'. In M. Paranjape (ed.), *Nativism: Essays in Criticism*. New Delhi: Sahitya Akademi, 1997, pp. 153–176.

Parker, A., Russo, M., Sommer, D. and Yaeger, P. (eds), *Nationalisms and Sexualities*. New York and London: Routledge, 1992.

Payne, L.A. *Unsettling Accounts: Neither Truth nor Reconciliation in Confessions of State Violence*. Durham and London: Duke University Press, 2008.

Petryna, A. *Life Exposed: Biological Citizenship after Chernobyl*. Princeton, NJ: Princeton University Press, 2002.

Phillipson, R. *Linguistic Imperialism*. Oxford: Oxford University Press, 1992.

Pope, A. *The Poems of Alexander Pope*. Ed. John Butt. New Haven: Yale University Press, 1963.

Porter, D. 'Chinoiserie and the Aesthetics of Illegitimacy', *Studies in Eighteenth-century Culture* 28 (1999): 27–54.

Porter, D. 'Monstrous Beauty: Eighteenth-Century Fashion and the Aesthetics of the Chinese Taste', *Eighteenth-Century Studies* 35.3 (2002): 395–411.

Poster, W.R. 'Hidden Sides of the Credit Economy: Emotions, Outsourcing, and Indian Call Centers'. *International Journal of Comparative Sociology* 54.3 (2013): 205–227.

Povinelli, E. 'A Flight from Freedom'. In A. Loomba *et al.* (eds), *Postcolonial Studies and Beyond*. Ranikhet: Permanent Black, 2008, pp. 145–165.

Pradeu, T. and Carosella, E.D. 'The Self Model and the Conception of Biological Identity in Immunology', *Biology and Philosophy* 21 (2006): 235–252.

Prakash, Gyan. 'Subaltern Studies as Postcolonial Criticism'. *American Historical Review* 99.5 (1994): 1475–1490.

Prendergast, C. (ed.). *Debating World Literature*. London and New York: Verso, 2004.

Puar, J. *Terrorist Assemblages: Homonationalism in Queer Times*. Durham and London: Duke University Press, 2005.

Puar, J. 'Homonationalism As Assemblage: Viral Travels, Affective Sexualities', *Jindal Global Law Review* 4.2 (2013): 23–43.

Puri, S. *The Caribbean Postcolonial: Social Equality, Postnationalism, and Cultural Hybridity*. New York: Palgrave Macmillan, 2004.

Rabasa, J. 'Allegories of Atlas'. In B. Ashcroft, G. Griffiths and H. Tiffin (eds), *The Post-colonial Studies Reader*. London and New York: Routledge, 1999, pp. 358–364.

Rabasa, J. 'The Comparative Frame in Subaltern Studies', *Postcolonial Studies* 8.4 (2005): 365–380.

Ramanathan, V. *The English-Vernacular Divide: Postcolonial Language Politics and Practice*. Clevedon, UK: Multilingual Matters, 2004.

Ratti, M. *The Postsecular Imagination: Postcolonialism, Religion, and Literature*. London and New York: Routledge, 2013.

Razack, S. 'Domestic Violence as Gender Persecution: Policing the Borders of Nation, Race and Gender', *Canadian Journal of Women and the Law* 8 (1995): 45–88.

Razack, S. *Dark Threats and White Knights: The Somalia Affair, Peacekeeping, and the New Imperialism*. Toronto: University of Toronto Press, 2004.

Rejali, D. 'The Real Shame of Abu Ghraib', *Time* 20 May 2004. http://content.time.com/time/nation/article/0,8599,640375,00.html. 5 September 2014.

Richardson, A. 'Darkness Visible? Race and Representation in Bristol Abolitionist Poetry, 1770–1810'. In T. Fulford and P.J. Kitson (eds), *Romanticism and Colonialism: Writing and Empire, 1780–1830*. Cambridge: Cambridge University Press, 1998. 129–47.

Rifkin, M. 'Representing the Cherokee Nation: Subaltern Studies and Native American Sovereignty', *boundary 2* 32.3 (2005): 47–80.

Robbins, B. 'Is the Postcolonial also Postsecular?' *boundary 2* 4.1 (2013): 245–262.

Rose, N. and Novas, C. 'Biological Citizenship'. In A. Ong and S.J. Collier (eds), *Global Assemblages: Technology, Politics, and Ethics as Anthropological Problems*. Malden, MA: Blackwell, 2005, pp. 439–464.

Rosenthal, L.J. 'The Queen of Sorrow and the Knight of the Indies: Cosmopolitan Possibilities in *The Recess* and *The New Cosmetic*', *Eighteenth-Century Fiction* 25.1 (2012): 9–35.

Rothberg, M. *Traumatic Realism: The Demands of Holocaust Representation*. Minneapolis and London: University of Minnesota Press, 2000.

Rousseau, G.S and Porter, R. 'Introduction'. In Rousseau and Porter, *Exoticism in the Enlightenment*. Manchester: Manchester University Press, 1990, pp. 1–22.

Rushdie, S. 'Commonwealth Literature Does Not Exist'. In *Imaginary Homelands: Essays and Criticism, 1981–1991*. London: Granta, 1991, pp. 63–70.

Rushdie, S. 'Fictions are Lies that Tell the Truth: Salman Rushdie and Günter Grass: In Conversation'. In Michael Reder (ed.), *Conversations with Salman Rushdie*. Jackson: University Press of Mississippi, 2000, pp. 22–25.

Safran, W. 'Diasporas in Modern Societies: Myths of Homeland and Return', *Diaspora* 1.1 (1991): 83–99.

Saglia, D. 'The Exotic Politics of the Domestic: The Alhambra as Symbolic Place in British Romantic Poetry', *Comparative Literature Studies* 34.3 (1997): 197–225.

Said, E. *Orientalism*. New York: Vintage, 1978.

Said, E. *Culture and Imperialism*. London: Vintage, 1993.

Sáiz, A.V. 'Globalization, Cosmopolitanism and Ecological Citizenship', *Environmental Politics* 14.2 (2005): 163–178.

Sarkar, S. 'The Decline of the Subaltern in Subaltern Studies'. In *Writing Social History*. Delhi: Oxford University Press, 1997, pp. 82–108.

Saro-Wiwa, K. *A Month and a Day: A Detention Diary*. Harmondsworth: Penguin, 1995.

Sassen, S. 'Spatialities and Temporalities of the Global: Elements for a Theorization', *Public Culture* 12.1 (2000): 215–235.

Schaffer, K. 'Colonizing Gender in Colonial Australia: The Eliza Fraser Story'. In G. Castle (ed.), *Postcolonial Discourses: An Anthology*. Cambridge, MA: Blackwell, 2001, pp. 358–373.

Schipper, M. *Unheard Words: Women and Literature in Africa, the Arab World, the Caribbean and Latin America*. London: Allison and Busby, 1984.

Scott, D. 'The Social Construction of Postcolonial Studies'. In A. Loomba *et al.* (eds), *Postcolonial Studies and Beyond*. Ranikhet: Permanent Black, 2008, pp. 385–400.

Scrivener, M. *Jewish Representation in British Literature, 1780–1840: After Shylock*. London: Palgrave-Macmillan, 2011.

Sharpe, J. *Allegories of Empire: The Figure of Woman in the Colonial Text*. Minneapolis: University of Minnesota Press, 1993.

Sharpe, J. 'Postcolonial Studies in the House of US Multiculturalism'. In Henry
  Schwarz and Sangeeta Ray (eds), *A Companion to Postcolonial Studies*. Malden,
  MA: Wiley-Blackwell, 2008.
Sheller, M. *Consuming the Caribbean: From Arawaks to Zombies*. New York and
  London: Routledge, 2003.
Shiva, V. *Staying Alive: Women, Ecology and Survival in India*. New Delhi: Kali for
  Women, 1988.
Shohat, E. 'Notes on the Postcolonial'. *Social Text* 31/32 (1992): 99–113.
Shome, R. 'Thinking Through the Diaspora Call Centers: India, and a New
  Politics of Hybridity'. *International Journal of Cultural Studies* 9.1 (2006):
  105–124.
Singh, H. 'Insurgent Metaphors: Decentering 9/11 in Mohsin Hamid's
  The Reluctant Fundamentalist and Kamila Shamsie's *Burnt Shadows*', *Ariel* 43.1
  (2012): 23–44.
Singh, J.G. *Colonial Narratives: Cultural Dialogues: "Discoveries" of India in the
  Language of Colonialism*. London: Routledge, 1996.
Singh, J.G. (ed.). *A Companion to the Global Renaissance: English Literature and
  Culture in the Era of Expansion*. Malden: Wiley-Blackwell, 2009.
Singha, I. *A Despotism of Law: Crime and Justice in Early Colonial India*. 1998.
  New Delhi: Oxford University Press, 2000.
Sinha, M. *Colonial Masculinity: The "Manly Englishman" and the "Effeminate Bengali"
  in the Nineteenth Century*. Manchester: Manchester University Press, 1995.
Slaughter, J.R. 'Enabling Fictions and Novel Subjects: The *Bildungsroman* and
  International Human Rights Law', *PMLA* 121.5 (2006): 1405–1423.
Slaughter, J.R. *Human Rights. Inc.: The World Novel, Narrative Form and
  International Law*. New York: Fordham University Press, 2007.
Slemon, S. 'Monuments of Empire: Allegory/Counter-Discourse/Postcolonial
  Writing', *Kunapipi* 9.3 (1987).
Slemon, S. 'Magic Realism as Postcolonial Discourse'. In L.P. Zamora and W.B.
  Faris (eds), *Magical Realism: Theory, History, Community*. Durham and
  London: Duke University Press, 1995, pp. 407–426.
Soyinka, W. 'Telephone Conversation'. In J. Reed and C. Wake (eds), *A Book of
  African Verse*. London: Heinemann, 1964, pp. 80–82.
Soyinka, W. *Death and the King's Horseman*. In Soyinka, *Six Plays*. London:
  Methuen, 1984, pp. 144–220. (First published 1975).
Spivak, G.C. 'Three Women's Texts and a Critique of Imperialism', *Critical Inquiry*
  12.1 (1985): 243–261.
Spivak, G.C. 'Can the Subaltern Speak?'. In C. Nelson and L. Grossberg (eds),
  Marxism and the Interpretation of Culture. Urbana: University of Illinois Press,
  1988, pp. 271–313.
Spivak, G.C. 'Poststructuralism, Marginality, Postcoloniality, and Value'. In P.
  Collier and H. Geyer-Ryan (eds), *Literary Theory Today*. London: Polity, 1990.

Spivak, G.C. 'The Burden of English'. In G. Castle (ed.), *Postcolonial Discourses: An Anthology*. Malden, MA: Blackwell, 2001, pp. 53–72.

Srivastava, N. *Secularism in the Postcolonial Indian Novel: National and Cosmopolitan Narratives in English*. London and New York: Routledge, 2008.

Stein, R.L. 'The Ballad of Sad Café: Israeli Leisure, Palestinian Terror, and the Post/colonial Question'. In A. Loomba *et al.* (eds), *Postcolonial Studies and Beyond*. Ranikhet: Permanent Black, 2008, pp. 317–336.

Stepan N.L. *Picturing Tropical Nature*. Ithaca and London: Cornell University Press, 2001.

Stoler, L.A. *Carnal Knowledge and Imperial Power*. Berkeley: University of California Press, 2002.

Suleri, S. *The Rhetoric of English India*. Chicago and London: Chicago University Press, 1992.

Sunder Rajan, K. *Biocapital: The Constitution of Postgenomic Life*. Durham: Duke University Press, 2006.

Sunder Rajan, R. 'Writing in English in India, Again', *The Hindu* 18 February 2001, http://www.thehindu.com/2001/02/18/stories/1318067m.htm/. 5 September 2014.

Sunder Rajan, R. 'Dealing with Anxieties – II', *The Hindu* 25 February 2001. http://www.thehindu.com/2001/02/25/stories/1325067a.html/. 5 September 2014.

Takagi, D. 'Maiden Voyage: Excursion into Sexuality and Politics in Asian America'. In L. Russell (ed.), *Asian American Sexualities: Dimensions of the Gay and Lesbian Experience*. New York and London: Routledge, 1996, pp. 21–35.

Taussig, M. *Shamanism, Colonialism and the Wild Man: A Study in Terror and Healing*.

Teltscher, K. '"Maidenly and Well Nigh Effeminate": Constructions of Hindu Masculinity and Religion in Seventeenth-century English Texts', *Postcolonial Studies* 3.2 (2000): 159–170.

Terranova, T. 'Free Labor: Producing Culture for the Digital Economy', *Social Text* 18.2 (2000): 34–58.

Thomas, N. *Colonialism's Culture: Anthropology, Travel and Government*. Cambridge: Polity, 1994.

Thussu, D. (ed.). *Electronic Empires: Global Media and Local Resistance*. London: Arnold, 1998.

Tidrick, K. *Empire and the English Character*. London: I.B. Tauris, 1990.

Trivedi, H. 'Reading English, Writing Hindi: English Literature and Indian Creative Writing'. In S. Joshi (ed.), *Rethinking English: Essays in Literature, Language, History*. New Delhi: Trianka, 1991, pp. 161–180.

Trivedi, H. 'Foreword'. In Rita Kothari and Rupert Snell (eds), *Chutneyfying English: The Phenomenon of Hinglish*. New Delhi: Penguin, 2011, pp. vii–xxvi.

Tsing, A.L. *Friction: An Ethnography of Global Connection*. Princeton, NJ: Princeton University Press, 2007.

Vishwanathan, G. *Masks of Conquest: English Literary Studies and India.* New York: Columbia University Press, 1989.

Vitkus, D. 'Adventuring Heroes in the Mediterranean: Mapping the Boundaries of Anglo-Islamic Exchange on the Early Modern Stage', *Journal of Medieval and Early Modern Studies* 37.1 (2007): 75–95.

Vizram, R. *Ayahs, Lascars and Princes: Indians in Britain 1700–1947.* London: Pluto, 1986.

Vizram, R. *Asians in Britain: 400 Years of History.* London: Pluto, 2002.

Walcott, D. *Dream on Monkey Mountain and Other Plays.* New York: Farrar, Straus and Giroux, 1970.

Waldby, C. and Mitchell, R. *Tissue Economies: Blood, Organs, and Cell Lines in Late Capitalism.* Durham and London: Duke University Press, 2006.

Waldron, J. 'Minority Cultures and the Cosmopolitan Alternative'. In W. Kymlicka (ed.), *The Rights of Minority Cultures.* Oxford: Oxford University Press, 1995, pp. 93–119.

Walker, K. 'We are Going'. In J. Thieme (ed.), *The Arnold Anthology of Post-colonial Literatures in English.* London: Arnold, 1996, pp. 223–224.

Walsh, J. *Domesticity in Colonial India: What Women Learned When Men Gave them Advice.* Lanham, MD: Rowman and Littlefield, 2004.

Watson, C.W. *Multiculturalism.* New Delhi: Viva, 2002.

Werbner, P. 'Vernacular Cosmopolitanism', *Theory, Culture, and Society* 23.2–3 (2006): 496–498.

White, H. 'The Forms of Wildness: Archaeology of an Idea'. In E. Dudley and M.E Novak (eds), *The Wild Man Within: An Image in Western Thought from the Renaissance to Romanticism.* Pittsburgh: University of Pittsburgh Press, 1972, pp. 3–38.

Whitlock, G. *Soft Weapons: Autobiography in Transit.* Chicago and London: Chicago University Press, 2007.

Williams, J.R. '"Doing History": Nuruddin Farah's *Sweet and Sour Milk*, Subaltern Studies and the Postcolonial Trajectory of Silence', *Research in African Literatures* 37.3 (2006): 161–176.

Willis, M. '"The Invisible Giant," *Dracula*, and Disease', *Studies in the Novel* 39.3 (2007): 301–25.

Wolfe, C. *What is Posthumanism?* Minneapolis: University of Minnesota Press, 2010.

Yaeger, P. 'Toward a *Female Sublime*'. In Linda Kauffman (ed.), *Gender and Theory.* Oxford: Blackwell, 1989, pp. 191–212.

Yeğenoğlu, M. *Colonial Fantasies: Towards a Feminist Reading of Orientalism.* Cambridge: Cambridge University Press, 1998.

Young, R.J.C. *White Mythologies: Hybridity in Theory, Culture and Race.* London and New York: Routledge, 1995.

Young, R.J.C. *Postcolonialism: An Historical Introduction.* Oxford: Blackwell, 2001.

Young, R.J.C. 'Postcolonial Remains', *New Literary History* 43.1 (2012): 19–42.

Yudice, G. '*Testimonio* and Postmodernism', *Latin American Perspectives* 18.3 (1991): 15–31.

Zoustopil, L. *Rammohun Roy and the Making of Victorian Britain*. London: Palgrave Macmillan, 2010.

Zutshi, C. '"Designed for Eternity": Kashmiri Shawls, Empire, and Cultures of Production and Consumption in Mid-Victorian Britain', *Journal of British Studies* 48.2 (2009): 420–440.